COMMUNITIES OF LUDLOW

COMMUNITIES OF LUDLOW

COLLABORATIVE STEWARDSHIP AND THE LUDLOW CENTENNIAL COMMEMORATION COMMISSION

Edited by

Fawn-Amber Montoya and Karin Larkin

UNIVERSITY PRESS OF COLORADO
Louisville

© 2022 by University Press of Colorado

Published by University Press of Colorado
245 Century Circle, Suite 202
Louisville, Colorado 80027

 The University Press of Colorado is a proud member of the Association of University Presses.

The University Press of Colorado is a cooperative publishing enterprise supported, in part, by Adams State University, Colorado State University, Fort Lewis College, Metropolitan State University of Denver, Regis University, University of Alaska Fairbanks, University of Colorado, University of Denver, University of Northern Colorado, University of Wyoming, Utah State University, and Western Colorado University.

∞ This paper meets the requirements of the ANSI/NISO Z39.48–1992 (Permanence of Paper).

ISBN: 978-1-64642-227-2 (hardcover)
ISBN: 978-1-64642-228-9 (ebook)
https://doi.org/10.5876/9781646422289

Library of Congress Cataloging-in-Publication Data

Names: Montoya, Fawn-Amber, editor. | Larkin, Karin, editor.
Title: Communities of Ludlow : collaborative stewardship and the Ludlow Centennial
  Commemoration Commission / edited by Fawn-Amber Montoya and Karin Larkin.
Description: Louisville : University Press of Colorado, [2022] | Includes bibliographical references
  and index.
Identifiers: LCCN 2021045196 (print) | LCCN 2021045197 (ebook) | ISBN 9781646422272 (hardcover)
  | ISBN 9781646422289 (ebook)
Subjects: LCSH: Ludlow Centennial Commemoration Commission (Ludlow, Colo.)
  | United Mine Workers of America—History—20th century. | Coal Strike, Colo.,
  1913–1914—Anniversaries, etc. | Coal Strike, Colo., 1913–1914—Personal narratives. |
  Memorials—Colorado—Ludlow. | Coal miners—Colorado—Ludlow—History—20th century.
Classification: LCC HD5325.M616 1913 C66 2021 (print) | LCC HD5325.M616 1913 (ebook) | DDC
  331.892/8223340978896—dc23
LC record available at https://lccn.loc.gov/2021045196
LC ebook record available at https://lccn.loc.gov/2021045197

Cover art: "Ludlow: Miners Camp." Painting by Lindsay Hand. Image courtesy of Colorado Springs Pioneers Museum.

This book is dedicated to all those who have sacrificed and dedicated their lives to continuing the story of the Ludlow Massacre. We remember the people who died on that day, including: Elvira Valdez, 3 months; Frank Petrucci, 6 months; Lucy Petrucci, 2 years; Lucy Costa, 4 years; Cloriva Pedregone, 4 years; Joe Petrucci, 4 years; Onafrio Costa, 6 years; Rodgerlo Pedregone, 6 years; Mary Valdez, 7 years; Eulala Valdez, 8 years; Rudolfo Valdez, 9 years; Frank Snyder, 11 years; Primo Larese, 18 years; Frank Rubino, 23 years; Fedelina (Cedilena) Costa, 27 years; Louis Tikas, 30 years; Private Alfred Martin, 30 years; Charlie Costa, 31 years; Patria Valdez, 37 years; James Fyler, 43 years; and John Bartolotti, 45 years.

We also acknowledge the survivors of the 1913–1914 strike and Ludlow Massacre and their descendants. We recognize the United Mine Workers of America, union members, coalminers of southern Colorado, and their descendants as the children of Ludlow. They are the ones who have heard the story and continued to tell it for the past 100 years.

Contents

Figures and Tables

FIGURES

TABLES

Acknowledgments

This kind of book is impossible to put together without the contributions of and support from our colleagues, families, and institutions. We have had the opportunity to build strong collaborative relationships with community organizers, labor leaders, and scholars throughout the state of Colorado, the nation, and the world. We had much interaction, support and inspiration from the descendent community of coalminers and other working families in southern Colorado. Many people shared their family's histories and memories of the coal camps with us. They welcomed us in solidarity with labor's struggle. We hope the readers of this book get a glimpse into the spirit of collaboration they possess.

The most important and rewarding aspects of our research came from our collaboration with the United Mine Workers of America (UMWA) and with the working people of southern Colorado. The UMWA Local 9856 and Women's Auxiliary Local 9856 maintain the Ludlow monument and host the annual memorial. The work of the UMWA is actively supported by Mike and Yolanda Romero and Robert "Bob" Butero. Their dedication to preserving the massacre site is exhibited in their daily lives.

The work of the Colorado Coalfield War Archaeological Project (CCWAP) formed one of the large communities of interest that contributed to our commemorative efforts. From the beginning, the CCWAP tried to build a program that speaks to multiple audiences, in understandable languages, in accessible formats, and about aspects of the past of interest to them. The work of the Colorado Coalfield War Archaeological Project would not have been possible without the vision and dedication to inclusive scholarship of Dean Saitta, Randall McGuire, and Philip Duke, as well as the Ludlow Collective. The collective included Dan Broockmann, Donna Bryant, Sarah Chicone, Bonnie J. Clark, Philip Duke, Amie Gray, Claire Horn, Michael Jacobson, Kristen Jones, Jason Lapham, Karin Larkin, Randall McGuire, Summer Moore, Paul Reckner, Mary Rudden, Dean Saitta, Mark Walker, and Margaret Wood. We conducted fieldwork at Ludlow with the permission of District 22 (now Region 4) of the United Mine Workers of America, Local 9856 of the UMWA, and the Women's Auxiliary of Local 9856. CCWAP received funding from a number of sources. The principal source of funding for the project was through History Colorado's State Historical Fund. They provided grants to the project every year from 1997 until 2004. The Walter Rosenberry Fund and the Humanities Institute of the Division of Arts, Humanities, and the Social Sciences at the University of Denver provided funding for site interpretation and public education programs. The Colorado Endowment for the Humanities funded two Summer Teacher Institutes on labor history for our project. A number of community institutions including the Colorado Digitization Project, the Trinidad History Museum, and the Steelworks Museum (then the Bessemer Historical Society) aided our work with in-kind contributions and their archival resources.

In addition to the CCWAP, the Labor and Working-Class History Association's efforts in establishing the Ludlow Tent Colony as a National Historic Landmark laid a foundation for the model of collaboration between academics and the UMWA. The association's collaborative spirit and forethought allowed the Ludlow Centennial Commission to think outside of Colorado and assisted the commission members as part of a broader national and international dialogue.

The members of the Ludlow Centennial Commemoration Commission were integral in this work, including Thomas Andrews, Robert (Bob) Butero, William Convery, Dawn DiPrince, Karin Larkin, Victoria Miller, Fawn-Amber

Montoya, Adam Morgan, Jonathan Rees, Dean Saitta, Maria Sanchez-Tucker, and Josephine Jones. They understood the importance and significance of this work but also the spirit of collaboration and respect; that collective commemoration and remembering was more important than the work of an individual. They assisted in creating a space where all voices and perspectives were heard, understood, and honored.

Special thanks to the following:

- The United Mine Workers of America and particularly Robert Butero for continued support and collaboration around researching and interpreting the history and archaeology of the strike of 1913–1914, the Ludlow Massacre, and the events before and after that shaped our history.
- Colorado State University–Pueblo, University of Colorado–Colorado Springs, and James Madison University for contributing funding and time that allowed us to share this work.
- Elaine Callas-Williams, representing the Assumption of the Theotokos, Greek Orthodox church in Denver, Colorado, and the support from Metropolitan Isaiah to host a memorial service on April 20, 2014.
- Carolyn Newman's portrayal as Mother Jones has kept the story of Ludlow alive in classrooms throughout southern Colorado. Her work at the Walsenburg Mining Museum has created a welcoming space for visitors. Her writing for the *Huerfano World Journal* has provided readers with a reminder about the history of the region.
- Sarah Deutsch's and Maria Montoya's publications on southern Colorado serve as a foundation for the importance of this region and its history. Their willingness to come to Colorado to speak to our communities is always met with enthusiasm. There is great excitement when historians from Duke University and New York University come to small towns in Colorado to share the importance of the history of this region to the nation.
- Linda Linville for her willingness to share her family's painful past with generations of school children and her dedication to see that the Costa family story lives on and adds to the "official histories."
- Frank Petrucci was the living embodiment of how the Ludlow Massacre continued to impact the victims of the massacre for generations. Many of the commission members had the opportunity to meet and interact

with Frank. We like to believe he was Mary Petrucci's reminder of what she had lost at Ludlow and a symbol of hope.

- We thank our partners and our children, for whom the Ludlow Tent Colony has become a regular topic of conversation, pilgrimage, and destination. Their support allows us to continue to tell the story around our kitchen tables to other children, our families, and our friends.

We envision this book as a continuation of the work of the many stewards of the history of the Ludlow Massacre. We encourage future authors to take up the telling of this story. It is through these texts and tellings that the story of the Ludlow Massacre continues to live on.

The Ludlow Massacre

KARIN LARKIN

Howard Zinn (2004) once stated that "anybody who read about the Ludlow Massacre, anybody who heard about it was bound to be affected by it." Nothing could better describe the impact this event has on the people who experience and learn this history. The southern Colorado coal strike resulting in the Ludlow Massacre was one of the most violent strikes in US history. The strike resulted in an estimated sixty-six deaths, including twelve children and two women, and an unknown number of wounded. The Ludlow Massacre was a shocking event with far-reaching effects because of the deaths of women and children. It galvanized US public opinion, turned the Rockefellers into national villains, and eventually came to symbolize the wave of industrial violence that led to the "progressive" era reforms in labor relations (Andrews 2008; Crawford 1995; Gitelman 1988). For those who have not heard of this horrific event, this prologue offers a very brief summary of the history. It is followed by a personal account of the lasting impacts on a family who lived and died at Ludlow.

https://doi.org/10.5876/9781646422289.c000a

The strike was initiated in the southern Colorado coalfields by the United Mine Workers of America (UMWA) to address a number of problems related to the coalmines and coal camps in the region. The southern coalfield of Colorado supplied high-grade bituminous coal that fueled the steel industry, which supplied rails for the expanding US railroad transportation network. In 1913, Colorado was the eighth largest coal-producing state in the United States (McGovern and Guttridge 1972). A few large corporations heavily industrialized and dominated the area. The largest of these was the Colorado Fuel and Iron Company (CF&I) based in Pueblo, Colorado. The company was founded through a merger of the Colorado Fuel Company with the Colorado Coal and Iron Company in 1892. In 1903, the Rockefeller Corporation purchased the controlling shares (Andrews 2008). According to the *Engineering and Mining Journal*, approximately 10 percent of Colorado's population depended on CF&I for their livelihood, and by 1913, the company employed about 14,000 miners (Whiteside 1990, 8–9).

CF&I wielded formidable political clout in early twentieth-century Colorado. The company had nearly total control over the politics of Las Animas and Huerfano Counties. Most of the miners lived in company towns and houses. They bought food and equipment at company stores and alcohol at company saloons. The doctors, clergy, schoolteachers, and law enforcement were all company employees. The entries to most of the camps were gated and guarded by deputized armed guards (Beshoar 1957; McGovern and Guttridge 1972). The fact that the company controlled the camps and the surrounding communities had important consequences. For example, the sheriff of Huerfano County, Jeff Farr, was under CF&I influence. In the years 1904 to 1914, his handpicked coroner's juries found the coal operators to blame in only one case of ninety-five deaths related to mining accidents (Whiteside 1990, 22). The Colorado coalmines were notoriously unsafe and listed among the most dangerous in the nation, second only to Utah. Miners died in Colorado coalmines at over twice the national average.

The United Mine Workers of America made its first appearance in the western states in 1900, with a strike in Gallup, New Mexico (Fox 1990). In 1903, the UMWA led its first strike in the Colorado coalfields. This strike was successful in the northern field but failed in the southern Colorado coalfield. In 1910, the northern operators refused to renew the contract, and the miners struck for the next three years (Andrews 2008). In September 1913, the

UMWA announced a strike in the southern Colorado field when the mine operators refused to meet a list of seven demands, which included:

1. Recognition of the union.
2. A 10 percent increase in wages on the tonnage rates. Each miner was paid by the ton of coal he mined, not by the hour.
3. An eight-hour workday.
4. Payment for "dead work." Since miners were only paid for the coal they mined, work such as shoring, timbering, and laying track was not paid work.
5. The right to elect their own checkweighmen. Miners suspected that they were being cheated at the scales, and they wanted a miner to check the weight at these scales.
6. The right to trade in any store, to choose their own boarding places, and to choose their own doctors.
7. Enforcement of Colorado mining laws and abolition of the company guard system.

The crucial demand was recognition of the union (McClurg 1959; McGovern and Guttridge 1972). Approximately 90 percent of the workforce went on strike, equaling 10,000–12,000 miners and their families. Those who lived in the coal camps were evicted, and on September 23, 1913, the striking families hauled their possessions through rain and snow to about a dozen tent sites rented in advance by the UMWA to house them (figure 0.1). The tent colonies were located at strategic spots covering the entrances to the canyons that contained the coal camps and mines to intercept strikebreakers. Ludlow, with about 200 tents that housed 1,200 miners and their families, was the largest of these colonies (Beshoar 1957; Foner 1980; McGovern and Guttridge 1972).

The operators reacted quickly by bringing in strikebreakers and the Baldwin-Felts Detective Agency from West Virginia. The operators initiated a campaign of harassment against the strikers. This took the form of high-powered searchlights playing over the tent colonies at night, murders, beatings, and the "Death Special"—an improvised armored car that drove near the tent colonies and periodically sprayed selected colonies with machine-gun fire. The purpose of this harassment was to goad the strikers into violent action (Foner 1980; McGovern and Guttridge 1972). Amid steadily escalating

FIGURE 0.1. Photograph of Ludlow Tent Colony, 1914. *Courtesy*, Denver Public Library Special Collections, call number Z-193.

violence in the coalfields and pressure from the operators, Colorado's governor Elias M. Ammons called out the Colorado National Guard, which arrived in the southern coalfield in October 1913.

After a brief lull in hostilities, militia commander General John Chase essentially declared martial law in the strike zone. Highlights of this period of unofficial martial law included the suspension of habeas corpus, mass jailing of strikers in "bullpens," a cavalry charge on a peaceful demonstration of miners' wives and children, the torture and beating of prisoners, and the demolition of the tent colony at Forbes. Chase also enlisted a considerable number of mine guards as militiamen (Foner 1980; McGovern and Guttridge 1972; Papanikolas 1982).

As the cost of supporting a force of 695 enlisted men and 397 officers in the field bankrupted the state, all but two of the militia companies were withdrawn after six months (McGovern and Guttridge 1972). The militia companies that remained were comprised primarily of mine guards.

On the morning of April 20, 1914, after the miners at Ludlow had celebrated Greek Orthodox Easter the day before, gunfire broke out at the Ludlow Tent Colony. While the exact circumstances that initiated the gun battle are uncertain, we know that three Colorado National Guardsmen approached the striking coalminers at the Ludlow Tent Colony demanding the release of a man they claimed was held by the strikers against his will. This demand provided cover for militia men to set up a machine gun on a nearby hill and station men along a railroad grade near the tent colony. Then the Colorado National Guard troops initiated a deadly attack on the striking coalminers and their families. While their families fled or hid in their canvas tents and cellars dug under those tents, the miners who were armed took positions to draw fire away from the colony. The militia sprayed the tent colony with machine-gun and rifle fire. By the end of the day, the force facing the miners consisted of 177 militia and two machine guns. In the evening, a conductor stopped his train on the tracks between the militia and the colony, which permitted most of the miners and their families to escape the tent colony. By 7:00 p.m., the tent colony was in flames and the militia was ransacking the colony. When the smoke cleared the following day, two women and eleven children were found suffocated in one of the tent cellars. Another twelve-year-old boy was found shot in the head. Louis Tikas and two other strike leaders, Charles Costa and Frank Rubino, were captured and executed (McGovern and Guttridge 1972; Papanikolas 1982). Costa's wife and children were also killed in the cellar. The known fatalities at the end of the day totaled twenty-five people, including three militiamen, one uninvolved passerby, the striking miners, and their families. The cellar where the two women and eleven children were asphyxiated and burned became infamous as the "Death Pit" (figure 0.2). The event became known as the Ludlow Massacre.

When news of the Ludlow Massacre got out, striking miners at the other colonies and sympathizers went to war. For ten days, they attacked and destroyed mines and fought pitched battles with mine guards and militia along a 40 mile front in a skirmish called the 10-Day War. The fighting ceased when Colorado's desperate governor asked for federal intervention in the form of federal troops. Following the massacre and the 10-Day War, the strike dragged on for another seven months, ultimately ending in defeat for the UMWA in December 1914 (Andrews 2008; McGovern and Guttridge 1972). After the strike ended, mass arrests of miners were made. There were 408 in total, with 332 indicted for murder—including the main strike leader, John Lawson. While these trials dragged on until 1920, all of the charges were eventually dismissed with most of those charged never coming to

FIGURE 0.2. Ludlow Death Pit, or "Hole where bodies of 11 children and 2 women were recovered after fire at Ludlow Tent Colony," taken by Lewis R. Dold, 1914. *Courtesy*, Denver Public Library Special Collections, call number X-60481.

REMEMBER LUDLOW!

Charles Costa and Family, all of Whom Were Assassinated by the Brigands of the "Law and Order" League

FIGURE 0.3. Illustration from *United Mine Workers Journal*, June 1914. *Courtesy,* United Mine Workers of America.

trial. In contrast, the Colorado National Guard court-martialed and quickly exonerated ten officers and twelve enlisted men for their roles in the Ludlow Massacre (McGovern and Guttridge 1972).

The wake of the Ludlow Massacre had wide-reaching rippling effects. First, the massacre of women and children proved to be a public relations

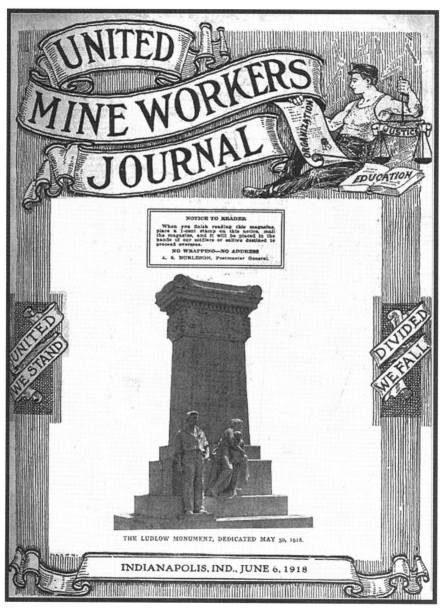

FIGURE 0.4. Illustration from the cover of *United Mine Workers Journal*, June 1918. *Courtesy*, United Mine Workers of America.

nightmare for CF&I and the Rockefellers (figure 0.3). This bad publicity prompted the Rockefeller company to initiate the first corporate public relations campaign in US history. The Rockefellers also instituted the Employee Representation Plan, otherwise known as the Rockefeller Plan, which provided a means for workers to air their grievances. This set in motion some basic improvements to the camps; however, most of the workers' original grievances were not addressed. Rockefeller's involvement in ending the cases against the miners was probably the result of his desire to cease discussion surrounding the massacre, which was tarnishing his name, as well as to create a more stable environment to initiate his new policies.

Another ripple effect involved the UMWA. They purchased the 40 acres containing and surrounding the site of the Ludlow colony. UMWA president John Phillip White officially proposed a memorial at the site during the 1916 convention, which passed. Later that year, several hundred coalminers met at the site of Ludlow and joined the union. Regular commemorations have been held at the site ever since that time. A monument to the fallen miners and their families was erected and dedicated by the UMWA on May 30, 1918 (UMWJ 1918) (figure 0.4). The "Death Pit" was preserved for people to walk into and pay homage to the women and children who sacrificed their lives for the cause.

In subsequent strikes in southern Colorado, the memory of Ludlow was invoked in mass meetings at the site. It also served as a safe ground for miners to meet. For the UMWA and other union members, Ludlow came to serve as an icon of industrial conflict and a rallying call. It was felt to mark a turning point in the struggle for union recognition. The United Steelworkers of America Union strikers from Pueblo marched to the site in 2001, illustrating the site's continued relevance.

The final ripple effect touched the families and descendants of the strike and massacre. The following account by Linda Linville, a descendant of Charles Costa and his family killed in the Ludlow Massacre, details this effect. Linda Linville's family moved to California to escape their heartbreak after Ludlow. In her personal essay, Linville talks about how she rediscovered this history and has spent her life studying and teaching it to another generation.

REFERENCES

Andrews, Thomas G. 2008. *Killing for Coal: America's Deadliest Labor War*. Cambridge, MA: Harvard University Press.

Beshoar, Barron B. 1957. *Out of the Depths: The Story of John R. Lawson, a Labor Leader*. Denver: Golden Bell.

Crawford, Margaret. 1995. *Building the Workingman's Paradise: The Design of American Company Towns*. London: Verso.

Foner, Philip S. 1980. *History of the Labor Movement in the United States, vol. 5: The AFL in the Progressive Era, 1910–1915*. New York: International Publishers.

Fox, Maier B. 1990. "United We Stand: The United Mine Workers of America, 1890–1990." International Union, United Mine Workers of America. Pamphlet.

Gitelman, Howard M. 1988. *Legacy of the Ludlow Massacre: A Chapter in American Industrial Relations*. Philadelphia: University of Pennsylvania Press.

McClurg, Donald. 1959. *Labor Organization in the Coal Mines of Colorado, 1878–1933*. Berkeley: University of California.

McGovern, George S., and Leonard F. Guttridge. 1972. *The Great Coalfield War*. Boston: Houghton Mifflin.

Papanikolas, Zeese. 1982. *Buried Unsung: Louis Tikas and the Ludlow Massacre*. Salt Lake City: University of Utah Press.

UMW. 1918. "Memorial Day at Ludlow." *United Mine Workers Journal* 6: 4.

Whiteside, James. 1990. *Regulating Danger: The Struggle for Mine Safety in the Rocky Mountain Coal Industry*. Lincoln: University of Nebraska Press.

Zinn, Howard. 2004. *You Can't Be Neutral on a Moving Train*. New York: First Run Features.

A Descendant's Story

LINDA LINVILLE

PROLOGUE

I was born and raised in California, but even as a child, I had a vague feeling that a mysterious distant place called Ludlow was lurking somewhere in the background, like a ghost. In the 1950s and 1960s, my large Sicilian family would gather at my grandparents' house in Los Angeles every Sunday for large family feasts. It was chaotic—my cousins and I running in and out of the house . . . my mother and her four sisters arguing over whether the pasta needed more anchovies . . . the three uncles and their brothers-in-law in the sunporch, sipping homemade wine and laughing over off-color stories . . . my grandfather sitting in his chair, his favorite western, *Hopalong Cassidy*, blaring on the TV.

After the heaviness of the midday meal, a stillness would fall over the house. The men would sit on the large porch for quiet companionship and keep watch over the neighborhood. My sated cousins and Grandpa would make their way to the sunporch couches for napping. The women, worn out from cleaning up the kitchen, would retire to the living room for coffee. I would

https://doi.org/10.5876/9781646422289.c000b

join them, feeling quite grown up with my mug of half-coffee, half-cream. It may have been during those times that I first heard snatches of conversations about a branch of the family that was left behind in Colorado—all five killed at Ludlow on April 20, 1914. When I was very young, my aunts shared only happy memories of their beloved aunt, uncle, and cousins. They laughed when they spoke of the jokes Uncle Charlie would play on them. Their eyes lit up whenever they mentioned Aunt Cedilena and her love for Charlie. They were proud that she was as "brave and fearless as any man." As they remembered their cousins, I visualized Lucy's blond curls bouncing as she ran the bases and her brother Onofrio's determined expression when he gripped the bat in anticipation of the pitch. I felt a strange closeness to these people who left the earth long before my entry. I knew them. We were bound by blood.

As I grew older, my questions about life in Colorado and what had happened at Ludlow became more insistent. I was eleven when my aunts and, to some extent, my grandmother became more willing to tell me about the nightmare the family had endured. They shared the story in bits and pieces, perhaps thinking it was too much for a child to handle. Thus, there are many questions that remain unanswered. I was the youngest grandchild, and by the time I was old enough to articulate more probing questions, the witnesses were gone.

Since that time, I have read numerous books and examined historical documents pertaining to Ludlow and the larger labor history, but they fail to address the personal element, how the trauma of Ludlow created ripples and waves in families such as mine.

I began to feel those repercussions the first time I set foot in Colorado when I was fifteen. It was summer, and my father's two-week vacation time was only three days away when my mother announced that she wanted to take a road trip to Colorado. My father, an easygoing guy, agreed and got down to the business of preparing the Ford Fairlane for the long drive. I was pleasantly surprised at Mama's sudden determination, as she was usually a long-term planner and was not very fond of travel. There was a sense of urgency about her desire. It would be her first and only journey back to the place of her birth and childhood. I didn't realize it at the time, but we were on a pilgrimage, and our destination was Ludlow.

It was a hurried trip along I-40. We made only one overnight stop in New Mexico and didn't check out any points of interest along the way. The car itself seemed hellbent on reaching Ludlow, or so it seemed to me. I sensed my mother's tension as we neared the site. She was uncharacteristically quiet as my father parked the car.

Upon exiting, we were met by a rush of hot, moist air. There was no sound except our footfalls over the brown weeds and scrub. I saw a dead bird on the ground. It was an oppressive, forbidding atmosphere. We stood before the monument, looking up at the three figures. None of us spoke. I glanced at my mother and saw that she was blinking back tears. The monument was larger and more lifelike than I expected. Relatives said the statues had been modeled after Charlie and Cedi, and I wondered if that were true or if the family only wanted to believe it to be so. We looked at the engraved names of those who had died in the massacre. My eyes fixed on the four names that were so familiar to me. I noticed with a degree of disappointment that Cedilena's and Onofrio's names were spelled incorrectly. I counted the names of children—there were eleven who never came close to reaching my own age of fifteen.

My father busied himself with loading the Brownie with film and began taking photos of the monument and the area. My mother, who was usually in charge of the camera, was oblivious to his activity. She seemed transfixed.

My father took my mother's arm as we walked over to the Death Pit where Cedilena and the children had been killed. A cloud suddenly obscured the sun, and it darkened, giving me an ominous feeling. My mother seemed spellbound as we peered down into the dark cemented hole. Somehow, I knew she would not descend the narrow steps with my father and me. She watched.

When we rejoined her, it seemed that out of nowhere a large black fly appeared and buzzed angrily in Mama's ear. No matter where she went, it followed her. She tried to swat it away, as did my father and I, but it would not stop its torment. The more she tried to get away from it, the louder and more insistent the buzzing, as if it were trying to chase her away.

Suddenly, she swayed back and forth and grabbed my father's arm. With a trembling voice, she told us she felt the ground thrusting upward beneath her feet, pushing her off balance. She had trouble standing. "We have to leave, my ancestors are telling me to go. They're trying to push me away from the blood in this ground . . . the evil." I realize now that my father, who had been driving for so long, must have been hoping to stretch his legs for a time, but he lovingly helped her into the car as she clung to him. I got into the back seat, shocked and fearful. I had never seen my matter-of-fact mother so shaken.

As we sped along the lonely highway, I thought about what it must have been like for Cedilena to be trapped in the cellar below the tent, at full-term pregnancy, with her children clinging to her—hearing the buzzing and cracking of bullets through the tent. . . . the sound of muffled screams of women and children outside the tent . . . the heavy thud of racing footsteps on the prairie ground above . . . the acrid odor of the smoke and fire engulfing the tent colony. I envisioned her in the corner of that ungodly black hole with her children pressed against her body. I wondered what her last words to Onofrio and Lucy were and if there was one horrific moment when she knew she and her children would die.

That road trip so many years ago may have been the beginning of my strong desire to learn more about Ludlow and the labor movement and to eventually become a teacher of US history. It left an indelible impression on me. My mother was a baby when the massacre occurred and only ten when the family left Colorado, and yet I realized how much that history, passed on to her by older relatives, had affected her.

I sensed that many other families must have been touched by the memory of Ludlow, yet it seemed that no one except my relatives knew anything about it. When you are very young, the historical event somehow doesn't seem real until you see it in print, in a substantial-looking hardcover book. I knew these stories were true, but it was a hidden history.

In my high school history class, I learned only about the great "captains of industry" who made our nation powerful and rich with rapid industrialization—no mention of unions, strikes, or immigrant workers. Our textbook lauded Rockefeller and Carnegie as "great humanitarians" with generous deeds of charity. One of my aunts told me otherwise—and quite emphatically—as we sat and enjoyed her homemade *cucidati* fig cookies one Sunday afternoon in the early 1960s. She was my oldest aunt, known for her sweet nature, never uttering an unkind word about anyone, let alone cussing. I had asked her about Ludlow and John D. Rockefeller, Jr. She remembered his presence in the coal camp during his public relations campaign after the massacre. Her voice rose when she related his attempt to "make nice" and dance with the Italian women. The veins on her neck bulged as she concluded her explanation. I paraphrase, but this is pretty close to what she said:

Rockefeller was a God-damn son-of-a-bitch. He thought he could put one over on us . . . that we would believe he knew nothing about what was going on in the coal camps. He thought we were stupid. We didn't want any part of it! This guy certainly wasn't the hero my teacher had been telling us about. I was beginning to understand that history depended on who was telling the story, and it was definitely the rich and powerful who had control of this one. My family's history, and the larger labor history, was being brushed under the rug, locked away. I wanted the story to be told.

THE STORY

My grandfather, Nicola Costa, and his younger brother, Charlie (Pasquale), were from a small village in Sicily, Palazzo Adriano. They came to America with their mother in 1893. Their father, Onofrio, had migrated five years before, finally saving enough money as a coalminer to finance their trip. Nicola was twelve and Charlie almost ten when they arrived. Shortly thereafter, the boys joined their father in the coalmines of southern Colorado.

When they reached adulthood, marriages were arranged. Nicola wed Luigia in 1902, one month after she arrived from Bisacquino at the age of seventeen. In 1905, Charlie married Adelina Mastri, a woman from the mountain village of Faeto in Puglia. She had arrived in America in 1901 with her mother and brother; her father had been working in the mines for years. My family called her "Delina," but she was known as "Cedi" or "Cedilena" by friends.

Nicola and Charlie believed the stories they had heard in Sicily that the streets of America were paved with gold, that everyone had an equal opportunity for a good life. They had great hope. However, they soon found that they and the three siblings born in America were trapped in a form of industrial slavery. They were paid in scrip, making it mandatory to buy wares at the company store. Earnings were dictated by the amount of coal they hauled out, not by hours worked, and they were often cheated at the scales. They lived in company houses with paper-thin walls and leaky roofs that failed to keep the chilly wind and snow outside. I heard many family stories about accidents involving runaway mine cars, collapsing shafts, fires, and tragic explosions. My grandmother and Cedi would hear the alarm that signaled a mining disaster and rush out to wait at the gate, praying that their husbands would emerge alive. Many of the accidents could have been prevented had the mine inspection law been enforced. Also, the company refused to pay the miners for "dead work"—safety measures, such as reinforcing the mine shafts. Owners cared only about getting the coal out as cheaply and quickly as possible. Two stories of mining accidents stand out in my memory.

There was a cave-in, and my grandfather was trapped underground for hours. My grandmother was traumatized as she waited. When he was brought out alive, she was relieved and thankful. However, he was in tremendous pain; his leg was broken. The company doctor prepared to amputate. Luigia burst into the railroad hospital car and argued with the insistent doctor as he proceeded to prepare Nicola for surgery. I can imagine her fury—she had deep, dark eyes that, when angry, seemed to bore a hole through your being. She called him a "butcher" and prevented him from going forward. Enlisting the help of friends, she somehow managed to get Nicola onto the train bound for a town where there was an Italian doctor. She begged him to save her husband's leg, telling him they had five children who would starve if their father could not work. The doctor set the broken leg, and it healed in a shorter time than expected. It galls me when I think about the cavalier attitude of the company doctor and how my grandfather could have been maimed for life under such company "care." It was indeed true that the company valued its mules more than the men, who were easily replaced by other poor immigrants desperate for work. I wonder how many unnecessary amputations were done. During the time Nicola was recuperating and couldn't work, his brothers took care of the family, for there was no such thing as workmen's compensation while convalescing. The company said the men "assumed the risk" when they agreed to go underground and claimed the accidents were the miners' fault. They were "off the hook" from any semblance of responsibility, financial or moral.

Another mining accident came to my attention because of my childhood curiosity over a framed picture on my grandparents' bedroom wall. I was drawn to the mysterious painting of a beautiful lady in a white gown. She was holding a tray of eyeballs, seeming to extend them to the viewer. I was afraid to look at it for very long. I asked my mother about it, and she told me it was Santa Lucia, the saint who protected eyes and who had saved Grandpa's. A mineshaft he was working in collapsed, and he was hit on the head with such force that it knocked him out. When he gained consciousness, he was blind. The doctor held out no hope of recovery.

My grandmother prayed to Santa Lucia for weeks, promising that she would honor the saint's day, December 13, for the rest of her life if her husband's vision was restored. One morning, he opened his eyes and, although his vision was blurry, he could see. Each day his vision improved more, and it eventually returned to normal. Luigia called the restoration of his eyesight "the miracle of Santa Lucia." She named her fourth daughter after the saint and kept her side of the bargain by celebrating the saint's feast day until she was no longer able to physically handle the preparations. However, Santa Lucia's picture remained in place until her death—a constant reminder of life in Colorado, as well as a tribute to the saint.

Nicola and Charlie had endured the hardships of mining for twenty years by the time the United Mine Workers of America (UMWA) began recruiting members. The four Costa brothers realized they had no recourse to gain their rights and dignity as human beings except to unionize. The coal companies reigned supreme over the state government and most of the press.

Charlie became a union organizer in the Aguilar area. Cedi was his partner in the struggle. My aunts had vivid memories of Saturday night parties when the miners' families would gather for music and dancing. They remembered my grandmother dancing the tarantella, something I couldn't picture as a kid. There was a dance band, and Charlie played the harmonica. I sensed their pride as they reminisced about how everyone pitched in, bringing food to drop into the big pot on the fire—mostly beans, potatoes, macaroni. They wondered if their childhood memories of how delicious the taste and savory the aroma were had more to do with how hungry they might have been.

As children, they hadn't realized that the parties were used to recruit union members. Charlie would talk union to the men, while Cedi encouraged the women to support their husbands in the fight to make better lives for their families. With unity, the miners renewed their hope in the promise of America.

One aunt remembered the excitement in the air when Mother Jones spoke so passionately in Trinidad; she remembered the roaring applause and boisterous, happy shouting. There was a UMWA convention in town, and she was proud that Charlie was one of the delegates who made a speech detailing the miners' grievances.

The company refused to negotiate with the union, so the delegates voted to call a strike. When it began on September 23, 1913, the miners were evicted from the company houses. Union tents became their homes, and the people in the tent colony became their family. It is an inspiring story of different immigrant and ethnic groups overcoming language barriers and prejudices to form a community with a shared goal.

Cedi and Charlie were tough and resilient. I remember snatches of family conversations about Cedi's defiance of the mine guards, such as using a broom to shoo a guard out of her tent, cursing him loudly as she chased him away. Aunt Josephine related, with a degree of awe, that Cedi carried a pistol for protection anytime she left the colony. She remembered Cedi's admiration of Mother Jones and her belief that the women had a responsibility to fight as hard as the men. Cedi was "no shrinking violet," and Charlie was proud of his wife's strength. However, my grandmother became increasingly concerned that Cedilena was taking too big a risk with her activism. Uppermost was protection of family.

The strike had gone on for almost seven months, with no end in sight. The situation was becoming more tense and violent. Aunt Josephine described seeing two bodies hanging from a tree outside the colony. She was horrified as she recognized a Mexican boy she knew from school and his father. They had been traveling in a horse-drawn cart piled with wood. Militiamen stopped them and searched the cart. Underneath the wood, they found rifles that were bound for the tent colony. They shot the boy and his father and hanged their bodies as a warning to anyone giving aid to the strikers. My aunt had tears in her eyes as she related how horrifying this was—she had nightmares that she would be killed.

Luigia was convinced that she needed to take action to protect her family. When the militia had first arrived, she was relieved, thinking they were there to protect the strikers, but she soon realized that many were thugs hired by the company owners to break the strike by any means necessary—even if it meant killing children.

She had a premonition that all hell would soon break out. Fearing the boiling point was near and the militia would attack, she resolved to leave the area with her five daughters, but first she had to convince her sister-in-law to come with her. She couldn't leave Cedi and the children behind (figure 0.5). Just two weeks before, Cedi had yet another confrontation with a militiaman, and with Charlie a union leader, she was afraid her sister-in-law would be targeted. Cedi was months along in her pregnancy—her delivery time was near. Charlie and Cedi had lost their youngest son, Tony, only last August.

FIGURE 0.5. Costa family, ca. 1914. *Courtesy*, Linda Linville.

The poor baby was only two years old when he was struck with fever and died. The family could not bear another loss.

My determined, stern grandmother made her way to Cedi's tent. She announced that they would go to a cousin's ranch where it was safe and commanded Cedi to round up the children and pack a bag. Cedi refused in no uncertain terms—she would not leave. Luigia then tried to persuade her to stay at the ranch just until she gave birth; then she could return. Cedi countered with the argument that there were midwives in the colony—babies were being delivered with no problems. They argued back and forth until Luigia realized she would never leave Charlie. In desperation, she asked Cedi to allow Lucy and Onofrio to come with her. Cedi wouldn't hear of it, saying the union was their family, and they had to stay united and strong. She and the children would remain with Charlie. She was not going to abandon the cause; she would not give in to fear and would fight for the America she had been promised—that was how she would "protect her family." Luigia gave up. That was the last time she saw her sister-in-law alive.

The next day, Luigia and her five daughters boarded the train at the Trinidad depot. Aunt Angie had vivid memories of that train ride. The train stopped abruptly at some point in the journey. As she looked out the window, she saw soldiers with rifles surrounding the train. Luigia stiffened as she roughly grabbed Angie's hand and jerked her body forward. In a commanding whisper, she forbade her daughters to look out the window. My aunt couldn't say how long the train was stopped, but it seemed like time stood still. Everything—even breath—seemed suspended in the train; the fear was palpable. All they heard were the muffled sounds of soldiers' gruff voices outside. They were rooted to the seats, facing forward, not daring to steal a glance outside. Finally, the train started to move; only then did Luigia's tense body soften. She dropped Angie's hand. It took a while for the red marks on her wrist to disappear. My grandmother and her children would escape the carnage.

The violence my grandmother had predicted arrived shortly after her departure, on April 20, 1914. Charlie was killed at age 31, shot in the head. As bullets flew over the tents, he was one of the men running out of the colony in the hope of drawing fire away from the women and children. On that same day, Cedilena was killed in the cellar beneath the tent. She was 27. Onofrio (age 6) and his sister Lucy (age 4) died as they clung to their mother in that black hole. The death of the unnamed infant has gone unacknowledged for over 100 years (see figures 0.5 and 0.6). There is no death certificate or mention in the official record, not even in the cemetery's record book. The infant was buried in the coffin with Cedilena. The entire family—all five were killed. Unimaginable grief. This was not the American dream; it was a nightmare.

The next time my grandparents saw Cedilena, Charlie, and the children was in the Trinidad mortuary, when they had to identify the bodies. Cedilena's body had been bayoneted. The death certificate reports asphyxiation as the cause of death, but there is nothing in the official record about the wounds. Interviews with eyewitnesses tell a different story. Victor Bazanelle, in an interview conducted by Eric Margolis in 1976, talks emotionally about Cedilena's pregnancy and the bayonet wounds. I ask myself if the bayonet wounds were the cause of her death—her murder—or was her body mutilated after she died? The bodies were in the Death Pit for three days before even the Red Cross was allowed to recover them. The National Guard made the area off-limits. Why? I am convinced that there was much to hide that has never come to light—these deaths were not "accidental." It has been argued that it's not true if it does not appear in the official record of the time. I can't accept the validity of that argument—at the time, the official record was controlled by a corrupt system that was on a mission to whitewash as much of the tragedy as was possible. I believe the eyewitnesses and the oral histories left behind.

My grandfather went back to work in the mines after the strike ended in December 1914. He had no other option, and his family was growing. My grandparents' first son and sixth child was born on November 13, 1914. They named him "Pasquale" and called him "Charlie" to honor the memory of my grandfather's brother.

Cedilena's family left Colorado sometime in the late 1920s. Her parents, Antonio and Raphaela Mastri, had four children; when they left, they had only one, Joe. Peter died in a mining accident at age 18 in 1911, and August died of "carditis" at age 16 in 1921. It is painful to consider the magnitude of their loss: their daughter, two sons, four grandchildren, and a son-in-law within a span of ten years. They moved to Connecticut and never spoke about their lives in Colorado again. I searched for and found the descendants of Cedilena's brother Joe. They knew nothing of their family's time in the coalfields of Colorado, had never heard of Ludlow and their brave great-aunt, Cedilena. I was sad that Cedilena's life had been erased from her family's memory. Once I found them, I had imagined that we would share stories about Ludlow and Cedi. I was eager to hear what history had been passed down to them. I wanted her family to know her and to remember. However, after my initial disappointment, I understood that her parents and Joe did what was necessary to cope with the trauma and pain of remembering such violence and loss. They had to leave her behind.

After the massacre, my grandmother was determined to save enough money to get out of Colorado—everything around them was a reminder of what they had lost, and Nicola's health was declining. She pinched every penny for nine years. In 1923, they were finally able to move to Los Angeles and tried to leave the pain of Ludlow behind, but it was impossible. The grief and loss followed them. It welled up like waves that ebb and flow, never disappearing no matter the distance.

EPILOGUE

After the family's witnesses were gone, I felt alone in my closeness to Ludlow. I wanted to know more. So many questions were unanswered. Relatives dispersed geographically; we lost touch. I wondered if anyone would remember Charlie's family and what they sacrificed. I passed the history of Ludlow along to my high school students and some of my younger relatives, but it wasn't until I discovered a community in Colorado that I renewed my hope that their story, and the larger labor history, would be preserved and honored.

In 1999 a friend sent me information about a week-long teachers' seminar on coal mining history to be held at Trinidad State Junior College. I had to go, and luckily my principal okayed the time off for a trip to Colorado. It was at this seminar that I met individuals who were as interested in the history and its resonance as I was. I learned a great deal about the historical context from historians and scholars. I witnessed archaeologists and their students digging up artifacts that revealed details of the miners' daily lives in the Ludlow Tent Colony. I sat in a Trinidad café, drinking coffee and talking to locals about their family histories, sharing mine as well. It was during the lunch break one day that Randy McGuire, a professor of archaeology at Binghamton University, suggested we drive to the Trinidad Catholic Cemetery to find the Costa gravesite. We went to the office and looked at the handwritten record book from April 1914. I felt a chill when I saw their names. We found the gravesite, but it was unmarked, the union's wooden crosses disintegrating after so many years. When I arrived home in California, a cousin and I

IN LOVING MEMORY OF THE
COSTA FAMILY
WHO LOST THEIR LIVES
IN THE LUDLOW MASSACRE
APRIL 20, 1914
CHARLIE COSTA AGE 31
CEDELINA COSTA AGE 27
LUCY COSTA AGE 4
ONOFRIO COSTA AGE 6
AND BABY TONY WHO DIED
BEFORE THE MASSACRE

THEIR COURAGE WILL LIVE
IN OUR HEARTS FOREVER

FIGURE 0.6. New Costa family grave marker located in Trinidad, Colorado. *Courtesy*, Linda Linville.

arranged to have a permanent marker installed for the Costa family (figure 0.6). I don't know why I had never thought of finding their gravesite, and I have always been grateful to Dr. McGuire for his suggestion, for caring.

I have returned to southern Colorado many times since 1999, visiting mining museums, attending the annual Ludlow commemorative events, listening to lectures, panel discussions, musical performances. I have had the pleasure of meeting a host of people from all over the world—historians, writers, professors, archaeologists, union leaders and members, musicians, playwrights, artists, curators, filmmakers, and many others—who care about the story of Ludlow and bring it to a wider audience in a variety of creative ways.

I owe a big debt of gratitude to the United Mine Workers of America and the many people in the state of Colorado who have worked tirelessly to preserve the memory of Ludlow and to raise public awareness of its relevance to issues of today. I feel a strange and wonderful kinship with this community.

I am most grateful to my family for sharing their stories of Ludlow, wanting me to know about what happened there, to remember Charlie and Cedi, and to honor the memory. That precious gift, that legacy, shaped my sense of identity and continuity with those who preceded me. It inspired my quest to learn more about hidden histories and shaped who I am and how I look at world events. Ludlow makes us remember that our rights were not freely given. They were won at great cost by the people who came before us. Perhaps we honor them best by remaining ever-vigilant in the protection of the rights for which they fought so bravely.

COMMUNITIES OF LUDLOW

1

Commemorating the Ludlow Massacre

The Power of Collaborative Scholarship and Stewardship

KARIN LARKIN AND FAWN-AMBER MONTOYA

The story of the Ludlow Massacre has traditionally been told as a tragedy of striking miners that occurred in the western United States during a turbulent time in US labor relations. It is much more than that. The Ludlow Massacre comprises the story of perseverance, solidarity, community, memory, collaboration, and stewardship that spans over a century. It relates the tale of a diverse community that rallied together to keep this history alive. The story is as much about place, tragedy, and the "American Dream" as it is of resilience and cooperation. It features working-class men, women, immigrant groups, and children, as well as scholars, artists, authors, museum professionals, and lawmakers. Ultimately, this is a tale of triumph. The story did not end with the cessation of the strike; instead, its aftermath and influence continues over a hundred years after the events. This longevity illustrates that Ludlow is a story of stewardship, collaborative scholarship, and social memory. This book highlights these stories through the work of the Ludlow Centennial Commemoration Commission (the Commission). The collective chapters relate this tale of collaborative stewardship around the memory

https://doi.org/10.5876/9781646422289.c001

and story of Ludlow and illustrate how this collaborative stewardship has transformed public scholarship.

REMEMBERING THE LUDLOW MASSACRE

The history and impact of the Ludlow Massacre continue because people and stakeholders have invested time and effort into keeping this history alive and relevant. Although the strike ended in an apparent defeat for the United Mine Workers of America (UMWA), the miners won some short-term battles and the long-term war. The state of Colorado sought to end the strike, the company tried to ignore the demands of the strikers, and the Colorado National Guard wanted to erase the blight the massacre left on its record. However, the collective actions of stewards have created a narrative of the endurance, sacrifice, and suffering of strikers and their families that not only persists but has been retold and remembered for generations.

Like the strike and massacre itself, the memory of this tale has been fraught with adversity and oppression. The state of Colorado chose not to accept or to remember this embarrassing, complicated, and upsetting episode in history. How do you tell an audience of schoolchildren learning Colorado history that their state leadership was complicit in the deaths of innocent mothers and children in collaboration with the Colorado National Guard? These institutions are supposed to protect Colorado's citizens, not sit idly by while state-sanctioned militia and business leaders terrorized workers and their families. Their lack of action allowed the circumstances that led up to the Ludlow Massacre. Despite the embarrassing history surrounding the Ludlow Massacre, remembering this past allows us to see how it resonates with issues in contemporary society.

For over 100 years, people have made pilgrimages to the Ludlow Massacre Memorial site to remember the dead, to place themselves within a larger narrative of labor history both past and present, and to learn about what occurred there. The story of the Ludlow Massacre has survived because families and advocates from throughout the United States and around the world have shared their stories.

There are many stewards of the memory of the Ludlow Massacre. The United Mine Workers of America is an important steward and the biggest advocate of the memory of this story. The UMWA's actions and stewardship have ensured that there is a place to commemorate. The UMWA owns and maintains the site of the massacre, erected and cares for a monument commemorating the event, and has hosted services to facilitate memory making for over a hundred years. It is the main steward. But there are many others. Families and lineal descendants also act as stewards, sharing their stories. Some of these stories recall loved ones who lived in southern Colorado and worked in the mines; some relate their connection to the strikers; still others lost loved ones in the struggle for their rights. Finally, scholars have also acted as stewards for decades. Scholars have studied the events leading up to, during, and after the strike and massacre to put them into a context that can be understood today. These various stewards have collaborated to guard the history and memory of the event.

COLLABORATION AND STEWARDSHIP

Collaborative scholarship and stewardship are intimately linked. To be good stewards, scholars should collaborate with various stakeholders, particularly descendant communities. In recent years, scholars have been increasingly practicing public scholarship that engages descendant communities and other stakeholders in new and increasingly collaborative ways. Collaboration simply means the act of working together, but the process can be much more challenging. For scholars to collaborate with descendant communities or other stakeholders, they must be flexible, open to alternative ideas, research agendas, and methodologies. Despite these challenges, more scholars are practicing collaborative scholarship. Chip Colwell-Chanthaphonh and T. J. Ferguson (2008, 1) edited a volume on collaboration in museums and archaeological practice in which they describe collaboration as "a global phenomenon." They note, "Collaboration is increasingly seen as a way for scholars to become involved with local stakeholders, moving beyond confrontational claims over who 'owns' the past while maintaining the principles of scientific inquiry. Collaboration is now seen as an explicit methodological model" (Colwell-Chanthaphonh and Ferguson 2008, 1). While they are referring specifically to anthropology museums and archaeology, the concept and methodological model apply to a multitude of disciplines and scholarly approaches.

Local stakeholders take a variety of forms, from descendent communities to scholars to interested members of the public. In the case of the Ludlow

Massacre, these stakeholders include a wide range of interested parties, but perhaps the most invested are the United Mine Workers of America and the lineal descendants of the strike and massacre. To collaborate with these descendant communities, scholars had to first establish a relationship that embodied a model in which they worked with these communities to achieve a common goal.

Collaboration in practice can take many forms, employ a wide range of strategies, and have varying degrees of success. These new relationships have exposed the complications that can arise over who controls the narratives of the past and who should be allowed the authority to construct narratives. When issues of control are coupled with complexities around the validity of these narratives, offered by both scholars and descendants, tensions increase. Recently, scholars in multiple disciplines have begun to explore how to share this authority and develop richer, more nuanced, and balanced interpretations to share with the various publics (see, for example, Reason and Bradbury 2012; Colwell-Chanthaphonh and Ferguson 2008; Peers and Brown 2003; Ames 1992; Smith 2012; Harrison 1992; Limerick, Cowell, and Collinge 2009; Mallon 2012). Colwell-Chanthaphonh and Ferguson (2008, 1) recognize collaboration as a continuum that ranges "from merely communicating research to descendant communities to a genuine synergy where the contributions of community members and scholars create a positive result that could not be achieved without joining efforts." Synergistic collaboration necessitates a willingness to be open, actively listen, and advocate for stewardship. Synergistic collaboration also requires humility and diplomacy.

Creating this type of collaboration involves time and trust to develop truly two-way relationships. The scholars who worked on the statewide commemoration committee and later on the Commission began developing relationships with the various stakeholders and descendant communities decades before the 100-year anniversary commemoration planning began. The Commission would not have been possible without these already established collaborative relationships. The humble, grassroots origins of the Commission foregrounded the interests and goals of these stakeholders and worked closely with them to create meaningful commemoration events. In this way, the work of the Ludlow Centennial Commemoration Commission falls on the synergistic end of the collaboration continuum. This volume outlines the synergy created by the collaborative efforts of the various stewards of Ludlow.

ESTABLISHING COLLABORATIVE RELATIONSHIPS

Relationship building around the scholarship of the Ludlow Massacre began decades before the establishment of the Commission. Scholars from various disciplines and institutions began creating relationships with the United Mine Workers of America and lineal descendants to embark on projects that ultimately contributed to the commemorative events. While the types of projects range from scholarly research to public outreach, we focus on the importance of two of these efforts: the archaeological excavations undertaken by the Colorado Coalfield War Archaeological Project (CCWAP) and research projects by historians that ultimately led to a National Historic Landmark nomination of the site. These two projects formed the foundation of the collaborative relationships that led to the development of the Commission.

The Colorado Coalfield War Archaeological Project

The Colorado Coalfield War Archaeological Project (CCWAP) formed to focus an archaeological lens on the social and material conditions of laborers and their families in the southern Colorado coalfields during a turbulent time of widespread industrial growth and corporate imperialism in America. The CCWAP itself began as a collaboration among three academic institutions (the University of Denver, SUNY Binghamton, and Fort Lewis College) and the United Mine Workers of America (UMWA). The three principal investigators—Dean Saitta, Randall McGuire, and Philip Duke—spent two years planning the project and establishing a working relationship with the UMWA prior to beginning any archaeological work. The first step was to establish that the project leaders and participants were sympathetic to and supportive of the goals of the union, since they would need to collaborate with the UMWA and unionized workers in southern Colorado (McGuire and Larkin 2009). The relationship with the UMWA spanned all levels, from the Local 9856 to the Regional District 22 (now Region 4) up through the national level. We would like to specifically mention several people who facilitated the collaborative efforts. First, Michael and Yolanda Romero, leaders of the Local 9856 and its Women's Auxiliary, were instrumental in setting up the project. The Romeros were union activists, caretakers to the site, and heavily involved in the annual memorial service. At the Regional District 22 level (now Region 4), Robert Butero facilitated access to the site, supported the archaeological project in a number of ways, and invited project leaders to speak at annual memorial services. In forming this collaboration, project archaeologists began a multi-year quest to study the material culture of class conflict associated with industrial America in a collaborative and inclusive way. All the archaeologists on this project were interested in moving away from official histories and looking more deeply into the impacts of this history on working-class men, women, and children. Project archaeologists undertook excavation at the Ludlow Tent Colony site and the Colorado Fuel & Iron coal company camp at Berwind to dig into the daily lives of these workers and explore their material realities. These excavations were funded by a series of State Historical Fund grants through History Colorado (then the Colorado Historical Society).

The project was designed to foster collaboration, address past inequities in representation, and affect contemporary practice and policy. Dean Saitta (2007) has called the project an "emancipatory archaeology." In doing so, he alludes to the collaborative work project archaeologists have attempted with the descendant communities. Project archaeologists were interested in using archaeology to examine a very different aspect of industrialization: the social, political, and economic conditions surrounding labor unrest; the efficacy of the collective action of multiple social and ethnic groups that resulted in the strike; and the strike's impact on the people who participated. In other words, the CCWAP sought to critically examine the material conditions surrounding social and economic inequality, the impact of collective action on the dominant forces of capital, and the economic impact of the strike on everyday life using the archaeology of this labor strike. The project resulted in numerous academic articles, two books, a mock trial program for high school students, various museum exhibits, interpretive signage at the Ludlow Tent Colony and Massacre site, dozens of public presentations, invitations to participate in annual memorial services, a digital atlas, a website, teachers' workshops and lesson plans, a traveling trunk, and the continued care of the collections through a Memorandum of Understanding (MOU) between the Department of Anthropology at the University of Colorado at Colorado Springs and the UMWA. These are discussed further in chapter 5. The collaboration of the CCWAP and the UMWA resulted in a Stephen H. Hart award for historic preservation from History Colorado in 2013. The

Ludlow Collective (the group of archaeologists who have worked on the project over the years) spent years unearthing the remnants and daily lives of those who had engaged in the 1913–1914 strike. The CCWAP began with the goal of practicing a public archaeology that was very successful and continues today (Duke and Saitta 2009).

National Historic Landmark

An act of vandalism to the monument set a foundation on which to build a National Historic Landmark nomination. In the spring of 2003, vandals desecrated the Ludlow Tent Colony site. They severed the heads of the man and woman and removed one arm and a vase from the monument (figure 1.1). This desecration became national news. The Labor and Working-Class History Association (LAWCHA) responded by forming an ad-hoc committee to prepare the paperwork for the Ludlow Tent Colony to be designated a National Historic Landmark. In January 2004, the president of the organization, James (Jim) Green, appointed Elizabeth Jameson and Zaragosa Vargas to co-chair this committee. The committee worked closely to establish a relationship with UMWA leaders Robert (Bob) Butero and President Cecil Roberts. In addition, community members, labor organizers, and academics contacted their elected leaders to support this designation. The nomination relied heavily on historical documents, the work of historians related to the significance of the site, and the archaeological investigations of the CCWAP. Legislation was passed and on June 28, 2009, the site was designated a National Historic Landmark. The work of the LAWCHA in collaboration with the CCWAP established a model of collaboration for how academics could engage with various stakeholders and elected officials throughout the United States to enact legislation. For more information on this process, see Green and Jameson (2009).

The establishment of the Ludlow Centennial Commemoration Commission was possible because of these previously formed relationships through the archaeological project and the successful National Historic Landmark nomination. Because these relationships had been maintained, it was easy to approach the UMWA about becoming involved in the commemorative events. The scholarly efforts tied to both the LAWCHA and the CCWAP resulted in tangible results related to stewardship but also created lasting

FIGURE 1.1. Desecrated Ludlow Memorial Monument. *Courtesy*, Randall McGuire.

connections between the stakeholders. The relationships built during these projects paved the way to partner with the UMWA in commemorating the centennial anniversary of the Ludlow Massacre. In addition, the site's National Historic Landmark status provided the historical credibility needed to allow the governor to declare a commission to commemorate the event.

From Collaboration to Partnership

The collaborative spirit begun during the previously mentioned projects continued among scholars throughout the state of Colorado, which, in turn, sparked conversations around the 100-year anniversary. These various groups joined together with community members to form a grassroots committee dedicated to commemorating the anniversary. The original grassroots committee formed to commemorate the centennial anniversary of the Ludlow Massacre began meeting and planning in 2012. Committee members organically assembled from interested stakeholders and community members throughout southern Colorado. Each member of the committee (and later Commission) had an established relationship with the stakeholders or the history surrounding the Ludlow Massacre. Many of those relationships initially involved collaboration with the United Mine Workers of America as the main steward of the site and history and expanded with the National Historic Landmark designation efforts. These community members and stakeholders self-selected to partner with the UMWA and each other in creating a ceremony fitting for the 100th anniversary and spreading information about the Ludlow Massacre and the upcoming anniversary. Each came with ideas based on their individual expertise and experiences, and the word spread. Every participant and group who was interested in participating in some way contributed to the generation of commemoration programming. Participants' interests ranged from sponsoring an event to creating public programs to developing exhibits to supporting other groups in doing those things.

At the beginning of these conversations, there were numerous meetings during which each member of the committee shared their expertise, their personal experiences with telling the history, and the creation of relationships. This communal sharing both strengthened long-standing relationships and forged new ones. The structure and inclusiveness practiced in the grassroots committee and during the work of the Commission transformed these collaborative relationships into a true partnership focused on sharing the narratives. All partners united with the common objective of advancing the descendant communities' messages and goals. Everyone in the room brought their own expertise, all of which meshed to create a strong foundation for a year-long series of commemorations. Robert Butero was at many of these meetings representing the UMWA and openly listened to and supported this wide range of suggestions and ideas. However, ultimately, it was the UMWA's interests and goals of keeping the memory and importance of the Ludlow Massacre alive that drove the discussion.

For over a century, the UMWA has been doing commemorative work during its annual remembrances. The UMWA, through its stewardship of the site—whether by the national leadership, regional leaders, or local coalminers and their families—has allowed visitors and scholars to freely visit the site. During the memorial events, the UMWA forged and strengthened relationships within working communities in southern Colorado and beyond and built a legacy that has lasted over 100 years. Their spirit of inclusion and cooperation has welcomed scholars of all disciplines from all over the world. The annual memorials feature speakers, musicians, politicians, descendants, and scholars who speak about the impact of the massacre in modern times. The event is open to the public at no cost and concludes with a barbeque sponsored by the UMWA in the spirit of commensality. This event has created a community that embraces a collective consciousness of that history, which continues to be told, remembered, and made relevant to contemporary society.

THE LUDLOW CENTENNIAL COMMEMORATION COMMISSION

The model of inclusiveness adopted by the original grassroots committee informed the approach and practice of the Commission. The Commission grew out of this grassroots, informal statewide committee, which had been meeting since the summer of 2012. The committee included an eclectic mix of union representatives, public historians, artists, archaeologists, museum personnel, and descendants who felt this anniversary was the ideal time to reignite interest in this often ignored epoch in Colorado history. It was also a committee of people who had worked on academic scholarship about the Ludlow Massacre for a much longer time. The committee offered an open forum to consider a wide variety of ideas on how to commemorate the 100-year anniversary of the strike and massacre in southern Colorado. Two committee members, Fawn-Amber Montoya and Dawn DiPrince, lobbied their state representative, Angela Giron, to make this informal committee a formal commission (figure 1.2). They succeeded. In 2013, John Hickenlooper, governor of the state of Colorado, appointed the Ludlow Massacre Centennial Commemoration Commission.

FIGURE 1.2. Commission advocates (*left to right*): Angela Giron, Dawn DiPrince, and Romaine Pacheco. *Courtesy*, Dawn DiPrince.

A diverse group comprised the twelve appointed members of the commission: Thomas Andrews, Robert (Bob) Butero, William Convery, Dawn DiPrince, Josephine Jones, Karin Larkin, Victoria Miller, Fawn-Amber Montoya, Adam Morgan, Jonathan Rees, Dean Saitta, and Maria Sanchez-Tucker. Robert (Bob) Butero represented the United Mine Workers of America as regional director. Dean Saitta and Karin Larkin were part of the archaeological project to excavate the Ludlow Tent Colony site. Karin Larkin with Randall McGuire edited a volume titled *Archaeology of Class War: The Colorado Coalfield Strike of 1913–1914* on the research produced by these excavations. Historian Thomas Andrews, author of *Killing for Coal*, spent years researching the history of the massacre and how the social, natural, and political environment impacted it. Historian Jonathan Rees studied the impact of the massacre on John D. Rockefeller's creation of an Employee Representation Plan. Victoria Miller and Maria Sanchez-Tucker worked at the Bessemer Historical Society (now Steelworks Center of the West), the nonprofit organization that houses the archives of the Colorado Fuel and Iron (CF&I) Company. The Bessemer Historical Society was formed in 2000 to preserve the buildings and archives of CF&I. The Steelworks Center of the West opened its doors in 2007 as the interpretive center for the archives. It now acts as a steward, using its archives and collections to tell the story of the CF&I. Adam Morgan, a historian for the Colorado National Guard, researched and shared the perspective of what the National Guard learned after the Ludlow Massacre. Dawn DiPrince, as curator of El Pueblo History Museum, worked with History Colorado to create an exhibit of the children of Ludlow at the museum. Historian Fawn-Amber Montoya edited the book *Making an American Workforce: The Rockefellers and the Legacy of Ludlow* and studied the impact of the Ludlow Massacre on labor relations. William Convery spoke about the impact of the Ludlow Massacre in the state of Colorado in presentations and documentary appearances in his role as Colorado's state historian from 2008 to 2015. Josephine Jones's experience facilitating humanities programming throughout the state for Colorado Humanities created opportunities for the Commission to better enable statewide programming. Each of these commission members brought a different perspective, area of expertise, and representation to the commemoration planning.

Of the commission members, the one with the most lived experience with coal mining and the Ludlow Massacre memorial events was Robert (Bob) Butero. Butero has been the UMWA District 4 representative for more than twenty-three years. He has organized the annual events at the Ludlow Massacre site for over two decades. Bob has overseen the physical site, approved the archaeological digs, identified speakers for memorial events, presented the UMWA's perspective of this history to the public, and kept the UMWA and communities of southern Colorado aware of anything related to the massacre site. His work and that of other UMWA representatives have kept access to the site open to thousands of visitors each year.

These commission members have touched artifacts of the Ludlow Massacre, spoken in the massacre's sacred spaces, and written the books that now stand as the official histories of a story the state of Colorado tried to erase. They have told the story of Ludlow over and over again in lecture halls, discussion groups, museum tours, and at their kitchen tables. The centennial brought all of those voices together, along with those of thousands of people across the world who took the time to reflect on what had occurred on

April 20, 1914. The commemoration created a space to allow them to remember the ghosts of the past. The commemoration events provided a platform to acknowledge that their story was important to those who had not heard it or had failed to remember the story. The overarching goal of the Commission was to help create spaces for commemoration and reconciliation while at the same time trying to find new and innovative ways to get the story and messages out to people who had never heard of the Ludlow Massacre.

The Commission as Collaboration and Partnership

The composition of the Commission embodied the collaboration discussed above. The members of the Ludlow Centennial Commemoration Commission were appointed to facilitate, coordinate, and oversee the memorial events surrounding the 100th anniversary of the Ludlow strike and Massacre in partnership with the UMWA. Members were also charged with using the anniversary to raise awareness of the story of the strike and the massacre. However, the Commission members did not see themselves as the gatekeepers of the story. Instead, they endeavored to collaborate and assist with facilitating the many stories related to Ludlow. They had already heard some of these stories, but they also knew many more were out there. The Commission members recognized that all of these stories need to be told and retold so the sacrifices of the miners and their families in the Ludlow Tent Colony and during the Ludlow Massacre would be remembered for another 100 years.

Governor John Hickenlooper appointed the Commission by Executive Order B 2013 003 on April 19, 2013 (appendix 1, this volume). This Executive Order established the Commission's mission, duration, and membership. The Commission members then formed an executive board and drafted bylaws (appendix 2, this volume). The mission of the Commission as outlined in the Executive Order can be paraphrased as follows:

> To raise awareness of the tragedy at Ludlow and the events surround-
> ing it; to explore the themes that underscore the Ludlow Massacre and
> the Colorado Coalfield War [. . . and] examine how this localized history
> impacted national and international labor relations . . . and continues to have
> modern-day relevance; . . . to expand community outreach . . . so that the
> stories of the individuals involved in these incidents can be heard[;] . . . to

reconcile the past and reflect on its relationship to the state of Colorado and the United States today.

In addition to a formalized structure and mission, the Ludlow Centennial Commemoration Commission recognized and acknowledged that organizations and individuals who wanted to share their perspective and participate in the commemoration of Ludlow should be encouraged and included to fully participate in all commission meetings. This resulted in a large statewide committee with representation from over forty organizations throughout the state of Colorado (see appendix 3, this volume). This inclusive dual structure allowed the Commission to expand its collaborative efforts through partnerships.

The Commission members agreed that while the Ludlow Massacre occurred in April 1914, the massacre was not a separate event from the strike that lasted from September 1913 to December 1914. Thus, the Commission members decided to enlarge the scope of commemoration events to include events preceding and following the massacre. As a result, a year-long series of commemorative events was planned to mirror that time frame.

To accomplish this goal, the Commission kept its meetings open to any interested parties and widely advertised upcoming meetings. Beginning in May 2013, the Commission hosted monthly meetings up and down Colorado's Front Range. Locations for the meetings were based on organizations that offered to host, and travel time was considered. For instance, one meeting might be held in Denver while the next two meetings would happen in Trinidad and Colorado Springs. This fluid arrangement ensured that all communities up and down the Front Range felt included and had opportunities to participate. Commission members felt that meeting planning must consider all individuals and organizations and ensure that they all had a voice. Beyond that, Commission members wanted to make sure that each participant in hosting commemoration events, no matter its size or location, felt its contribution was seen as equivalent to others, relevant, and impactful.

There was no dedicated budget from the governor's office for commemoration events. Each organization covered the costs of its event, and, if possible, monetary resources were pooled. Colorado Humanities and History Colorado assisted with the dissemination of material and advertising. In addition, Colorado Humanities collected and administered all incoming donations related to the commemoration. The Commission sunset in December 2014, after which a full report was drafted for the governor that outlined the purpose, activities, and impact of the Commission's work (appendix 4, this volume).

Scholarship as Stewardship

Academic institutions along the Front Range of Colorado also collaborated to create meaningful commemoration events. Scholars from the University of Colorado at Boulder (CU Boulder), the University of Denver (DU), the University of Colorado at Colorado Springs (UCCS), and Colorado State University–Pueblo (CSU-Pueblo) all participated in the commemorative events in a number of ways. Historians and archaeologists from CU Boulder, DU, UCCS, and CSU-Pueblo participated in a Colorado Speakers Bureau organized by the Commission (figure 1.3b). The University of Colorado at Colorado Springs organized an "All Campus Reads" series of events that spanned the 2013–2014 academic year and focused on Colorado Poet Laureate David Mason's verse novel *Ludlow*. The series of events included students in the First Year Experience program's courses reading and discussing the book, a humanities course on the topic, presentations by authors and scholars, exhibits, plays, and music concerts sponsored in part by the UCCS Daniels Ethics Fund. CSU-Pueblo hosted an academic symposium dedicated to the topic in April 2014, in addition to having classes dedicated to the topic. Finally, Elizabeth Jameson spoke at the Centennial Memorial Service hosted by the UMWA. For a full listing of events and attendance numbers at events, see appendix 5 (this volume).

A National Speakers Bureau furthered the Commission's collaborative efforts and brought in scholars from across the United States and Canada to address issues related to labor struggles in Colorado (figure 1.3a; appendix 5). Speakers presented at a variety of venues, including Colorado State University-Pueblo, the University of Colorado at Colorado Springs, and the Trinidad, La Veta, and Rawlings libraries. This series resulted from the pooling of resources. Colorado Humanities facilitated a Memorandum of Understanding between hosting sites in which the overall cost of the speakers was divided based on what each host site could provide. This cut the cost for each location because the cost of travel was shared and the speaker was paid one honorarium for multiple speaking engagements. Speakers included:

FIGURE 1.3a. Flyer of Colorado and National Speakers Bureau sponsored by the Commission. *Courtesy*, Fawn-Amber Montoya and Karin Larkin.

- Anthony DeStefanis, history professor at Otterbein University in Ohio, presented "The Road to Ludlow: Breaking the 1913–1914 Southern Colorado Coal Strike."
- Maria Montoya, New York University professor, presented on Josephine Roche's response to the 1927 strike.

FIGURE 1.3b. Flyer of Colorado Speakers Bureau sponsored by the Commission. *Courtesy*, Fawn-Amber Montoya and Karin Larkin.

- Sarah Deutsch, Duke University professor, addressed research from her book *No Separate Refuge*.
- Scott Martelle, author of the book *Blood Passion: The Ludlow Massacre and Class War in the American West*, presented on the research related to his book.
- The speaker's series ended with UMWA president Cecil Roberts's presentation "The Ludlow Massacres Echo in Today's Labor Movement."

The speakers bureau illustrated the collaboration among the many voices on the statewide committee and provided an opportunity for university students and rural communities to hear about the Ludlow Massacre in a broader context.

In addition to the speakers bureau, the Commission collaborated with local area museums to create exhibits that told the story of the Ludlow Massacre. The Colorado Springs Pioneers Museum mounted an exhibit titled *Memories of a Massacre: Perspectives on Ludlow* that paired artifacts from the excavations of the Colorado Coalfield War Archaeological Project with artwork by local artist Lindsay Hand. Hand reimagined the historical photographs of the 1913–1914 coalminers' strike in southern Colorado on a massive scale. The exhibit opened on Saturday, April 19, 2014, during an all-day event that drew hundreds of people. The museum also sponsored lectures and events throughout the run of the exhibit highlighting a variety of perspectives from artists, descendants, scholars, and musicians. El Pueblo History Museum, a community museum of History Colorado located in Pueblo, Colorado, mounted an exhibit called *The Children of Ludlow* that opened in September 2013, with more than 400 people in attendance at the opening reception. Labor leaders, politicians, retired steelworkers, retired miners, and families of those present at the Ludlow Massacre attended. The exhibit, which was slated to close in December 2014, was still open at the time of the writing of this book.

In April 2014, the Commission hosted a weeklong series of events throughout the state of Colorado. Events included speakers, a concert held at Pueblo's Memorial Hall, the previously mentioned Academic Symposium, a Greek Orthodox Easter celebration, and a memorial service at the Ludlow Tent Colony site (figure 1.4). The memorial service was held on April 20—100 years to the day after the massacre. Hundreds of people came from all over the nation and the world to remember the lives lost. The next day, History Colorado hosted a panel discussion with Thomas Andrews, William Convery, Bob Butero, Adam Morgan, and Fawn-Amber Montoya reflecting on the commemoration events and what can be learned from Ludlow.

One of the most impactful events to arise from the collaborative efforts happened on Tuesday, April 22, 2014. On that day, the Colorado House of Representatives issued Resolution 14–1005 and proclamation, which read:

FIGURE 1.4. Greek Orthodox Easter celebration, April 20, 2014, Ludlow, Colorado. *Courtesy*, Dawn DiPrince.

Be it Resolved by the House of Representatives of the Sixty-ninth General Assembly of the state of Colorado:

... (a) Commemorate the 100th anniversary of the Ludlow Massacre and convey our sympathies to the families of the men, women, and children who lost their lives on that fateful day;

(b) Recognize the tragic events of the Ludlow Massacre as a pivotal event in American history; . . .

(c) Remember the people who died on that day, including: Elvira Valdez, 3 months; Frank Petrucci, 6 months; Lucy Petrucci, 2 years; Lucy Costa, 4 years; Cloriva Pedregone, 4 years; Joe Petrucci, 4 years; Onafrio Costa, 6 years; Rodgerlo Pedregone, 6 years; Mary Valdez, 7 years; Eulala Valdez, 8 years; Rudolfo Valdez, 9 years; Frank Snyder, 11 years; Primo Larese, 18 years; Frank Rubino, 23 years; Fedelina Costa, 27 years; Louis Tikas, 30 years; Private Alfred Martin, 30 years; Charlie Costa, 31 years; Patria Valdez, 37 years; James Fyler, 43 years; and John Bartolotti, 45 years.

In this proclamation, the state recognized the need to remember the events and victims of the Ludlow Massacre. This was the first public acknowledgment of sympathy and recognition by the state and was the direct result of the Commission's collaborative efforts.

Throughout this process and our long-standing work, academics have been allowed to enter the sacred spaces of the original stewards both physically and emotionally. We were able to forge personal as well as professional relationships with these stewards, such as Mike and Yolanda Romero, Bob Butero, and Linda Linville. We were allowed to share their stories and their work and pass them along to larger audiences. The relationship-building process has created a mutual respect, where the scholars have become learners and the public has become educators. These stewards of the story shared their expertise with the importance the centennial commemorations needed to leave a permanent mark that would guarantee that the story of the Ludlow Massacre would live for another 100 years.

Commission members agreed that space would be created for all voices to be heard in the format the organizers felt comfortable with and that was appropriate for their intended audience. This led to an eclectic mixture of events, including art exhibits, performances, memorials, readings, and speakers. The two events mutually agreed upon were the UMWA annual memorial on May 18 and a memorial service held on April 20. The 100th anniversary coincided with Easter Sunday and Greek Orthodox Easter. Many committee members felt apprehensive about scheduling an event on this day due to the religious significance. In the fall of 2013, at a statewide committee meeting, Elaine Callas-Williams asked what event would be held on the exact day of the memorial, April 20. Committee members responded that no event was planned. Callas Williams suggested a Greek Orthodox Easter service at the site hosted by Assumption of the Theotokos, Greek Orthodox Church of Denver, Colorado. Her religious community had discussed this idea and received support from Metropolitan Isaiah. Upon her suggestion, the room, which held more than twenty-five people of different beliefs and affiliations, fell silent. Slowly, many nodded their approval; others vocally shared that this seemed a fitting way to remember the event. The significance of this was not lost on any of those in attendance. The committee felt that a memorial service would be appropriate since it was focused on the loss of life at Ludlow and because it had been 100 years since the strikers and their families had celebrated Greek Orthodox Easter (Slevin 2014).

The open and collaborative nature of the Commission's work transformed the experience for everyone involved. Representatives from community organizations were respected and valued alongside academic scholarship. Locations that did not have the financial resources to support presentations were supplemented with resources from other organizations. Memory and unofficial history meshed with archaeology and history and have come to form a broader and more stable foundation. The Commission was able to create a space that pieced together a deeper narrative than what is typically available in primary documents or the archaeological record alone. Now, it is not just about who died at the site. The site has become a sacred space to share remembrances and visions for the future. As scholars and partners, our investment has increased, as we have accountability and have become stewards in partnership with the UMWA.

OVERVIEW OF THE BOOK

This book furthers these commemorative efforts by discussing how the various stewards of the memory of the Ludlow Massacre collaborated on and continue to work toward creating new and creative spaces for commemoration. We use our work on the Ludlow Centennial Commemoration Commission as a potential model for how synergistic collaboration can create lasting, impactful, and inclusive scholarship that reaches outside the hallowed walls of academia and captures the interest of the public. As scholars, our audience is typically confined to other academics and students. This project has moved the dialogue outside of these realms and shared authority with various stakeholders. The open and inclusive design created spaces where we as scholars benefited from exposure to new and varied perspectives. No matter how much research scholars have collected or how much they think they know about the subject, this inclusive and collaborative design exposed us to new perspectives, ideas, and stories. Being open to these new perspectives and histories allowed us to strengthen our public scholarship and forge connections to the present.

Chapters in this book weave these perspectives together with models for practicing public scholarship. The volume is divided into three parts. The first highlights the work of the UMWA as stewards of the memory of the Ludlow Massacre. We felt strongly that their voices should be heard first and without a scholarly filter. The oral histories presented in this section along with Linda Linville's powerful narrative in the prologue privilege the perspectives of descendant communities. We use "communities" specifically, as we acknowledge lineal descendants of the strikers and coal miners in southern Colorado as well as the UMWA as descendants and communies of interest. This section allows these stakeholders to share their views and construct narratives through their stewardship in their own words. The second part of the book highlights the methodologies explored and utilized to practice public scholarship and remembrance through the work of academics studying the event and the Commission's work. These chapters provide potential models or templates to expand scholarship beyond academia into the public realm and engage diverse audiences. The third section explores the importance of and potential methods for teaching this history through both traditional and nontraditional means. These chapters focus on outreach and pedagogical issues related to teaching this difficult history both in and out of the classroom using Ludlow as a case study. The chapters highlight our collaborative efforts during the work of the Commission. These stewards are composed of a diverse group of stakeholders, yet the goals are aligned. The goals include diversifying the narrative, correcting misconceptions, filling in omissions in the historical record, and using this past to negotiate the present and future. We conclude by exploring the impact of the commission by looking back over Commission members' experiences and looking toward the future by making suggestions on future collaborations and commemorations around the Ludlow Massacre.

This book explores the intersections of public scholarship, advocacy, and personal experience. Contributors to this book broke down the walls surrounding academia and worked outside the box to create new and powerful narratives. The book illustrates the power of creating spaces for sharing ideas and information in an environment that encourages creativity, open dialogue, public outreach, political action, and alternative narratives. Using the Ludlow Centennial Commemoration Commission as a springboard, we discuss how this became a platform for sharing stories and opening the narrative to reach wider audiences and create more diverse and inclusive narratives.

We envision this book as an open and inclusive narrative that weaves together many perspectives and tellers of the story. These tellers range from lineal descendants and the UMWA to scholars, artists, poets, and more. The history and the story of the Ludlow Massacre have been maintained for over 100 years through oral tradition, community promotion, scholarship, and commemoration that lives beyond textbooks and state-sanctioned narratives. The Ludlow Massacre is important to the history of our state, nation, and world not just because of the lives lost but also because of what their deaths have inspired and communicated to people regarding labor relations, community building, collaboration, and the power of communal memory. The spirit of collaboration the UMWA fosters allows everyone to work together to create an inclusive, diverse, and accessible narrative. We hope this structure both highlights the importance of a more pluralistic approach and offers practical models for practicing public scholarship.

REFERENCES

Ames, Michael M. 1992. *Cannibal Tours and Glass Boxes: The Anthropology of Museums*. Vancouver: University of British Columbia Press.

Andrews, Thomas. G. 2010. *Killing for Coal: America's Deadliest Labor War*. Cambridge, MA: Harvard University Press.

Colwell-Chanthaphonh, Chip, and T. J. Ferguson. 2008. *Collaboration in Archaeological Practice: Engaging Descendant Communities*. Lanham, MD: Altamira.

Duke, Philip, and Dean Saitta. 2009. "Why We Dig: Archaeology, Ludlow, and the Public." In *The Archaeology of Class War: The Colorado Coalfield Strike of 1913–1914*, edited by Karin Larkin and Randall H. McGuire, 351–362. Boulder: University Press of Colorado.

Green, James, and Elizabeth Jameson. 2009. "Marking Labor History on the National Landscape: The Restored Ludlow Memorial and Its Significance." *International Labor and Working-Class History* 76: 6–25.

Harrison, Faye V. 1992. *Decolonizing Anthropology: Moving Further toward an Anthropology for Liberation*, 2nd ed. Vol. 40. Arlington, VA: American Anthropological Association.

Larkin, Karin, and Randall McGuire, eds. 2009. *The Archaeology of Class War: The Colorado Coalfield Strike of 1913–1914*. Boulder: University Press of Colorado.

Limerick, Patricia Nelson, Andrew Cowell, and Sharon K. Collinge. 2009. *Remedies for a New West: Healing Landscapes, Histories, and Cultures*. Tucson: University of Arizona Press.

Mallon, Florencia E. 2012. *Decolonizing Native Histories: Collaboration, Knowledge, and Language in the Americas.* Narrating Native Histories. Durham, NC: Duke University Press.

Montoya, Fawn-Amber, ed. 2014. *Making an American Workforce: The Rockefellers and the Legacy of Ludlow.* Boulder: University Press of Colorado.

Peers, Laura L., and Alison K. Brown. 2003. *Museums and Source Communities: A Routledge Reader.* New York: Routledge.

Reason, Peter, and Hilary Bradbury. 2012. *The Sage Handbook of Action Research: Participative Inquiry and Practice,* 2nd ed. London: Sage.

Saitta, Dean, 2007. *The Archaeology of Collective Action.* Gainesville: University Press of Florida.

Slevin, Colleen. 2014. "Easter Service Marks Colorado Massacre Centennial." *Washington Times,* April 21. Washington, DC. Accessed April 21, 2019. https://m.washingtontimes.com/news/2014/apr/21/easter-service-marks-colorado-massacre-centennial/.

Smith, Linda Tuhiwai. 2012. *Decolonizing Methodologies: Research and Indigenous Peoples.* London: Zed Books.

PART I

Continuing Ludlow

For the past 100 years, communities of southern Colorado have continued to preserve the story of the Ludlow Massacre. Their active stewardship has allowed the story of what occurred on April 20, 1914, to live on in community and family memory through oral tradition. This method of telling not only allowed the stories of those who died at Ludlow to live on, but it set these individuals in the broader context of working-class and immigrant history. Since the massacre in 1914, two distinct yet interconnected groups have acted as stewards. They consist of lineal descendants of the striking miners and others who participated in the strike as well as the "community of interest," to borrow a phrase from Robert Butero of the United Mine Workers of America (UMWA). The "community of interest" includes miners, steelworkers, and, of course, the UMWA. Linda Linville's story presented in the prologue to this book offers a very personal and touching account of stewardship. Here, we privilege the "community of interest's" stories.

The stories of the coalminers' sacrifices have lived on through their lineal descendants. Today, their children, grandchildren, and great-great-

https://doi.org/10.5876/9781646422289.p001

grandchildren continue to come to southern Colorado to visit the remnants of these mining communities. The Ludlow Massacre site has become a pilgrimage to visit the place where their families lived and worked.

Since 1918, the UMWA has been the steady steward of the memory of Ludlow as a "community of interest." The UMWA not only tends to the physical site of the Ludlow Tent Colony but also keeps the spirit and memory of the collective action at Ludlow alive. After the 1913–1914 southern Colorado coalfields strike ended, the UMWA purchased the land surrounding the original site and the "Death Pit." In 1918, the organization erected a monument to those who died in the massacre and has held regular memorial services at the site since that dedication. This community of interest has preserved the physical site that is considered sacred ground. In 1985, it helped list the Ludlow Massacre site on the National Register of Historic Places. In 2009, the organization successfully nominated the site as a National Historic Landmark, cementing the importance of this history to the nation. The UMWA Local 9856 has physically maintained the site for visitors to be able to make that pilgrimage.

The UMWA also actively commemorates the event and uses this memory to illuminate and address contemporary problems, such as issues with healthcare (black lung, lack of, cost of), disparities in pay, worker safety, capital/labor relations, the problems immigrant laborers face, and others. The UMWA starts from a platform of inclusion that recognizes the benefits of collective action. This mind-set has impacted every project or person who works at Ludlow. The UMWA's vision, openness, and positive attitude have set the tone for remembering and invoking the past to address the present. The organization has created an accessible atmosphere that influences all those who remember, study, and interpret Ludlow. The UMWA District 22 has also been generous in facilitating researchers interested in the events surrounding the strike, massacre, and aftermath. From the support of various projects to choosing diverse speakers and hosting numerous events at the site, the UMWA illustrates that the spirit of solidarity and inclusion that pervaded the Ludlow Tent Colony during the strike lives on. Robert Butero, UMWA regional director for District 4; Mike Romero, president of Local 9856; and Yolando Romero, then president of the Women's Auxiliary of Local 9856, have led the stewardship efforts to commemorate this history.

The chapters in this section privilege these descendant communities' voices through mostly unedited interviews. In the spirit of sharing authority

FIGURE 2.1. Yolanda and Michael Romero in Trinidad. *Courtesy*, Yolanda Romero.

in creating narratives around the history of Ludlow, this section presents the words of these descendants as they shared them without a filter. The narratives include an interview with Robert (Bob) Butero and Yolando Romero. These interviews were conducted at the Southern Colorado Coal Mining Memorial and Museum in Trinidad, Colorado. The interview with Butero occurred on June 4, 2019. The interviewers, Karin Larkin and Fawn-Amber Montoya, have known and worked with Bob for over ten years on a variety of projects related to the Ludlow Massacre site. They have spoken at the site and assisted Bob as he facilitated the events for the Ludlow Massacre Centennial in 2013 and 2014. The interview with Yolanda Romero took place on June 12, 2019.

The Southern Colorado Coal Mining Memorial and Museum in Trinidad, Colorado, is the entry into a much deeper richer history than can be discerned from just a sign on Interstate 25. The community of interest that

FIGURE 2.2. Southern Colorado Coal Mining Memorial and Museum and Louis Tikas statue image, Main Street, Trinidad, Colorado. *Courtesy*, Yolanda Romero. Photo by Karin Larkin.

came together to build this museum has been part of the annual memorials for more than thirty years. Yolanda and Mike Romero are known in the community of Trinidad for their contributions to small business, their labor organizing, and their strong desire to preserve the rich heritage of coal mining in the region (figure 2.1).

In chapter 2, Yolanda Romero shares what motivated her to find out more about the Ludlow Massacre and the history of coal mining in the region. As the wife of a coalminer and living in a community of coalminers, Yolanda felt connected to the women at Ludlow. She understood the danger miners faced but also the hardship women encountered when sending their husbands and sons into the coalmines. Yolanda's story also illustrates how the Women's Auxiliary of the UMWA assisted in times of economic turmoil in the community and how her support of her husband's work with the UMWA has kept the memory of Ludlow alive. While much of the Romeros' work has centered on the Ludlow Massacre site, in more recent years the Romeros and other families have organized to make the mining history of Trinidad, Colorado, central to the community's history. With the building of a miners' memorial that includes statues of a canary, Louis Tikas, and a museum, the work of the Romeros will leave a lasting imprint on this community and its tourism for decades (figure 2.2).

Mining created a togetherness in the community. As miners worked in the mountains, their labor and working conditions created a tight bond. Their families understood the danger of the work, and communities formed based on their shared economic status, dangerous working conditions, and rural living. These communities included nuclear and extended families as well as the creation of bonds across ethnic groups. Following the Ludlow Massacre, some families shared their experiences with their children and grandchildren. The Ludlow Massacre was not just about those who died but also those who lived to tell of the horrors that had occurred and to also embrace the wins and come to understand that it was the labor of the men and women of these communities that solidified and strengthened their community ties.

It is these interviews with stewards of the story that humanize this history and make it relevant. We share their stories unedited as the acknowledgment of their narratives and the power and strength of these communities and their stories that have lived on in their homes. The story of the Ludlow Massacre has been kept alive for over 100 years because those present at Ludlow shared their tragedy, the coalminers of the region have continued to build these communities, and the UMWA purchased and maintained the land.

2

Yolanda Romero

INTERVIEW BY FAWN-AMBER MONTOYA AND KARIN LARKIN

Interview conducted on June 12, 2019, by Fawn-Amber Montoya and Karin Larkin at the Southern Colorado Coal Mining Memorial and Museum in Trinidad, Colorado.

FAWN-AMBER MONTOYA: How old were you when you first started coming to Ludlow, or what made you come to Ludlow for the first time?

YOLANDA ROMERO: For the first time, it was in the early 1970s, when Mike became a coalminer. [He] was a coalminer back then. It drew our interest, my interest. He was involved from the very beginning. With the encouragement of local retirees and the older coalminers to be involved and to be shown what work needed to be done and to be involved as an officer. At the local level it was more at the encouragement of our elders who were here. Most of them are gone now, but I became involved at that point in time. Anything that had to do with Ludlow or had to do with coal mining. Because of [Ludlow] we began a Women's Auxiliary back then. I can't give you an actual year but I would say the early 1970s as well. We began an organized Women's Auxiliary with I believe eight other women. I have

https://doi.org/10.5876/9781646422289.c002

FIGURE 2.3. UMWA Women's Auxiliary for Local 9856 from *United We Stand* by Patrick Donachy, 1990, Trinidad, Colorado. *Courtesy,* Yolanda Romero. Front row *(left to right)*: Louise Montano, secretary, Julia Dominguez, treasurer, Leola Saiz, vice president, Yolanda Romero, president. Back row *(left to right)*: Josie Rael, Ascension Mendoza, Jennifer Schuster, Chris Gettler, June Wakefield, Esther Aragon, Vicky Colangelo. Not pictured: Cindy Poole, Gloria Chavez, Lorraine Renner, Margaret Chavez, Myra Baca, and Marie Avila.

the exact names in the publication over there. [It is] a photo of the women who were involved then, that we organized with back then (figure 2.3). Anything that was about Ludlow and its history and its heroes, we thought was important to keep it alive and, because we knew nothing of Ludlow, we knew nothing of union history. We knew nothing [about what] brought those folks together here at the time. It was a learning for all of us that we never gained in public education or locally, anywhere. Not in church, not in school, not anywhere. Our learning began then. Along with the United Mine Workers and the local coalminers and the local union at that time. That's when the auxiliary began.

When the auxiliary began, we were able to connect with others who had a history about Ludlow, and of course they would contact us, and then we would [sit down and talk], like we're doing today. We have done

[that] with the Greek community [around] Louis Tikas. It was a vehicle for us to contribute and to connect with others and learn ourselves at the same time. [We learned] about the union, the United Mine Workers. We attended conventions to learn. We assisted with the dig at Ludlow and got to know folks out there, and still yet, if there's something that needs to be done here or there, we work to facilitate that. I guess if that's the answer that I need that's the one I'll give, but that's how it was back then. I don't know if I'm off track here.

FAWN-AMBER MONTOYA: No, you're fine, you're totally on track. What was it about the site that made you want to become so involved? Was it because you were the wife of an officer, or was it something else?

YOLANDA ROMERO: It was more the history of Mother Jones and what she did. It was more the fact that women were not involved at that point at all locally. No women involved with matters of [the] union, coal mining, or Ludlow and the history of Ludlow. It was that that drew me to it and wanting to be involved because it was something that I was close to because of having a husband who was a coalminer, families that were coalminers, and friends that were coalminers. The fact that it was such a big thing. It was the lifeblood of this community way back in the early years, and that was important to me. The other thing that was important was the fact that coal mining history might be lost because of the closures of the mines. That was important to me to keep it alive and to keep going with whatever involved the history of coal mining in our community.

KARIN LARKIN: I was curious about you guys starting the museum here. What led to that, how you organized it? How is it run?

YOLANDA ROMERO: In July of 2018, I think it was 2018, we were contacted by the foundation of Helenis. The president of that nonprofit, Cervos Mikos, Michael! Michael, it's Mikos Cervos, that's his last name. I was always confused and always called him Cervos, but his name was Mikos, Michael. Wanting to know what we thought about the work that could be done to have the statue of Louis Tikas. Because of being a labor leader, he lived, worked, and died here. I didn't realize the work that had to be done if that was going to take place. I said sure, that would be wonderful for our community, and it's fitting that it should be here in that Louis Tikas played an important role in our community along with other families that were here. [He] worked to get what they needed here, their livelihood, and other things that they worked and strived to get because of the strike. I said yes, I think it can be done.

I said, it's a wonderful thing for our community. It would bring folks here to visit and to view the memorial and to understand our history here. I agreed that I would go ahead and help and work with others to get it done. Communication was constant with him. The work began and continued with him through their foundation, with the city, with the county, and with anybody else who was close to the project. In June of 2018, the dedication was realized. There was a dinner. The public was invited. City and county officials and other local officials [were invited] to attend and the general public. That memorial that sits out there was dedicated that day. That's how it all began. That's how it all happened.

I don't think, well, I'm not sure, but I don't think people realize the magnitude of and the importance of coal mining here. [Or] the union, the importance of the union here. We're hoping that with that they realized it. It was a good thing for the community. It was important for our kids and our families. It all happened for a good reason that was in regard to the Louis Tikas memorial.

In 2013, this building was vacant. Nothing was being done with it. We had been told that a woman from Chicago owned the building. She and her estate. Apparently, nobody wanted it. I thought, well, it'd be nice if we could get it and do something with it. We did not know what was going to ultimately happen to the building if someone didn't do something with it. I wrote to, I believe her name was Carmen Mendez. I worked through her attorney. She said [we needed] primarily just a letter of request asking to be considered. She said okay, no strings attached. We did a quick claim deed for the building. She said it's yours if you take it as is. The guys, the retired guys, started getting together and pulling it together. We did some fundraising to get the paint [and] the flooring. [To] get all the things done that it needed, and we still need more but that's going to take more work. That's how it all began. It took three years to finish it, get it open and dedicated. That's how that all began with that.

The Coal Miners' [Memorial], yes, that project began in 1992. That was a project of the Trinidad Las Animas County Hispanic Chamber [of Commerce]. We wanted something to do that we could be proud of. The elders were still alive as well; that kind of guided us. We talked about it with our board [and] decided that would be something that would be important for the community. We began fundraising at the local level doing numerous kinds of things, raising money for it. It was dedicated in 1996. At that time, Harry Sayer was the mayor. I don't remember who the whole city council board was at that time, but with his support and encouragement [we proceeded with the project]. He thought it was important as well that they dedicated the park area to us. They were going to give us an area down by the tracks. I thought, "No, we can't camp down there because the highway's there." My worry was that changes would be made to the highway setup, and we might be out of luck at some point or have to be moved. I asked, what about this area, right here [area adjacent to the museum]? He didn't have a problem with it, and we went with it. We got the area, and it was just weeds and bushes there. People would throw cans and stuff in there, trash. We thought it would be nice to have a memorial there. It's part of the historical district. We began with that. Our board would take visits up to Pueblo, to Renaissance Bronze. [We worked] with David Durham up there. [We worked] to get all the pieces of those different coalminers there that were models for that project. It took numerous trips to keep approving what was going on. Because we wanted to make sure that it was the right thing and that he was gonna finish it. It was just our concern to get it finished and to have a project in place.

That was dedicated in 1996, and the city was pleased with what it was. They thought it was just going to be a small kind of thing, but that's what we wanted and we got what we wanted. There's a time capsule there that could be opened in 100 years, and it's all about mining equipment and a lunch pail. Different kinds of things that were donated by different coalminers. An auger. Different kinds of things are sealed there. The project with the inscriptions, which still come in today, brings us still a little bit of money for the maintenance and upkeep of the project. That's what happened there, and that was our branch from the Hispanic chamber to become a 501(C3) nonprofit and do the fundraising for [it]. [We] continued fundraising for that project. The canary also came about because it was an important part of the history as well. We thought it would be symbolic of what the miners felt [was] important. We used the canary and the canary is in place, the mules as well; at that point in time our money is dwindling because we had raised quite a bit of money in the beginning. Little by little, you know, spending it on the project piece by piece, it goes. The mules are made of cast aluminum, but they're in place and are reflective of that part of history, symbolic of that part of history.

Company people viewed the mules as very important, but as well, they assisted the coalminers in the mine. Of all the things that are there, the children find them the most interesting, and the canary. Nevertheless, it's all important. The building came after all that, the dedication of the building here. The fact that it was donated to us. After that, the city purchased the portraits and donated them to the museum.

It took Lindsay Hand, who is the artist, it took her as many years to paint all of them as it took the coalminers to work and finish this building (figure 2.4). When we came together to dedicate the building, it was exactly three years. She three years and us three years. We have the building in place and [are] proud of it. We could do more and we're going to do more. Provided we get more funds, we'd like to do a mural out there, the width and the distance of the wall to incorporate all [the] history of working people. If we can do that, we want to do that. Incorporate everyone. Everything that's a part of our history here, with the work of artists.

Donating their time to paint, but there is money there for artists. We could facilitate that through the tourism board. Getting that in order, maybe it'll tie in. I think it'll tie in with Art Space over there, and we would like to get that done.[1] We would like to have our signage done; above our building we have drafts of what we want it to look like. We need money for that.

Every year we plan and work with the United Mine Workers, Bob specifically, to facilitate the Ludlow services out there. For us it's not a whole lot of work anymore, other than to invite the general public and that kind of thing. But in the beginning, what we did with the auxiliary was to facilitate the work of the painting of the building and the canopy and the cement pad that's out there. The steel enclosure that recognizes the donors out there, then, of course, Randy McGuire got a hold of us at the time to work with the union summer kids out there,

FIGURE 2.4. *Ludlow: Miners Camp*, 100 × 72 inches, oil on canvas. Painted from Ludlow Tent Colony photograph for *Perspectives on Ludlow* exhibit at the Colorado Springs Pioneers Museum. Painting by Lindsay Hand, donated to Colorado Springs Pioneers Museum. *Courtesy*, Colorado Springs Pioneers Museum.

and our work was to bring food and water and stuff to the kids out at Ludlow.

A lot of the bigger parts of the project are funded with the United Mine Workers and facilitated out there. We use that event to fundraise for this building and just sell donuts. [We sell] something small, donuts, publications, coffee, at one time we used to have vendors who would come out there. The Indians from Gallup [NM] and a lot of other folks wanted to be vendors out there, and that made for a fun day. Then we'd have our dinner, we'd dance after and have a good time. Once everything was over, we'd dance on the pad. At the time when there wasn't a pad, we were dancing on the dirt and the rocks, but we had fun. It was all family fun and that's what we do with Ludlow. Or have done in the past.

FAWN-AMBER MONTOYA: At the site and at the museum, how do you see them either working together or why do you feel the two spaces are important? Can you maybe tell me a little bit about that or maybe for you the need to have the museum in addition, not just having the site?

YOLANDA ROMERO: There was talk that the museum should be at Ludlow. It would've been difficult, I thought, for us to manage it from here to there. We remained here because we were able to get the building donated, and the importance is that we can house [these items], like the portraits. We can house things, histories, oral histories that we have. It would be a place for us to meet. The mine workers meet here every Sunday for their meeting, and it was something we never had before. I would always say, we sure could do with having a building for us. It finally came to pass. We jumped on it to get this building. This is where they can meet, where we can meet, where we can have students come yet still take them down there. We were taking them out there anyway. The kids from the fire museum down here, we would meet them out there and visit them out there and talk about Ludlow. Now what we can do is we can house more children here to come and view history, plus offer the history at Ludlow and take them out there. I guess because it is one [and] the same to me, it's a way to bring about history together but in an enclosed space here and then do oral histories here. We'll be doing an upcoming one in August or September with the guys that are here now.

I don't know. I think it's a good thing overall, for all of us, because we can utilize this building to provide the same kind of knowledge about Ludlow as the historical value here. The fact that this town was built with the coalminers. Its economy and the livelihood here was because of coal mining. I'm glad that that area was donated, to have the monument there, and rightly because that's where the fight was. That's where those folks lived, in and around that area. That's the appropriate place for the Ludlow monument. Still, visitors come by [in] great numbers there to visit and comment about Ludlow. It's important to keep both going.

FAWN-AMBER MONTOYA: What is your role for the commemorations every year? What has been your experience in the past with the annual events?

YOLANDA ROMERO: I think it's more moral support. It's being a coalminer's wife, I guess, that cares about the local mining history here. Involving families to that end and encouraging the public to realize the importance and attend. That's how I see our role. It is moral support and valuing the history and saving it. And hanging on to it. Teaching others about why it's important. It's important to our community, it's important to me, keeping it alive, wanting people to understand why we're proud of our community and why we're proud of coalminers, their families, and others who lost their lives. Even if they're gone, we're still proud of them. We still want people to acknowledge labor and the importance and value of work and the importance of unions and [how] they've helped the oppressed and why it's important to continue with that.

FAWN-AMBER MONTOYA: Do you feel [that running the museum is different] from what you were anticipating? Has it been what you were anticipating at all? What have been some of your experiences working on running a museum and working on a nonprofit?

YOLANDA ROMERO: It's been quite a job. It's an extensive job that requires time, money, upkeep. I guess someone told me once about it being a labor of love. It is, it is, and it's a lot of commitment but really important. Because it is important to keep it alive and to keep it well and to keep it going, to me. We have volunteers that care, volunteers that help. It's just a very important part of life for me.

FAWN-AMBER MONTOYA: Do you think the community of Trinidad understands the importance of the Ludlow Massacre? Or do you think it's something that you're still educating your own home community about?

YOLANDA ROMERO: Yeah. I don't know that newcomers realize how important it is to the rest of us. But I think because of the work that's been done here, because of the statues that are in place and the other things that continue to happen, they've learned over time. I think they've come to appreciate what we do. There's going to be those that don't value what we do and don't see the importance of what we've done. We had conflict over the canary and it was this constant bickering about having a canary on Main Street, but not the value of coal mining, not the value of the canary to the coalminer, the link that's there [is] about coal mining. I think it's been an awakening for those that want to learn and that are going to live here that this is a part of who we are. To accept it as it is, understand it, and appreciate the work that we do to keep it alive. Some will, some won't. We always invite them to come to Ludlow to learn about the history of Ludlow or come in here. We've had clubs and organizations that are local that have come now to understand what this history is, and they'll have their meetings here. That's a good thing. Now they know there is a place, and they know why we value our history. It's been a good thing for learning for all, even us, that we didn't know anything about Ludlow way back when it happened. It really should have been part of our academics, but it wasn't; it never was.

FAWN-AMBER MONTOYA: Were you originally from southern Colorado?

YOLANDA ROMERO: Yes.

FAWN-AMBER MONTOYA: You grew up in southern Colorado and had heard nothing about Ludlow until you got married?

YOLANDA ROMERO: Yeah, none of the schools, I believe, taught anything about Ludlow. It was sort of a silent kind of thing until I became involved in the 1970s. [I realized] there was more to our community than we knew.

FAWN-AMBER MONTOYA: When you began work with the Women's Auxiliary, was [it] your own personal quest within the auxiliary to learn more about the massacre? Were there stories that stood out to you over the past almost fifty years that you have been doing all this work? Were there any stories that stuck out to you that you either feel compelled to tell, or stories that stayed with you to help you frame the importance of it?

YOLANDA ROMERO: It's been the history of Ludlow. The fact that those people suffered to make a living. That to me was the most important thing. That touches my heart and that is important to me. It's the history, what happened there. That it should have never taken place. I mean, those people suffered through the hardest times. That's why we enjoy what we enjoy. Whether people chose to believe it or not, it's created the basic workday and the pay that people get. If people choose not to work, well, that's their choice, but that's why they worked. They strived to make a better living so they could survive. To me, that's important. Knowing many families that were coalminers. Kids we went to school with that were children of coalminers. We're together in this community. Along with the ranching and farming children and all the others that came here. We were all together, but lots of families who united in activities as families. The coalminers did that, they came together as families to do other things in the community. They had their baseball teams. They were family. United is what it was and it was important, and it still is to me.

KARIN LARKIN: What would you consider something that you're most proud of, in all this work you've done over the past fifty years?

YOLANDA ROMERO: This, this project, it started way back.

KARIN LARKIN: The museum?

YOLANDA ROMERO: No, the entire thing because we started with that project out there. I'm the last founding member of the Hispanic chamber that began way back in 1988. It's been this project that stands out that's the most important because it's an important part of our history. Because it belongs to the community. It belongs here. It belongs to Ludlow. Ludlow belongs here. It incorporates all the other families that have left. The names on the memorial are many families that had to leave because the mines closed, but nevertheless, we're in contact with them when they come and bring their families to visit. It's important because they say when they come, they're so happy that it's here. They're so happy that there's something here to remind them of how hard their dads worked and how proud they were of their fathers for doing the work that they did. I think that's it. It's this whole entire project.

FAWN-AMBER MONTOYA: The whole site.

YOLANDA ROMERO: Yeah.

FAWN-AMBER MONTOYA: You said it's still connected. Then to Ludlow as well.

YOLANDA ROMERO: Yes.

FAWN-AMBER MONTOYA: It's the visitor's center, the entryway to everything else.

YOLANDA ROMERO: Right   •

FAWN-AMBER MONTOYA: It's bigger than Ludlow. It's a story that is bigger than Ludlow. Ludlows a piece of it or a cornerstone. Maybe the center of it, but there's all these other [places].

KARIN LARKIN: It's the whole community, and this is the part that's in the community.

YOLANDA ROMERO: Right

FAWN-AMBER MONTOYA: And that's accessible.

YOLANDA ROMERO: Yes. This is where they would quite possibly see it first. Unless they get off the road and go on. We can continue to tell the story here and get visitors there. What would be ideal is if we could have the trolley that would go to Ludlow. We had talked about [how] that would be another piece. Maybe visit some of the more accessible coal camps that might still be intact and a little bit of the ruins. That might be a good thing. It would be a good thing if we could get it coordinated where we could just get the trolley here, then go on out to Ludlow. Some of the little coal camps that still exist. And any of the ruins that are out there.

FAWN-AMBER MONTOYA: What do you see as next steps?

YOLANDA ROMERO: It's to continue raising money, that's important. We need our signs. When people walk by, they know what this building is about. To continue to do whatever work that it takes to assist Bob and the United Mine Workers out at Ludlow. To get the mural in place. I would like to see the mural in place. Maybe that back part of this building, which is sectioned off with a wrought iron back there next to what was the Chronicle News. That's part of this park, but we thought we could do a little theater there. Outdoor, with a canopy, and maybe have mining stories or different kinds of entertainment to coordinate out there. It's all part of this area. I don't know if there's enough time left or not, but there's still more work to be done. There's a lot of good work to be done. It's just getting there.

FAWN-AMBER MONTOYA: Now you're kind of the elder.

YOLANDA ROMERO: Yeah, that's what we say. We're the old people now.

FAWN-AMBER MONTOYA: Is there another generation that you feel is going to take on the stewardship of all the work that you've been able to do? Do you have younger members that are [interested]?

YOLANDA ROMERO: I'm not sure, but I'm hoping with the learning that takes place, that it'll spark. Like it did with us with our elders. Some type of pride, [people] wanting to do it and seeing how valuable and important it is to see it forward. Whether that will happen or not, we'll see. Because it did with us, but we come from a different generation. But there's still kids out there that we try to impress upon when they come here and we give them the history. Bob gives them history. Mike, Jerry, all the guys that come give them a complete history of their work, what they've done, what others have done, and why they've done it, why we have what we have today, the importance and value of work, and the importance of Ludlow, the importance of [the] union. That kind of thing. We're hoping that, at least I do, hope that one day that it will leave an impression in their mind[s] that it is important and why it's important to continue. I'm thinking there will be, but we'll see. It did with us is all I can say.

FAWN-AMBER MONTOYA: Of all the visitors you've had in the past couple of years, were there any visitors that stood out to you. People that you were surprised that either where they come from or why they came, or are there patterns that you're kind of seeing across whoever does come?

YOLANDA ROMERO: Yeah, there were visitors from Russia. We talked about how things are no different for working people. I mean, working people still suffer and are oppressed in one way or the other. People from New York and young people who see the value of what's going on here and they're in tune with what history is about. They value history, and then again, some that know not a thing about coal mining or coal. We give the kids coal; they don't know what coal is. [It's] learning for young people. We had a teacher come from New York who came and is a teacher but wanted to come and live here, but she wanted to know more about the history. This was one of the places that she chose to come and learn about the local history because she wanted to bring forth to her students something of what she learned. It was a way for her to learn and be able to teach it. I think she was going to be a teacher at the high school level. That's important.

KARIN LARKIN: Are there any sort of resources or things you can think of or ways that the universities here can [help]? Is there anything you can think of that you might need moving forward that we can help with?

YOLANDA ROMERO: Can you let me know what's there?

KARIN LARKIN: Most of the stuff that we excavated from Ludlow, except for one or two boxes that I have to go back up to DU to pick up, they're all there. We have the bedsteads and the washboards and all that.

YOLANDA ROMERO: Okay. Yeah, we could put that up. We have room downstairs.

KARIN LARKIN: Yeah, if there's stuff that you can think of that you want to put on display. Some of the broken stuff, like the broken dishes and things, we used in lab class. We figured you're not going to want to display those, they're not, I mean they're cool, we've got tons of them. But if you can think of anything you need to help, you let me know.

YOLANDA ROMERO: (pointing to a display case at the front of the museum), That's why we have the stuff that we had.

KARIN LARKIN: Is that stuff from Diggers?[2]

YOLANDA ROMERO: That was from the archaeological dig. Bob brought those all in boxes. Okay. Okay, yeah, that's what we have. But it's real important when people come to see that. They want to see that display and it's real important.

KARIN LARKIN: You said you have a lot of kids' groups that come through. What age group are they?

YOLANDA ROMERO: The last group we had was from kindergarten and older. They all wanted to come together. We said okay and there were around thirty-four, thirty-five people. Kids are very smart, maybe a little one will pick up on something. They were very interested.

KARIN LARKIN: At DU we used to have a trunk that had artifacts from the excavations at Ludlow that kids [could handle and] pass around, touch them. It got dismantled. I don't know where some of that stuff is, but we could always put something [like] that back together. If you think that would be a useful thing for you to have some of the stuff from Ludlow and from the excavations at Berwind [and] from the coal camp as well.

YOLANDA ROMERO: Sometimes kids are not aware of what that was for. Those serve as learning tools for them.

KARIN LARKIN: I mean, it's fun to pass things around and [ask,] what do you think this was used for? They come up with the craziest stuff.

YOLANDA ROMERO: We leave coal around because they don't know what coal is. [They get] to touch it, to see it, and to understand where it came from is good. Learning, some kids, they enjoy learning that way. Even the teachers and the parents came because there was many of them. We took them in shifts, but they all had fun, it was a great group.

KARIN LARKIN: At one point, Dean Saitta got money from Colorado Humanities to put together some teacher workshops. Some of those teachers gave us a couple of lesson plans for various age groups. I don't know if that's something that [could help]. We can easily share that, it's all up on our website, we could send you some of those lesson plans. I don't know if teachers contact you [asking] what could we do with this stuff or whatever, but if you need any of that, we can send that down, too. If you don't want it, that's fine.[3]

YOLANDA ROMERO: Okay. Now that would be appropriate for teaching.

KARIN LARKIN: That would be something you would share with the teachers before they come in that they're a little primed before they come. Maybe they will know what coal is.

YOLANDA ROMERO: Okay. Now that would be appropriate for teaching? That would be helpful for them, and I'm sure they'd appreciate it.

KARIN LARKIN: I'll dig those up. All this stuff.

YOLANDA ROMERO: Yeah, anything. Because we could use some more stuff downstairs. That would be helpful. These artifacts as well in there, the photos. The photos, portraits, anything that's here. That coal car is the one that was the model for the one outside. Those coalminers were the models who the artist placed in certain locations around the coal car to get his idea of how to do the bronze of the coalminers. He used that coal car and those coalminers up there, they were the models for the one outside. Yeah, the three gentlemen there. Yeah, it's all with learning, kids don't know what a coal car is.

KARIN LARKIN: Right.

FAWN-AMBER MONTOYA: Is there anything that you would want to add, as far as the importance of either the Ludlow Massacre site or the museum, that you think people would want to know or that you would want to share? Or even about the work that you and Mike have worked on all these years.

YOLANDA ROMERO: Always, it's my personal opinion that I feel it's important to our community and it's important nationwide. Coal is still here, and we have a massive coalfield out there. I don't know if coal will be utilized anymore for anything as it was in the past. Nevertheless, it built the community and brought various nationalities here who had to learn to work together and be together as families.

I guess to me, that's important. That people here were able to get along under some of the hardest times, and during times when they could've given up, they didn't. They continued to strive to work together to raise their families and to care about one another. I think that's important. In a community where they all spoke different languages and were under difficult situations where it would have been easy to get up and leave but they chose to stay. I value that and I find that important.

FAWN-AMBER MONTOYA: I like that you [mentioned] that community piece. I think for me, the Ludlow story stayed alive because of Trinidad, because of the United Mine Workers, because people came to the site year after year after year. Because of the people sharing the story. I think it's that piece that you said, it's the connectedness of both this location and Ludlow. That you're teaching people their history. It's not just about Ludlow, it's about coal mining, it's about all the people that came here. It's this much broader, larger story. But it is, it's the community and I think it's the work of that Women's Auxiliary that came together and said we have to know our history.

YOLANDA ROMERO: Right, that was the value of learning about it. I remember a time when our buildings were empty. I mean, downtown at the time there were all the shops. With all the shops that were downtown, they employed around 666 people downtown, and the town was alive. People were walking down the streets. They were working. People were working. It seemed as though families were happier back then and the work was important. It strengthened families in terms that they were able to get their families what they needed. Take them out to eat, to a movie, whatever. They made a good living to do that. The shops were all busy and they employed people during that time. It was alive and active, but then when all that fell apart, because people had to relocate, no more jobs.

We were asked to take a window, take one of the shops downtown, and do something with it. I don't know if I have any pictures of that. I said, well, we'll take the Jolten's building, that building where Bella Luna was. We chose that area because we thought that would be where we want our presence known. We made, I don't know if it was out of papier-mâché or what it was, a Mother Jones. I think it was like a little campfire and Mother Jones with coalminers. I don't know if we used the mannequins or what we used, but we were given that space. That was the saddest part for me because to me, that was [the reality that there was less work]. Why do we have to fill our windows with this, other than the meaning to me was important. But it was sad that we didn't have no more. I mean it was no more. There was no clerks in there, nobody working, the dust had just taken over, and the windows were dirty. I can't remember how long that lasted that was our window. It wasn't a window of joy, I mean, it was sadness because they told us there are no jobs, there's no more happy people, nobody shopping, nobody walking the streets.

That was part of our auxiliary works, way in the beginning, was to fill a window. Other people were doing the same thing with what window they had. I think it was to make that part of the downtown look alive. But it was just what we did, Mother Jones and that was our window. It wasn't a good thing, but it reflected how everything had disappeared, everything was gone. Anyway, that was our window, it was about mining and it was about Ludlow and Mother Jones.

Then within the framework of the auxiliary we gave out what we titled the Mother Jones award to women that were part of the auxiliary. Every year we'd give a woman member an award. It was called the Mother Jones award. That's another part of the project I think that would be important that I didn't mention, to have Mother Jones also out there. As part of the memorials to have her up there as well. I forgot to mention that, but that's another piece of the project that was important and I think should be out there.

Visitor enters

YOLANDA (Speaking to visitor): Hello! Come on through. Would you like to sign the guest book there? It's right there on the, there you go.

YOLANDA ROMERO: We get various people coming in here, and the city planted us some flowers in that planter. Over there and back here. That's a washer out there, that round tub. When they used to wash coal, back when. I forget what they call it. But anyway, that's where we plant our flowers. Of course, the city did it this year, that's real nice for us. Then we just water the trees out there. We carry buckets of water and water our trees so they'll look nice. Then we'll ask the city to maintain the weeds at the other area, back there. Then our job is to maintain the memorial. We wanted to get that painted before they turn the water on, but then Mike got sick and here we are. But we'll get it painted again next year, but ours is the upkeep and maintenance of the park as well [and] of course this building.

FAWN-AMBER MONTOYA: I lived in Hoehne when I was a kid, and I had an uncle that would hang out at the park before it had been changed.

I remember when you put up the monument. It definitely adds a different . . . it's much different now.

YOLANDA ROMERO: Then the city did the brick work. I think Purgatory Valley did the brick work and they put a sundial. It's supposed to be a sundial there and they did that. Topar Welding designed, and I forget to mention that, but he designed and built the cage for the canary.

FAWN-AMBER MONTOYA: It seems like you've gotten a lot of support from the Hispanic chamber and the city to help with maintenance and upkeep.

YOLANDA ROMERO: Yes, yeah. They do. We've got coal mining friends still working for the city that help us, which is a good thing because they care. It's part of their history, their fathers and their grandfathers. Michael [will call] saying when are we going to get the water on. We want to paint before we get the water on. [They'll say] okay, we'll wait till you get your painting done and we'll come. We have a star at Christmastime up on the cage, above the cage, as a decoration that lights up. It was welded. We put lights in it, just to be part of the decorative holiday season. They'll come and put it up. Yeah, it helps to have friends or family that work for the city or the county. The county goes out every year and they get the grounds ready. We just need to call them and tell them when the services are. The porta-pot service, they call, "When do you need me out there?" They come and provide the porta-potties and get them out there for us.

FAWN-AMBER MONTOYA: Do you feel a lot of that's been the relationship and the community that the United Mine Workers and you and Mike and Bob have built over the years? If I remember correctly, for years it was Mike doing a lot of the work out there. Now for the county to be prepping it. They are paying attention.

YOLANDA ROMERO: Yeah. I think as they do it, the new folks. I mean, what's to argue about? When in Rome, do as the Romans do. They come and they learn, and then, there's nothing wrong with learning and helping. Yeah, even if we do have new employees that are not folks from here, they've come over time to learn that it's important. They're doing their job, yes, yeah, in the beginning, always the guys were out there.

I didn't want to be left out, and that's why I said I'm going to get involved, I'm going to be there, I'm going to do what I have to do. I wanted to be a part of it way back, and I did. The same with the Hispanic chamber. I thought it was proper for people to remember who began this project, why it's important. We put the plaques up there to recognize those people because that's with who it all started. We continue. It's been important to a lot of people who don't say a whole lot. But ask for money, they'll help you. If you need a sponsored event or whatever, they're more than willing. Because you've proved yourself. You've done what you said you were gonna do. The trust is there.

Now that you mention that, there was a couple of young women that came here last summer, or it was late in the fall I think. But they were from South Dakota and somewhere else in Colorado, Rifle? Where's that place that's real cold in Colorado?

FAWN-AMBER MONTOYA: Rifle?

YOLANDA ROMERO: I think she said Rifle but anyway, when they were here learning about Ludlow because they knew nothing of Ludlow and they were young, I imagine they were in their mid-twenties, maybe early twenties? But she said, Ludlow? Did you say Ludlow? I said yes, and she said "One of my favorite songs is about Ludlow." I said oh, how ironic is that because we're just in here talking, it's by Houndmouth? Or it's a different young group, I said "It's about Ludlow, the Ludlow?" and she said "yes, yes," she found it on YouTube for me, and we listened to it. But I didn't know of a younger group that was making music about Ludlow, but she said yes, and she had me listen to it. I said, "Well, put it on my phone because I've never heard of that group!"[4]

FAWN-AMBER MONTOYA: That's great, especially a young group.

YOLANDA ROMERO: Yeah, yeah, Houndmouth or something about hound.

FAWN-AMBER MONTOYA: There's a group, my uncle is Jimmy Montoya, his son does the coal train, the coal camp, the coal town songs. He sings a song about Ludlow, I heard him perform at the Ludlow site probably four years ago. But I remember, he was in Denver, but he had been here, and just how the music has carried through in ways that the books don't.[5]

YOLANDA ROMERO: We had them here early on, and now they're doing a lot more things, but yeah, they were here. Oh, I can't remember what event they were here for, and they sang up on the memorial, were you here? It wasn't the dedication. Yeah, it was some event. And they played out here for it.

FAWN-AMBER MONTOYA: I'm trying to think, it might have been the dedication. Was it when you first opened, it might have been the weekend that you first opened.

YOLANDA ROMERO: It was some event and they played out here for it. It was nice.

FAWN-AMBER MONTOYA: Does the city do a First Friday Art Walk or different things like that?

YOLANDA ROMERO: They do. They have the First Friday Art Walk, from 5–7. We participated last year, we got a few people in, and, of course, what we do is have desserts of the day. We had *sopa de arroz*, the sweet rice, we had *biscochitos*. We thought those would be something that we thought would be appropriate. We had cookies that day, of the time, and we had the sweet rice, and, of course, we had to go searching to see who was old enough to remember the types of food. The desserts mostly because we said we'd do desserts. It worked out, though. The cookies [were] okay, but they wanted the sweet rice. Apparently, they've eaten it before. That's what we had. We did good that night, we had fun, the people that came in, of course, they got something to eat, then they got a little history. We got a little history from them. It was all good . . .

FAWN-AMBER MONTOYA: We wanted to thank you. We really appreciate it. Our plan is that we're going to get [this interview] transcribed, then as we get further in the publication process, we'll send you a copy.

NOTES

1. Art Space is also known as Trinidad Space to Create. It is part of a state-led initiative called Space to Create Colorado, which is focused on creating workforce housing and workspace in rural Colorado communities. This space in Trinidad is across the street from the Southern Colorado Coal Mining Memorial and Museum. https://www.artspace.org/trinidad.

2. Reality TV series *Diggers* by Half Yard Productions and distributed by the National Geographic Channel dedicated an episode to the Ludlow Massacre site. The hosts, Tim Saylor and George Wyant, filmed Season 4, Episode 4 at the site. The episode initially aired on July 27, 2015.

3. du.edu/ludlow/.

4. Houndmouth's song "Ludlow" was part of their album *From the Hills below the City*, released in 2013. https://www.houndmouth.com/.

5. "Blood and Coal," http://www.coaltownreunion.com/. "Ludlow Massacre's 101st Anniversary Recognized" by Marty Mayfield on June 15, 2015. http://krtnradio .com/2015/06/15/ludlow-massacres-101st-anniversary-recognized/.

3

Robert (Bob) Butero

INTERVIEW BY FAWN-AMBER MONTOYA AND KARIN LARKIN

Interview conducted on June 4, 2019, by Fawn-Amber Montoya and Karin Larkin at the Southern Colorado Coal Mining Memorial and Museum in Trinidad, Colorado.

FAWN-AMBER MONTOYA: When did your work at the Ludlow site begin, whether it was organizing or even visiting the site, how young were you?

BOB BUTERO: I first went out there probably in the late 1950s, early 1960s with my dad. My dad was a coalminer, for twenty-three years he worked in the coalmines. Then at the end of 1959, when the Frederick or Valdez mine shut down, he wasn't rehired at the mine and he bounced around on a couple jobs and then eventually got hired by the state highway department. When he wasn't a miner anymore, he still used to attend the [memorial] services out there.

I went out there with him at an early age. Of course, this was before I ever got hired in the mines. I got hired in the coalmines in 1975. That's when I first became a member of the UMWA and started attending the services and things out there. When I first got hired back in the 1970s,

https://doi.org/10.5876/9781646422289.c003

I was a member of what they call[ed] District 15 at the time. There was two districts out here. One was District 22, which was Utah, Arizona, and the southwest corner of Wyoming. District 15 was Colorado, New Mexico, the northern part of Wyoming, Montana, North Dakota. District 15 was basically the caretakers; they were the people that put on the program on a regular basis at that time and the annual service. They did that part, and, of course, through the years we had different people or they not so much employed, a lot of it was volunteer, but they employed somebody to be the caretaker out there.

[I started helping with organizing] I'm thinking the late 1980s, early 1990s. Mike Romero was elected international executive board member at that time. He reached out to the different labor organizations within the state of Colorado, and that's how they built the canopy over it. One of the things, I just found this out talking to John Fatur who's kind of our caretaker now. He's the guy that lives right off of the exit there in the old gas station that's there. He was telling me his family is actually from Del Agua. He remembers he lived up in Del Agua till the mid-1950s or so when they closed that coal camp down. He remembers Ludlow not having the bandstand or whatever you want to call it there.

Now I have never been able to verify this for sure, but my understanding was that CF&I [Colorado Fuel and Iron] during that period of time, they had workers up at the Allen mine that were classified as carpenters. They still had a few company houses and these guys would take care [of the site], plus they would build things at the mine. During that time, CF&I was all basically self-contained, and supposedly they built that bandstand in the mid- to late 1950s.

[I started] being a part of taking care of [the site] probably around the early to mid-1980s. I got hired by the union in 1981; I went to work for the union as a safety inspector in 1981. Prior to that in 1978, it was either 1978 or 1979, I was elected vice president of Local Union 9856 at the time.

I was vice president and Mike Romero was president of the local. That's when the CF&I still operated the two mines. There was about 600 active miners, and we had about almost 900 retirees in the local, so it was one of the biggest local unions in the United Mine Workers. I did that for a couple years and then I was offered a job as a safety inspector for the union, an underground inspector. I went to work for them in 1991, but I kept working with Mike Romero through that period of time.

We had a strike here in 1985, 1984 or 1985, at the Golden Eagle mine or Maxwell mine. We had a little bit more involvement in that period of time. Basically, at that period of time a lot of the people that attended the service were people that really weren't born during the [massacre], but they were born shortly thereafter. They worked and like my dad [were] hired in the coalmines in 1936. His brother, who actually brought him into the mines, was hired in the late 1920s, early 1930s, right after the [Great] Depression started.

In them days if you got hired at the mine, they basically assigned you an area to work because it was hand-loaded. Then you chose your partner. That's how a lot of family members or brothers got involved. The older siblings would be the miner, and they would bring in the younger because it was easier for two family members to work together than two maybe neighbors because you got paid by what you loaded and you kinda had to share that.

And so that's how our service [was] at that time, a lot of the attendees were family members or members of those retirees because, like I said, Valdez closed down in 1959, Morley closed down I believe in 1954; most of those miners that worked at Morley got transferred up to the Allen mine. The Allen mine opened up in 1951 and 1952, and when they opened the Allen mine that was one of the first times they ever used mechanized mining. [They believed that using] machines to mine the coal [produced] more than [workers did]. Valdez and Morley were both hand-loaded mines. A lot of the people that attended the service, I call part of the greatest generation of miners. Most of the people that attended were either local people or people that were involved in the labor movement throughout Colorado. That's basically who was there at the different services, the different speakers, and stuff like that. The memorial [has] always been a priority within the union, and that was always part of that.

Then in 1983, Richard Trumka was elected president of the mine workers along with Cecil Roberts as vice president, and a gentleman by the name of John Banovic was the international secretary-treasurer. They made it a point in their administration that every year there would be one of the three of them to come out and be a part of our service. And so, you know, they did that.

That continued on that way, and we would go out there right before the service and help whoever was in charge of maintenance [and] clean the site up and make sure that the site was presentable, especially for the service and stuff, and we continued on with that.

In 1984 or 1985, we had the strike, and we used the Ludlow site and service to be a part of that to basically, for no better term, inspire the miners and the local people in that to participate. There was definitely a generational deal where the so-called greatest generation, they knew, and they owed their soul to the union. You know, they were different. I think that's what's bothering the labor movement today is that we had that generation of people that kind of let that slip through their fingers, where the older generation, you know, wasn't going to do that, and they didn't do that.

Then as those people started passing on and different people died and stuff, there was kind of a lull in there. Attendance, it just wasn't really the same as people [died]. We'd still have our annual service; we'd still have the different people come and speak and stuff. Then, like I said, we went through the 1980s; we kind of got a little bit of a spark by the international union sending somebody out there, you know, all the time.

Karin, when did you start your [archaeological] work?

KARIN LARKIN: It was Randy [McGuire] and Dean [Saitta] and Phil Duke at the time. The first testing was, I think it was 1997 or 1998. They got their first State Historical Fund grant to go out and check to see if they could do anything, I think that was in 1997. First year of field sort of investigations was in 1998.

BOB BUTERO: There was a little bit of a bump [in attendance] from that and stuff, and so we continued. Then in 1995, 1996, they merged District 15 into District 22. So there was no longer a district. The district was run out of the Price, Utah, office. They became kind of the overseers and stuff of that. I believe it was around 2000, I think, was the year that the steelworkers had the big strike up at Pueblo. I think that was about a six- or seven-year strike that they were a part of that, and they used Ludlow. They bused loads of people and we had our service down there. Again, that was another basic lift, you know, and then it continued on.

KARIN LARKIN: That was in 1999? That year, Randy and Dean, I think, participated in that march with the strike.

BOB BUTERO: Oh, okay, in 1999, and then it continued on. Then in 2003, of course, was when the monument was desecrated. Still today, we don't have solid proof of who did that. There was some theory that it was maybe [a] right-wing type group that was just anti-labor. There was a theory too that it had something to do with the steelworker strike. Could've been local vandals, there were just different theories and stuff. At the time, I was the regional director and I was living up in Denver. I was really surprised about the [numbers of people], not so much from locally but from across the country and even foreign people, expressing interest or expressing their sadness over it, wanting to know what they could do. There was just a very good outpouring of people and of stuff of that. We raised money or funding for it, and we raised over $90,000 to restore the monument (DeMario 2003; Terwillinger 2003).[1]

A gentleman out in California was the one that ended up doing the work. I think it was 2006 when we had the re-dedication of the monument. Since around that 2003 time forward, I've taken a more direct role. Myself and Mike Romero in setting up the program and running the program and stuff, and doing that. You know, we try to maintain the place out there and make it as presentable as possible. I think it was in 2006 we had the re-dedication. Cecil Roberts came out and spoke at that time. It was about that same time that a gentleman by the name [of] James Green and another, Betsy Jameson, basically started investigating, seeing what could've been done about making it a historical landmark. They started a lot of that work, especially Betsy Jameson, she spearheaded that, and we had some people that she was working with, [including] the National Park Service (Green and Jameson 2009).

And they did that. That was actually through the George Bush administration. I'm trying to think, it was right before [Ken] Salazar took over [as] interior secretary, or Secretary of the Interior, and I can't remember who the person was. With the help of some of our legal team and that, they finally did get it designated as a National Historic Landmark (figure 3.1).

We had a dedication of that in June of 2009. I can't remember if it was exactly that year or the year before, but we actually had George

FIGURE 3.1. Bob Butero (*right*) with Dean Saitta at Ludlow Tent Colony National Historic Landmark designation ceremony, Ludlow annual memorial gathering, June 28, 2009. *Courtesy,* Dean Saitta.

McGovern. [McGovern] was a speaker, he came out and spoke about Ludlow and stuff (McGovern and Guttridge 1996).

FAWN-AMBER MONTOYA: It was probably 2008 because I didn't go to the 2008 one and I don't remember him. I've never heard him speak, but in 2009, I was there.

BOB BUTERO: This is a little bit [off topic]. That next year there was a big push for what they called card check recognition, you know, throughout the country, that's when [Barack] Obama got elected. I was actually at a facility in Denver exercising, on the TV George McGovern came up and was speaking against it. It was a sad day for me, you know, because he'd been out there. Then also right about that time is when archaeology work was being completed. Shortly during that time of 2006 to 2009.

I credit the archaeology dig with revitalizing Ludlow. Up until that time, it was mainly a labor-type deal. [The archaeology dig was] a springboard into [it]; Dean [Saitta], that was probably a person I communicated more with. You know, he'd always tell me how many people would come there to the site thinking that it was an Indian massacre, and you still see that. The times that we've been out there, you see people drive up that have no idea what that is, but then when they start looking at it, some of them can't even believe that [it was a massacre of miners and their families (McGuire 2004; Saitta et al. 1999)].

Some of the most intense or best work that we did out there was [the 100th anniversary], started by, I think, mainly you [Fawn-Amber Montoya] and Dawn [DiPrince]. It was around 2010 when we first started meeting to start. I remember thinking [after] getting calls and saying, "Geez, we're three years away from that. What do we want to do now?" It was quite the journey; that three years or four years took us to a lot of places, even though it was all pretty much in Colorado. There was a lot of good speakers, a lot of good people that came out and, you know, talked about that. The other day there was a picture on Facebook of us being at the governor's office when he was signing that [the Executive Order establishing the Commission]. From there it just kind of really grew the attention and stuff of that nature (Montoya 2016).

Still today, I wonder how many people really know about Ludlow. There is a lot more people that do know about it, I think there's a lot more students being taught about it. I did an interview for a young woman. I think she's thirteen or fourteen years old out of Boulder, she did a documentary for Ludlow for her history project, and she did a great job with it.

I did a tour here the 4th of April. I think it was a private school, but they were out of New York City. They did a tour of the area and stuff. I think the Louis Tikas monument, because of being descendants of

Greek or Crete. Colorado Humanities that group or organization is kind of spread, and I think there's more people teaching or talking about it.

I remember, they had a summer program. It was kind of a history preservation summer camp type deal, and I believe there was fifty-six students. I received a call and they did three places—Pueblo, Bent's Fort out here, and they did Ludlow. They came and then they called me and they said they wanted to do a project. We had them paint the wrought iron fence out there, and then that Friday we got together. They were all from Colorado, and they varied from kids that have either finished the eighth grade or they had just graduated, and I think there was fifty-six of them and we [had] a roundtable there, and they were talking to us about our faults and stuff as far as history preservation. At the end, I said if I can, I'd like to ask you one question. Before you came here, before this was set up, how many of you had heard about Ludlow? Not one of them raised their hand. So out of fifty-six students from different areas [no one had heard of the Ludlow Massacre]. And even today, Trinidad being part of their heritage and stuff, some of this helps out. Last year we had the Greek community as a whole throughout the country, they raised the money and quite a bit of money, to erect that Louis Tikas statue. It was in order to honor them. They've kind of been pushing us to try to get a Mother Jones statue down here.

The mining industry [is] dying, especially around here and stuff. [It's a] big part of our heritage. You know, I was here early with my dad. [I] had a couple uncles, mainly one uncle that worked a lot in the mine. [They spoke] about my grandfather [who] came here shortly after from Texas. He'd come in the 1920s, shortly after Ludlow, and did work in the mines around here. Eventually, he retired from the railroads. I remember as a young kid, sitting around talking to him and that [is] why I say they understood unions and they understood what they did. I think too much of us have let that slip through our fingers over time, and we're paying a heavy price for it.

KARIN LARKIN: Yeah, we are.

FAWN-AMBER MONTOYA: Do you think that there has been a shift in audience, as far as who comes to the memorial now?

BOB BUTERO: Oh, I definitely do. [I am usually] trying to, hopefully, schedule a historian to kind of come and speak [on] their terms, Dean [Saitta] has spoken a couple times. We've had different authors, Thomas Andrews, and different people have come. Almost every author that I know of that's written something about Ludlow has come. Zeke Papanikolas, he was a speaker here and different family members, I'm trying to think of the woman who came from California, Linda Linville, she's [been] part of it. We've also tried to reach out to different people. The Petruccis has been a great story on this, you know, especially with [Frank]. That was amazing too [because] we kind of honored him during the National Historic Landmark dedication. When I first called him and told our people we were gonna honor this friend, they said, you got his name wrong because that was one of the children that died, you know, at Ludlow. Talking to him, come to find out that when his mom and dad had their first three children [after the massacre], they named [them] after the three that had died, you know. That was a good story.

Richard Bonacquisti and their family. That type of presence, but we tried to spread that out and, and last year we had a very good turnout from the labor movement statewide. We're hoping to have that again, but I think it's been more of a public interest. I think it was pretty much self-contained in the early days with just the labor movement, and now it's numerous people from different [areas], academia, family, historical groups, so it's spread out, which I think has been very beneficial. It brings better life to the situation.

FAWN-AMBER MONTOYA: You talked about having a more direct role in the program for the annual event starting in 2003. Was there a shift in what was done at the memorial site? I mean, now it's speakers and music; has it always been that sort of thing?

BOB BUTERO: There's been a little bit more labor people that came and spoke. As it progressed, I wanted it to be more of a community, so-called community of interest. To try to reach out to the different people, the different groups. There was a gentleman that was a judge here and he was kind of a historian. He used to talk to different [groups], and he was one of the speakers that I heard many years ago.

We tried to reach out to the community because I thought that [it was] necessary because people showed interest in the committee for the 100th anniversary. [Many] people made an effort, different communities [to be involved]. We had Florence get involved. We had different speakers. Pueblo was big, hosting different events. Colorado Springs, the paintings were up [at the] Pioneer Museum. History Colorado from Denver on down. Everybody was supportive and involved in it. We've tried to reach out to have different family members speak. We've had the Petruccis' cousin and a granddaughter speak there. We've tried to reach out to everybody on that and to so-called build that coalition of people of interest.

And with that [we've had] the different music. Different people have at least dedicated some of their music to that, and it's been well received. I think people who have been to the service and even with the music [we have expanded our outreach].

KARIN LARKIN: What would you like to see moving forward? What sorts of directions would you like to see, sort of the outreach or the stewardship or whatever move in?

BOB BUTERO: Right, probably one of my so-called biggest dreams or biggest on the bucket list or whatever you want to call it is I would really like to see some kind of a museum out there. I would think that that would be some kind of a situation out there where it tells more of a story where people can go and really get [an understanding of what occurred]. It would've been nice to so-called built this out there, but I think that would be one of the things I'd like to see. Hopefully, we could open up tours of different groups, you know, we've had educational groups, people come and do tours, and I think there would be a little bit more to offer than just kind of the site itself now. Where if we had a little video-type deal of some of it. It's going to be a labor slant on what happened there, what went on.

I've always told people I don't care, you may have thought that the coal companies were in the right, you may have thought the National Guard was in the right; you should still have interest in that because it is a part of our history, and people should be a part of that.

But that's what I would like to see, you know, happen. I'm sixty-six. As we get older, hopefully we have people that are willing to step up and take over the service and to have the United Mine Workers plan on doing that, plan on holding the yearly service. Maybe at some point in time it might be the Colorado labor movement that's gotta take over [or] historians or people that wanna see this move forward. [I'd] like to do a little bit better, but it takes funding, it takes money to try to do anything like that; and to try to set up something like that would be, would be great, you know.

Because there's a lot of people that come from the different [camps]. I myself, you know, I was born and raised in Sopris, which was a coal camp just east of town up here. It's where the dam is built now. Sopris was like different communities here in the area, part was company town and part was incorporated. So, as the company town shut down, then, like Valdez up the river. They had the railroad tracks that ran through it. What would be on the railroad tracks is all incorporated, and everything on the south side was company town. So, when Valdez shut down, all of that was either the houses were moved or they were torn down. Segundo [was] the same way, Segundo was a massive coal community and Aguilar. I mean there's a lot of history here, people, they came from those areas.

The greatest generation, they worked in the mines but they, they were kind of the middle class and they didn't want their kids in the mines. They wanted their kids to go out and get an education and stuff of that nature, so it was a lot like the Bonacquistas. Their dad made sure that both of his sons were able to get out and get educated and make a living outside of the mining industry. A lot of people like that have come back. One of the things that I'd like to do here even in Trinidad is set up like a so-called coal camp reunion. You set up in central park out here, which is kind of an open field where you have a Cokedale camp [or] a Sopris camp. [Like what we do now with] Sopris. Every five years, we have a reunion.

Little by little, people are passing on. I think a lot of people, especially with genealogy and stuff now, kind of want to know where they came from. We just had a woman come in here from, actually from Italy. I think [her] grandfather was from Grey Creek. She wanted to go up there; of course, that's all private property. It's hard to get up into that area. But she really wanted [to]. She came into the museum, we talked to her and stuff and like I said, even the people from New York that really didn't have [ties to the massacre]. You know, they had ties, you know, nationality-wise and stuff. I think in that it was basically some kind of private school mainly for Greek children.

[They have the] interest from [their own backgrounds]. Like Froosa just coming in [and making the film *Ludlow: Greek Americans during the Colorado Coal War* (Lewis 2017)]. They had the ties, you know, to Louis Tikas. They also had ties to Ludlow and stuff of that nature here. There's so many immigrants, and I think that was one of the issues. I think that when Ludlow happened, there was tremendous amount of gains made in the different areas, immigration, standard of living, different mine safety [laws], you know, there was a ton of that.

But in the same sense I think we've lost some of that, and we've actually taken a step back in a lot of those arenas. The greatest generation, they kept their nose to the grindstone and they made sure that a lot of these atrocities that happened weren't going to happen again. I think there's been too much think[ing] that we made such great gains. We've [taken] our eye off the prize, and I think we're paying a price for it.

You look at immigration now. You can look back at that time, I mean a lot of it, especially the so-called militia or National Guard's attitude toward a lot of these people was they looked down on them because they weren't so-called Americans. [That's] what's occurring today. [It] is sadly some of the same stuff. These people only came here to make a living. They had a tough time of it, 85 [percent], maybe 90 percent of the people that come here are promised a job.

They're brought in here by someone basically taking advantage of them. That's why I think a lot of times they won't, they don't want to deal with immigration. They want these people to be vulnerable and be able to take advantage of them instead of working to find a solution, but that doesn't mean so-called corporates. That's why they want to keep this anger fighting, that's what I've told people now, I say, do you want to solve this problem? All of these immigrants say, all right, give us five days, we're going home. We're striking. [Where there is] this nationwide strike. We're leaving our jobs, we're headed to Mexico, give us five days to get out of here. You'll see this economy crash. I mean, more so in Colorado and California, New Mexico, Arizona, but pretty much all over the country. Because these people are in Denver now. You go to any fast-food restaurant, it's almost 100 percent immigrants. You go to almost all your housing construction. The economy would just come to a screeching halt. It may be that's what shines the spotlight on what's really happening here.

I mean, from a worker's perspective I could see there'd be a little bit of anger because they look at those people. [They believe that] the reason we can't make high pay is because you guys are willing to do it for a lower pay, but they don't understand the whole dynamics of how it got there and why it's there. [It's] the same thing with a lot of trade agreements and stuff like that. To me, it's not so much about Japan or China wanting their companies to sell stuff here. It's these American companies that are taking our jobs and making products over in those countries and then selling them back to us. That's where the problem exists; [it] is more those people than as far as Chinese compan[ies] or Japanese compan[ies] or somebody like that selling products here. It's these corporations in this country taking advantage of cheap labor overseas.

KARIN LARKIN: Well, I was just going to ask one more [question]. So, in terms of sort of your long-term goals, it sounds like you're trying to figure out sort of a succession plan for how you're going to keep this going,

BOB BUTERO: Right.

KARIN LARKIN: The museum sounds awesome. All in favor of that. What is it that you think . . . we as academics could do to help further that or help . . . facilitate that?

BOB BUTERO: The number one is basically what you're doing now. Anything that you could do, whether it's a course on so-called labor history or like a month-long [lesson], you know, maybe in US history or Colorado history or whatever, be able to on a regular basis be part of the curriculum. So that no matter what your background is, no matter what [you think] those darned workers deserved, whatever the so-called attitudes is, but I believe that people oughta be taught or be a part of this. I'm not going to try to say it was as [important as] the Civil War or the Revolutionary War or anything like that, but it definitely had a big part in civil rights. You know, we had this debate, and I think there's some people that think that while it happened too long ago to have any effect on the passing of the Wagner Act and labor rights, but I don't agree with that.

Rosa Parks, when she sat on that bus in the mid-1950s [years before the passage of civil rights legislation]. Movements take time, you know, to move that way. [The Ludlow Massacre] had a big role. I think that's why it should be taught; I think that people should understand collective bargaining. The people should understand about, even within business classes [it should be taught].

FIGURE 3.2. Michael Romero (*left*) and Bob Butero celebrating Louis Tikas statue dedication, Trinidad, Colorado, 2014. *Courtesy*, Yolanda Romero.

That's another debate in this country is that we're kind of a consumer-driven country. Our people have got to be able to buy products. And when they, to me, when they made this jump from taking money out of people's pockets, you know, they bridged it with credit cards. If you remember back [then], you know fifteen years or so ago, I mean, every week in the mail you got an application for a credit card "You've Been Approved, You've Been Approved," and that continued on and people got into that habit with the credit cards. Then there was also people that got wise to the situation; they build up all this credit, file bankruptcy, clean their slate, you know, keep their nose clean for three or four years. Then start building this credit because they can file for bankruptcy every seven years. Well then, these people said, well, we can't have that anymore, we gotta have some controls, and so they start taking that cheap credit away from people and that's why we had the so-called crash in 2007, 2008.

In order to build a sound economy, you have to have people making a standard of living that they could buy these products and keep this economy going and stuff like that. Collective bargaining or labor history should be taught, and the struggles of different people (figure 3.2).

Civil rights, you know, should be an issue taught in schools. I think that's part of our so-called history or growth and how we went from basically a two-class system, society, to basically three classes. We're retreating backward. That's where I would think, especially people in academia and then even people that are authors or people that are just the general public that have an interest in it [or have] more of an academic background to when they write books and stories and stuff about it.

NOTE

1. In May 2003, the caretaker John Fatur discovered that the granite heads of the miner and his wife had been removed.

REFERENCES

DeMario, Dennis. "Memorial Desecrated." June 12, 2003. https://www.peoples world.org/article/memorial-desecrated/. Accessed November 20, 2019.

Green, James, and Elizabeth Jameson. 2009. "Marking Labor History on the National Landscape: The Restored Ludlow Memorial and Its Significance." *International Labor and Working-Class History* 76: 6–25. *JSTOR*. www.jstor.org/stable /40648508. Accessed April 6, 2020.

Lewis, Shanna. 2017. "Documentary Spotlights Greek American Miners in Shadow of Ludlow Massacre." *Colorado Public Radio*, April 19, 2017. https://www.cpr.org /show-segment/documentary-spotlights-greek-american-miners-in-shadow-of -ludlow-massacre/. Accessed September 3, 2019.

McGovern, George S., and Leonard F Guttridge. *The Great Coalfield War*. Niwot: University Press of Colorado, 1996. Print.

McGuire, Randall. 2004. "Letter from Ludlow: Colorado Coalfield Massacre." *Archaeology* 57 (6). https://archive.archaeology.org/0411/abstracts/letter.html. Accessed September 3, 2019.

Montoya, Fawn-Amber. 2016. "Report to the Governor of the State of Colorado Concerning the Ludlow Massacre Centennial Commission." Submitted to Governor John Hickenlooper, August 1.

Saitta, Dean J., Randall McGuire, and Philip Duke. 1999. "Working and Striking in Southern Colorado, 1913–1914." Paper presented in the symposium "Communities Defined by Work: Life in Western Work Camps and Towns," chaired by T. Van Bueren and M. Maniery. Society for Historical Archaeology Meeting, Salt

Lake City. https://www.du.edu/ludlow/working.html. Accessed September 3, 2019.

Terwillinger, Cate. "Almost Like They Massacred Them Again." June 26, 2003, 2–3. https://www.csindy.com/coloradosprings/almost-like-they-massacred-them-again/Content?oid=1119467. Accessed November 20, 2019.

PART II

Remembering Ludlow

When scholars allow themselves to engage with these spaces, stewards, and the memorial events, they become a part of the collective memory of the place and its history. The boundaries between scholarship and life become blurred, often to the point of becoming nonexistent. Scholars begin to see the humanity and complexities of these events, communities, and memories across space and time. The complexities become more than just words on a page or spoken lectures; they become lived experience. They are linked to contemporary people and events, which highlights the importance of emotion and foregrounds the need for understanding the connections to a longer history and a broader audience.

We, Karin Larkin and Fawn-Amber Montoya, have come to see our scholarship as public but also personal. As scholars, we were trained to be objective in our research and to approach our disciplines within the context of academic discourse. Our own interactions with the events surrounding the Ludlow Massacre and the stewards of this story have placed us into spaces where our disciplinary lines have become blurred with our lived experiences.

https://doi.org/10.5876/9781646422289.p002

In these spaces, we have created relationships and become advocates with other stewards to tell the story of the Ludlow Massacre. These relationships necessitated that we step outside the bounds of traditional academia. We have become public scholars emotionally connected to and invested in preserving the story for the next generation. This work has both blurred and moved the line between objective scholarship and activism, which we view as a positive development in our own work.

As scholars, we have found that our personal perspective and our subjectivity have become crucial to sharing and understanding the story of the Ludlow Massacre. This personal connection doesn't just help us to better understand the profound impacts of the events, it also allows us to connect it in our own lives and share it for posterity. When the events surrounding the Ludlow Massacre are approached with objectivity, it is easy to put brackets around the beginning and end of the strike, to limit the voices of the people present, and to place it within the context of national importance. This might be a cleaner method of categorizing the numerous voices, artifacts, and events that surround the massacre, but the complexity of the story can be lost. In addition, its longevity and communal storytelling can become undervalued when viewed through only an objective lens.

In the course of our scholarly work, we connected with the stewards of Ludlow, but it was really our part in the Ludlow Centennial Commemoration Commission that allowed us to become part of this broader community in a new intimate, and collaborative way. As scholars of Ludlow, we interacted with the stewards of the story, with other scholars, and with pilgrims to the site and annual memorial services during the course of our work. As commission members, we expanded our interactions to also include the audience and various publics that came from around the world to remember and learn about the massacre. We also became witnesses to the memory of the events while at the same time creating additional memories for the next 100 years. By being present at memorial events and speaking to audiences throughout the West, we met the descendants of victims and survivors. We have met individuals who shared how the massacre site or the story of the Ludlow Massacre has influenced their work and their lives. With memorial events held on weekends in June, our families and children have come to these events, visited the memorial site, and met these stewards many times. They have become intertwined with the story of Ludlow through these interactions. The authors of this next section have expanded our families and birthed and raised children as we have studied the history and stood at the base of the memorial reading off the names and ages of the dead mothers and children. These personal connections deepened our empathy and understanding of the Ludlow Massacre and embodied the significance of their sacrifice then and now.

By connecting the past to the present, we have been regularly reminded of the significance of the scholarly work, which impacts not only the academy but the stewards as well. Scholarly research and interpretations of the events can affect the various stewards both positively or negatively. Observing how Bob Butero and the Romeros have embodied the memory and relevance of the strike and massacre elevated us to a greater level of accountability to the descendant and scholarly communities. By our disciplinary training, we are charged with giving accurate, well-researched perspectives centered on artifacts or primary documents. However, this experience has forced us to question how we as scholars share the emotions we experience through our visits to the site, meeting with the descendant communities, or seeing the dedication of volunteers in their home communities sharing the history of Ludlow. How do we document these when our own experience has become part of the collective memory and the history?

As scholars, we know that the history of Ludlow should be shared in classrooms, public spaces, and homes. But our experiences on the Ludlow Centennial Commemoration Commission have shown that this is a more personal story that lives beyond our scholarly research. There is always more to learn. Through the work of the commission, the Ludlow Massacre came to us in different ways and through different perspectives: as children, as college students, in written form, lectures, songs, creative writing pieces, and museum exhibits. The 100th anniversary allowed us to share what we knew, but it also deepened our knowledge and understanding of the event and our relationship with the stewards.

Betsy Jameson's chapter is the speech she gave in 2014 for the centennial commemoration. The speech illustrates the connections of labor struggles before the Ludlow Massacre and, almost 100 years later, with the steel strikes in Pueblo. She also shares her interaction with Frank Petrucci, the younger sibling of those who were killed at Ludlow. Her ability to understand the richness of this history, not just from an objective and scholarly perspective but also from a personal, subjective view allows the reader to see connections over a 100-year time frame. This may have been lost if the story of Ludlow was only approached from a traditional academic perspective.

Karin Larkin explores the development of relationships through archaeological stewardship and the importance of social memory. Larkin expands the definition of archaeological stewardship and highlights the benefits of this expansion. She shares examples of how the work of the Ludlow Centennial Commemoration Commission fostered spaces for the collaboration of stewardship and memory sharing of the Ludlow Massacre.

Fawn-Amber Montoya's chapter recounts her experience working with the performance of *Song of Pueblo: An Oratorio* and the 100th anniversary events. She shares her experience of seeing the connections of poet Frank J. Hayes and corrido writer Elias Baca with actor and composer Daniel Valdez. This chapter illustrates the importance of music in the sharing of the history of the Ludlow Massacre as well as in creating spaces for non-academic venues and methods of sharing the story of the massacre.

All three of these chapters expand the boundaries of scholarship into the realms of emotion, personal connection, and advocacy. They illustrate the importance and impact of moving beyond objective scholarship and creating collaborative partnerships with descendant communities. They also explore the benefits of these partnerships in stewardship.

4

Remembering Ludlow

ELIZABETH JAMESON

This is an abbreviated copy of the speech given at the 2014 Centennial Commemoration.

I have been visiting the Ludlow site for almost fifty years. My first visits were pilgrimages to a site that had deep meaning for me as a historian of Colorado labor. I saw Ludlow in the contexts of other labor wars stretching back at least to Leadville in 1896. The nature of my visits changed in the wake of the vandalism that dismembered the statues on the Ludlow monument. I was privileged to speak at the annual Ludlow commemorations three times—in 2006, as chair of LAWCHA [Labor and Working-Class History Association] Committee to establish National Historic Landmark (NHL) status for [the] site; in 2009, at the official plaquing after we achieved NHL designation; and then in 2014 at the centennial celebration.

The events that followed the attack on the statues altered Ludlow's terrains of memory from a site preserved by the UMW [United Mine Workers] and through personal memory to a site of national and public recognition. Ludlow's history was kept by the UMWA, the annual memorial services, and

https://doi.org/10.5876/9781646422289.c004

the members of the Trinidad local who watched over the site and who collected the registers where visitors recorded their responses and their own memories. Here are just a few that I copied reading through old registers with Mike and Yolanda Romero:

September 18, 1993: We came with our family Tanya age 9 and Sergei, age 8. I told them this was a memorial for children killed in the struggle for human rights and dignity. Rosemary Zibort, Santa Fe, NM

October 12, 1991: . . . I'm passing through—just went to my father's funeral in California. He was Wesley J. Thompson who was born in Ludlow in 1907. He was 7 years old when the massacre happened. He saw it while he and family were in a wagon being shot at. He described the puffs of dirt popping up around the wagon from the bullets being shot at them.

July 3, 1994: I Frank Luchetta am related to Charles Costa. His brother Nicolas Costa was my Grandfather. He spoke of his Bro. Charles often. I'm 65 years old & this experience will last forever. May they rest in God's peace.

Before 2009, fewer than 2,500 sites were designated as National Historic Landmarks; only three were connected to labor struggles. Secretary of the Interior Dirk Kempthorne said when he made the official announcement that "the National Historic Landmark designation is the highest such recognition accorded by the nation to historic properties determined to be of exceptional value in representing or illustrating an important theme, event, or person in the history of the nation. Designation and national recognition encourages owners to protect and preserve the properties." At Ludlow, it worked the other way around. The UMW recognized the importance of the site immediately, bought the land in 1915, and dedicated the monument in 1918. For almost a century, Ludlow's history was kept by the union faithful and passed down privately from generation to generation. The National Historic Landmark designation, the act of Governor [John] Hickenlooper to create the Ludlow Centennial Commemoration Commission, and the outstanding work it did—these official recognitions shone light on Ludlow's history and helped make *public* stories long preserved as private family memories.

By 2006, when I first spoke at Ludlow, the dismembered statues had been repaired—had literally been re-membered. The annual Ludlow memorial service, the testimony of countless visitors who sign the registry at the Ludlow site, and even the violent disfiguring in 2003 of the figures on the Ludlow Memorial monument, all these acts testified to the power of memory. There was no reason to disfigure a monument that had no power to inspire.

The massacre inspired sympathy and outrage from the moment it happened in 1914. The UMW and labor supporters publicized the massacre nationally, focusing on the murder of women and children. That established Ludlow in popular imagination as a unique tragedy. Miners had died underground and had been killed, evicted, and deported in previous strikes, but the militia had stopped short of killing women and children, though they had always been part of the struggles. Kids threw rocks at scabs and yelled at the militia; women paraded, protected union men, raised money, and did the hard daily grubbing to care for their families on strike pay. Women in the 1913 Calumet, Michigan, copper miners' strike dipped their brooms in outhouses and poked scabs with them. Just four months before Ludlow, fifty-nine children died during the Calumet strike on Christmas Eve when someone yelled "fire" at a union Christmas party for striking miners' kids, causing a panic in which seventy-three people were crushed and suffocated in a crowded stairway. But before Ludlow, *state* actions hadn't directly killed women and children. The militia had threatened women but never killed them—perhaps because their names were not Petrucci or Vargas, Costa or Pedregone. They died partly because owners and militia leaders saw the strikers as ignorant, violent foreigners from southern Europe and as Mexicans, who they considered foreigners, although their ancestors settled Santa Fe long before the Rockefellers got to America. General Chase, who commanded the National Guard in Cripple Creek and Ludlow, saw the strikers as "Greeks, Montenegrins, Italians, Servians, and other recent arrivals from the southern countries of Europe . . . present for the one purpose of participating in any riot that might be started" (United States 1914, 10291). Ludlow vividly entered popular memory because women and children died there, yet their tragic deaths can overshadow the larger history of industrial conflicts in which they were embedded. Children died at Ludlow as their parents fought to make better lives for them, to keep the kids in school and the boys out of the mines at least until they grew up, to give their fathers a better chance of living to see them grown. Mother Jones charged that no one cared about the miners' conditions until women and children died. "Little children roasted alive make a front-page story," she said. "Dying by inches . . . does not" (Parton 1925, 191).

Each time I spoke at Ludlow, I ended with the story of Mary Petrucci, who has always epitomized for me the reason people struggled there and what they lost. Mary Petrucci, age twenty-four, born in a coal mining family in the shadow of the Victor-American mine tipple at Hastings, raised in a company house, educated at a company school, married at sixteen to Thomas Petrucci, who loaded boxcars for the coal company in Walsenburg. The morning of April 20, 1914, Mary Petrucci was doing the laundry when her tent in the southeast corner, front row, of the tent colony was set on fire. She ran with her children to the Pedregones' tent and got them safely inside the pit. When she regained consciousness, she was holding her dead infant, surrounded by the corpses of her friends, their children, and her own.

Mary Petrucci chose to be at Ludlow. She was not simply a powerless victim, but neither could she control the choices she had as a working-class woman. She joined three other activists—Pearl Jolly, Mary Thomas, and Margaret Dominiske—who traveled to Chicago, Washington, DC, and New York to speak at rallies and give interviews. Mary Petrucci broke down during the trip and returned to Colorado. She told her story to a reporter:

> "Perhaps," she said, "it seems strange to you that I want to go home, but I do. My man is there and my children are buried there . . . I have been so happy there . . . I used to sing around my work and playing with my babies . . . I'm 24 years old and I suppose I'll live a long time, but I don't see how I can ever be happy again . . . But you're not to think we could do it any differently another time. We are working people—my husband and I—and we're stronger for the union than before the strike . . . I can't have my babies back. But perhaps when everybody knows about them, something will be done to make the world a better place for all babies." (Huffaker 1915)

When Mary Petrucci testified before the US Industrial Relations Commission investigating Ludlow, the *New York Tribune* reported that the audience was in tears. She was born in Colorado, it wrote, "of Italian parents twenty-four years ago and married when but 16. She spoke good English," it marveled, "and impressed the audience as a woman of refinement above her station" (Huffaker 1915). *Above her station.*

In 2009, during the ten-minute ride from my hotel in Trinidad to Ludlow, I was informed that a ninety-year-old man named Frank Petrucci would attend the ceremony. I had not known that five years after the Ludlow Massacre,

FIGURE 4.1. Elizabeth Jameson with Frank Petrucci at the Ludlow Tent Colony site National Historic Landmark designation ceremony, Ludlow annual memorial gathering, June 28, 2009. *Courtesy*, Elizabeth Jameson.

Mary and Thomas Petrucci began having babies again. They named the first three after the children who died at Ludlow; Frank was named for the six-month-old infant who died in his mother's arms. Before the program, I introduced myself and asked Mr. Petrucci if it was okay for me to speak about his mother. Then, in the most extraordinary experience I have had as a historian, as I spoke, I could see nothing but Frank Petrucci's face—that held at that moment the legacy of the tragic past and of parents who dared to bring more babies into a still imperfect world.

I was privileged, after our meeting in 2009, to get to know Frank Petrucci, his niece, and his daughter and to record more family stories (figure 4.1). Mary Petrucci, according to her son and granddaughter, never sang again, but she risked enough hope to love more children. And she issued, I think, the dual challenge of this history encapsulated in her words: "perhaps when everybody knows about them, something will be done to make the world a

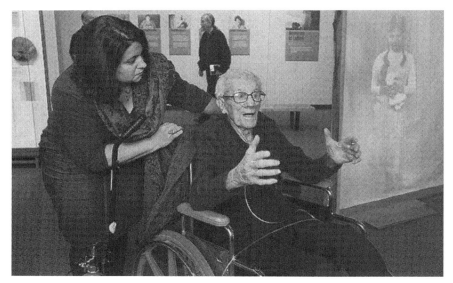

FIGURE 4.2. Frank Petrucci at *Children of Ludlow* exhibit opening at El Pueblo History Museum, Pueblo, Colorado, with Dawn DiPrince, 2014. *Courtesy*, Dawn DiPrince.

better place for all babies." We are challenged to remember and then to act. Ludlow's legacy resonates in a world not yet safe for all babies.

How we remember Ludlow and what we do with those memories may still, in some small ways, make history (figure 4.2).

REFERENCES

Huffaker, Lucy. 1915. "Women's Varied Interests Section: That the Sacrifice of Her Three Children's Lives May Count for Workers' Betterment, Mary Petrucci Goes about Telling Ludlow's Story." *New York Tribune*, February 4, 1915. https://chroniclingamerica.loc.gov/lccn/sn83030214/1915-02-04/ed-1/seq-7/. Accessed December 3, 2021.

Parton, Mary Field, ed. 1925. *The Autobiography of Mother Jones*. Chicago: Charles H. Kerr.

United States. 1914. *Congressional Record: Proceedings and Debates of the 63rd Congress Second Session*. Washington, DC: Government Printing Office.

5

Memory and Stewardship

Collaborative Archaeology in Remembering Ludlow

KARIN LARKIN

Why do communities work to remember and commemorate terrible trage-dies like the Ludlow Massacre? It seems logical that people would want to forget the horror that took place in that cellar where women and children went to escape the battle raging around them in their striking tent colony. Certainly, Colorado Fuel and Iron (CF&I—the company involved) and the state of Colorado actively tried to forget their roles in these horrific events. They took steps to actively address and expunge this episode from public mem-ory and history through their actions following the Ludlow Massacre. But the families and the United Mine Workers of America (UMWA) worked hard to make sure these events were and continue to be remembered, even today. The stewards of this history we highlight in the first part of this book actively strive to keep the memory alive because the event and what it represents still hold personal, cultural, social, and political significance. Due largely to the efforts of the UMWA, this memory not only lives on but is actively commemorated each year. The recent centennial commemoration of the Ludlow Massacre provided descendant communities and scholars alike with an opportunity to

https://doi.org/10.5876/9781646422289.c005

remind the public of the importance of this tragic event to American history. Their stewardship efforts illustrate the importance and purpose of situating this past within contemporary social and political contexts and the role social memory can play in shaping the future. In other words, stewardship provides a vehicle for exercising and engaging social memory with contemporary social issues. These communities view stewardship as not just maintaining the site of the massacre but as integrating the importance of this history into the contemporary social fabric. Archaeology, in contrast, generally defines stewardship much more narrowly; as to protect the site and its artifacts for a future generation. Here, I reflect on my experiences expanding the concept of stewardship in archaeological practice through my work with the Ludlow Centennial Commemoration Commission (the Commission). I include the good, the bad, and the ugly experiences.

THE ROLE OF SOCIAL MEMORY AND COMMEMORATION

What is social memory? We typically think of memory as a phenomenon that happens in an individual's brain where information is encoded, stored, and retrieved. The idea of social memory entails a collective encoding of past events, places, people, or traditions. In this way, memory can be understood as a cultural or social phenomenon as well as an individual one (Connerton 1989; Halbwachs 1992). Maurice Halbwachs (1992) argued persuasively in the 1920s that memory can be collective. Groups of people can encode the past into a social consciousness that can be referenced and retrieved when needed. Suzanne Vromen (1986, 57) succinctly states that "remembering this implies being tied to collective frameworks of social reference points which allow memories to be coordinated in time and space. Not only are memories acquired through society, they are recalled, recognized, and located socially."

Paul Connerton (1989) explores the idea of how social memory is both conveyed and sustained in his book *How Societies Remember*. He argues that collective memory has social and political power and is expressed through commemorative ceremonies as well as bodily practice. Collective memory, therefore, can use references to these past events, people, places, or ideas that can be enacted or embodied to influence the social or political present. These references can be expressed through commemorative ceremonies, material referents (like monuments), or practice. Understanding that memory can be situated within a large social context questions the purpose of social memory. George Gaskell and Daniel Wright (1997, 177) explain that "the reason why some memories are particularly vivid is that they play a significant function in the organization and structure of a person's identity." The same can apply to collective memory and identity. Commemoration not only helps communities remember significant people, places, and events; it creates a sense of social identity and unity through the communication and commemoration of these shared memories (Connerton 1989; Pauketat 2001; Mills and Walker 2008; Alcock 2005, 16; Van Dyke and Alcock 2003; Hobsbawm and Ranger 1983; Trouillot 1995; Eber and Neal 2001). These commemorations of the past not only create social unity but also inform contemporary social and political contexts (Hobsbawm and Ranger 1983). Because memory is not confined to the individual but can apply to a social group, this concept becomes useful for examining social ethos, attitudes, agendas, and dispositions. Scholars can use memory as a powerful tool for looking at what communities find significant, influential, and important in the present based on the way they utilize the past. Communities, particularly descendant communities, act as the stewards of these memories.

So back to my original question, Why do communities work to remember and commemorate terrible tragedies like the Ludlow Massacre? The answer lies in the purpose of social memories. Descendant communities, as stewards of the memories, utilize the past to help inform the present and shape the future. Tragic events, such as the Ludlow Massacre, offer powerful referents to rally around. In the case of the Ludlow Massacre, two distinct yet sometimes overlapping descendant groups hold collective notions of the events, places, and people involved in the 1913–1914 Southern Colorado Coalfield Strike and the Ludlow Massacre. The first group is comprised of the lineal descendants of the participants in the strike and massacre of 1913–1914. The second incorporates coal miners and unionized workers in southern Colorado and is epitomized by the UMWA as (to borrow a phrase for Bob Butero) a "community of interest" in the issues the strike represented. Each group negotiates and constructs narratives to link the past events and people to the present based on their collectively perceived needs and agendas. Since the fateful day of the Ludlow Massacre, both the UMWA and lineal descendants have referenced this event in various ways for a multitude of reasons. Lineal descendants reference the event to evoke the memories of their lost loved ones and the importance of their sacrifices, among other things. The UMWA invokes this past to commemorate the sacrifice these men, women, and children made while also informing contemporary labor and social issues with the goal of advocating for change. For the UMWA, the past acts as an object lesson on the present and a catalyst for action. However, memory is an elusive thing and needs consistent referents to remain in the collective consciousness and so we do not forget. The stewards of these memories work hard to ensure that these events remain in our collective conscience and continue to inform the present and the future.

How do communities such as the UMWA keep these memories alive? In the case of the Ludlow Massacre, there are multiple vehicles for reinforcing memory. The site of the Ludlow Tent Colony and the monument erected by the UMWA provide physical reminders or referents of these memories. The UMWA maintains a monument to the people whose lives were lost during the event. Monuments offer a material reminder of the tragedy as well as a physical space to unite (Alcock 2005, 16). In addition, the UMWA hosts an annual commemoration event at the monument each summer to act as a rallying point for discussing contemporary issues in reference to the strike and the massacre. The UMWA physically maintains the space and keeps the narratives of the people and events of the Ludlow Massacre in the collective public memory. Lineal descendants make pilgrimages to the site and monument, both on their own and as part of the annual memorial services hosted by the UMWA. Lineal descendants also use oral histories to keep these memories alive. Linda Linville's powerful essay at the beginning of this volume illustrates these efforts in a personal and poignant way.

Scholars also participate in reinforcing memory and stewardship efforts around the Ludlow Massacre. Historians dig into the archival record and offer narratives based on the historical accounts of the events in an effort to teach people of this past (McGovern and Guttridge 1972; Montoya 2014; Andrews 2008; Clyne 1999). And since 1997, the UMWA has allowed archaeologists of the Colorado Coalfield War Archaeological Project (CCWAP) to literally dig into the material remains of this past to help supplement the archival and historical record and offer other tangible reminders of the past through the artifacts they uncovered (Larkin and McGuire 2009). Archaeology is about storytelling, and telling stories of important past events is one method of reinforcing collective memory. Archaeologists take the clues left behind in people's material remains (things such as tools, clothing, household items, toys, and, when available, written records) to weave together very personal stories of past people, events, and places. Through these stories, archaeologists remind people of the past and the important lessons the past can teach.

This differs from historical accounts, which often leave out events or people the writers would like to forget. It is important to keep in mind that history is written by the literate, the wealthy, the powerful, and the victors. Their individual and collective memories are the ones that history codifies (Trouillot 1995). Because of this, history often leaves out the majority of the people and events that cast these writers in a negative light. Archaeologists who study the historical record can correct misrepresented ideas or memories in the record. The collective memory of the victors in an important event, while an important record, does not represent a complete or democratic narrative. Archaeology does not have this bias. Historical archaeology uses archaeology to evaluate the accuracy of written documents. Historical archaeologists test those documents against the material remains left behind and evaluate what was not recorded as well as what was recorded incompletely or inaccurately. These gaps often represent the collective memory of disenfranchised groups in history and help to democratize the memory. Practicing historical archaeology allows anthropologists to dig deeper into the social, political, and economic realities of all sectors of society because it concentrates on the intersection of identity, experience, and materiality. Archaeology can help fill in the big gaps left by history, allowing scholars to be better stewards of the past.

The Ludlow Centennial Commemoration Commission united descendants, scholars, artists, and the public to collaborate on stewardship efforts around the memory of this tragic event. The Commission, the UMWA, the CCWAP, lineal descendants, and historians have all acted as stewards of this past in helping to preserve the memory and convey the importance of this event. But what does stewardship really mean in the field of archaeology, and how have project archaeologists practiced stewardship? How did the Commission's work advance stewardship efforts?

STEWARDSHIP AND ARCHAEOLOGY

Archaeological practice not only offers an avenue for stewardship, but archaeological stewardship is also key to practicing archaeology ethically. In fact, stewardship is listed as Principle no. 1 in the Society for American Archaeology's (SAA's) code of ethics. The organization's website defines archaeological stewardship as "the responsibility of all archaeologists to work for the long-term conservation and protection of the archaeological record by practicing and promoting stewardship of the archaeological record. Stewards are *both caretakers of and advocates for the archaeological record for the benefit of all people*; as they investigate and interpret the record, they should use the specialized knowledge they gain to promote public understanding and support for its long-term preservation" (Society for American Archaeology 2019, emphasis added). This definition explains that stewardship is more than the conservation and protection of archaeological materials as generally practiced. Of course, a good archaeological steward acts as a caretaker to protect the material remains of the past and works to preserve them for the future. But good stewards also do much more. As noted in the definition above, archaeologists should be advocates for the past, promote public understanding, and garner public support for long-term preservation. I would argue that preservation extends beyond the physical preservation of the site and artifacts to include preserving the memory, relevance, and importance of the events and people who occupied the site. How can archaeologists achieve these lofty goals? While there are a variety of ways, this chapter focuses on just a few examples practiced during the Commission's work as well as during the original CCWAP fieldwork that involved reaching a wide and varied audience through inclusive and diverse public scholarship and advocating for changes in the present or the future using the past.

Reaching a wide and varied audience not only allows archaeologists to be advocates for the past; it also allows them to promote its relevance to a wider public, thereby practicing good stewardship. Creating an inclusive scholarship through a diverse and inclusive research design helps expand the benefits to "all people" to make the scholarship relevant to a more targeted, invested group. A wide body of literature on working with descendent communities has illustrated that inclusive scholarship should involve working with those communities and including not just their voice but also their agenda from the inception of the project design (Smith 2012; Saitta 2007; Oland et al. 2012; Denzin, Lincoln, and Smith 2008; Mallon 2012; Lonetree 2012; Colwell-Chanthaphonh and Ferguson 2008). Privileging the needs of the descendant communities has the added advantage of making archaeology relevant to contemporary issues. Descendant communities often want to see some utility to contemporary society in the archaeological work, thereby making that work relevant. Working with descendant communities allows archaeologists to redefine the relationship between academics and the public by creating a collaborative environment that is mutually beneficial.

Advocating for the present using the past involves making the past relevant by engaging with politics and social issues in contemporary society. This is an activity many traditional and academic archaeologists shy away from, for good reason (McGuire 2008; McGuire and Paynter 1991; Wood 2002; Leone 1995). Taking a political stance can impact site access and funding. However, archaeologists who practice public archaeology have seen the utility of relating the past to contemporary issues and politics (Blakey 1997; Clark and Amati 2018; Dalglish 2011; McGuire 2008; Saitta 2007; Wood 2002). Creating connections between the past and present offers possibilities for new innovative solutions to recurring problems by learning from past mistakes and triumphs. Using archaeology as a vehicle for understanding the relevance of the past to contemporary society is one of the main goals of public or community archaeology. Using the tools of public archaeology—which include the internet, non-scholarly books, academically vetted television programs, museum exhibits, and public lectures—academic archaeologists can widen their audience and be better stewards and advocates of the past while promoting understanding of the relevance of the past. The opportunities provided by the Ludlow Centennial Commemoration Commission allowed the CCWAP to further our role as stewards.

EXPANDING ARCHAEOLOGICAL STEWARDSHIP IN PRACTICE

As a member of the Ludlow Centennial Commemoration Commission, I was honored to work beside many stewards of this memory, including relatives of victims and survivors, union officials and members, politicians, scholars, a representative of the Colorado National Guard, and members of the public invested in furthering the memory of the Ludlow Massacre. As archaeologists, we rarely get the opportunity to make our work as relevant and impactful as this opportunity afforded. We also rarely get the quality feedback that allows us to contemplate reflectively on our practice and interpretations. Practicing collaborative public archaeology provides a powerful avenue to stewardship and has many benefits. However, it is not easy or without missteps. Using our experiences in the field and those of the Commission, I discuss both benefits and missteps while focusing on my experiences as part of the archaeological project and Commission.

Both the CCWAP and the Ludlow Centennial Commemoration Commission offered a unique opportunity and case study to explore public scholarship, academic and non-academic collaboration, and issues of inclusiveness and diversity in pedagogy. The CCWAP was founded on the principle of practicing public archaeology, and project archaeologists have been the archaeological stewards of the Ludlow Massacre since the beginning of the project in 1997. This project began as a collaboration between three academic institutions (the University of Denver, SUNY Binghamton, and Fort Lewis College) and the UMWA and resulted in a multi-year quest to study the material culture of class conflict associated with the 1913–1914 Southern Colorado Coalfield Strike and the Ludlow Massacre. In consultation with the UMWA, the CCWAP ran fieldwork and public education projects between 1997 and 2004. The founders of the CCWAP—Dean Saitta, Philip Duke, and Randall McGuire—initially sought to develop an archaeology both of and for the working class (Duke and Saitta 2009; McGuire 2008, 2014; Saitta 2007; Walker 2009). They worked hard with UMWA representatives to design a project that was mutually beneficial. They spent years developing and cultivating this relationship (Duke and Saitta 2009, 351; McGuire and Larkin 2009, 1; Saitta 2007), and the project grew over time into a large public archaeology program. In the process, all project archaeologists became stewards of the site and the story alongside the UMWA, descendant communities, and colleagues from other disciplines. I joined the project in 2001 and became the second project director. Funded by grants from History Colorado's State Historical Fund, the project wrapped up in 2004. At that point, the bulk of the fieldwork and interpretive efforts ended. In 2009, McGuire and I published an edited volume on the archaeological work (Larkin and McGuire 2009). In the summer of 2012, I joined a grassroots coalition of people interested in planning events to commemorate the 100-year anniversary of the strike and massacre. The Commission grew out of this grassroots, informal committee. Both Dean Saitta and I, from the original archaeological project, were named to the Commission by then Governor John Hickenlooper. The Ludlow Centennial Commemoration Commission gave project archaeologists a unique platform on which to continue this work practicing collaborative public archaeology and illustrating its relevance and importance to contemporary society.

THE IMPORTANCE OF COLLABORATION

The spirit of collaboration fostered by the UMWA allowed the CCWAP, other scholars, descendants, and communities of interest to work together to create an inclusive, diverse, and accessible narrative. The practice of archaeology benefits immensely from collaboration with the descendant communities. I would even go so far as to argue that archaeology is a meaningless endeavor without the guidance and feedback of people who have ties to these places and events, if available. However, that benefit needs to be reciprocated. Archaeological stewardship means being relevant to the community and promoting understanding of the community's interests and needs. The UMWA expressed the need to highlight the importance and impact of understanding labor history and collective action on workers' rights and laws. During our grassroots meetings in the summer of 2012, some community members expressed an interest in celebrating the roles of women and children in the fight for workers' rights. While other segments of the community were interested in particular ethnic group or immigration issues, all were interested in how to tell these stories in nontraditional and non-academic forums. These diverse perspectives challenged Commission members to think outside our respective boxes and work outside our normal venues to develop interdisciplinary or transdisciplinary collaborative efforts.

Transdisciplinary collaboration provides a powerful tool for stewardship. Take, for example, the roles of women and children in this history. One of the most moving and impactful aspects of Ludlow's story was that it involved families—in particular, women and children. Women and children had been an important force in all aspects of Colorado coal mining life, and they played active roles in the strike efforts as well. Women and children worked, organized, marched, fought, and went on strike alongside the men. The deaths of women and children catapulted this story to a national stage. Yet their stories of daily life and struggle are often untold and undervalued. Their presence is seen and felt in historical photographs of the time, but it is in the material culture excavated by the archaeological project that we begin to uncover their real, un-posed stories. The reality for the working-class laborers in the southern Colorado coalfields was that many women and children had to work to supplement household wages and often contributed substantially to the family's overall financial health. Child labor was prevalent in industrialized society, but few laws existed to protect children's rights prior to the strike. Combining historical accounts and the archaeological research clearly speaks to the work of women and children. Accounts tell horrific stories of boys working as "trappers" in the mines, opening and closing the large wooden doors as the carts came through. Photographs show groups of boys, grimy from working in the mines, posing with coal dust on their faces. In the CCWAP excavations of the cellars at the Ludlow Tent Colony, the children's artifacts were among the most touching and personal of those we uncovered. When we see their belongings, they look remarkably normal. The objects paint a scene of a typical domestic American life in contrast to the stories and photos. Things like a child's shoe, a porcelain doll's head, a fine set of china, toy tea sets, and a baby's bottle are touching, identifiable reminders of normalcy. They also emphasize the Victorian morals of the time espoused by middle-class American society and actively encouraged by company policy. However, these items were found in the burned remains of the cellars of the striking miners' tent colony. In this context, they re-paint the picture of normal everyday domestic life as one interrupted by violence and strife.

Commission members applied a transdisciplinary approach to this topic by highlighting a literary book that focused on a child and creating museum exhibits that both incorporate and highlight these stories. For instance, the material culture excavated from the archaeological project was incorporated into several museum exhibits, including the *Children of Ludlow* at El Pueblo History Museum (figure 5.1) and the Colorado Springs Pioneers Museum exhibit *Memories of a Massacre: Perspectives on Ludlow*. Both were mounted to commemorate the centennial anniversary but forefronted the communities' interests in these often untold stories.

I presented a talk at the Pioneers Museum in conjunction with its exhibit titled "Women in the Ludlow Tent Colony." At this talk, one of the lineal descendants who attended expressed her gratitude to me for highlighting women's contributions. I contributed an article to History Colorado's membership publication titled "Uncovering Families: Historical Archaeology and

FIGURE 5.1. *Children of Ludlow* exhibit entrance at El Pueblo History Museum, Pueblo, Colorado. *Courtesy*, Dawn DiPrince. Photo by Karin Larkin.

the Women and Children of the Southern Colorado Coal Camps." The University of Colorado at Colorado Springs's (UCCS's) professional theatre company, TheatreWorks, also sponsored a production of *Can't Scare Me: The Story of Mother Jones* in which the Obie award–winning stage and screen actress Kaiulani Lee brought her one-woman play to select Colorado theaters, including UCCS, in May 2014. These efforts arose from the desire of the community to foreground the roles of women and children and from the collaborative efforts of the community and the Commission to provide a variety of transdisciplinary products to reach a diverse audience outside the academy. When practicing public scholarship, the touching and tangible reminders of families available through the archaeological remains resonate with the public in ways history books and technical archaeological reports cannot. These collaborative efforts were very successful.

This example of diversifying interpretations and outreach through collaboration exemplifies good stewardship. Project archaeologists used our specialized skill set to refine and add to the collective memory and narration creation of this important historical event and distributed it more widely as part of the Commission. Adding the experiences, knowledge, and interests of the descendant communities enriched the quality and relevance of our interpretations of the past. By working with the UMWA and a diverse set of colleagues, project archaeologists were able to participate in crafting and advocating for the preservation and advancement of this important history.

PRIORITIZING DESCENDENT COMMUNITIES' VOICES AND ADVOCACY

The SAA code of ethics notes that stewardship involves being "advocates for the archaeological record for the benefit of all people." However, the interpretation of that statement does not dictate how the idea is applied. Coming from a museum and anthropological background and training, I personally interpret this statement as employing methodology that both prioritizes the needs and goals of the descendant communities and creates opportunities for advocating for those communities' issues, needs, and desires.

The UMWA understands political advocacy and actively uses the memory of the events surrounding the 1913–1914 strike and the Ludlow Massacre in retelling the hard truths of those events. It also actively evokes the past to address contemporary structural inequalities. In fact, the UMWA has a long history of using this narrative for political gains, going back to the 1916 convention when the then UMWA president John Phillip White successfully proposed a memorial for the site. The monument, dedicated on May 30, 1918, stands as a material reminder of the events at Ludlow and their importance (UMWA 1918). Using the archaeological data in conjunction with historical research and documents, the UMWA successfully nominated the site as a National Historic Landmark in 2009 (see figure 3.1). The project and UMWA won a Stephen H. Hart award for historic preservation as a result of the collaboration.

The yearly UMWA memorial service provides a venue to invoke the memory to illustrate the importance and relevance of this event to contemporary social and political issues. Many of the rights and freedoms the strikers and their families fought for then are still unresolved or have resurfaced in today's political, economic, and social landscape. Commission members sought to assist the UMWA in tying this past to present social issues. Xenophobia, apathy to working-class struggles, lack of adequate healthcare, and political disenfranchisement of the working-class and immigrant populations (to name a few) are all prominent problems discussed in today's news cycles.

Commission members and project archaeologists recognize that our work is a form of stewardship and advocacy, adding new depth and dimension to the political landscape and the narrative of the descendant communities involved. To this end, the Commission pulled together a speaker pool of scholars who focus on using this history to address contemporary issues. At UCCS, the anniversary and my position on the Commission allowed me to argue for campus-wide resources to develop and fund events and public outreach around these issues that would not have otherwise gained traction. I secured a Daniels Ethics Fund grant through the University of Colorado at Colorado Springs College of Business to bring a series of speakers developed by the Commission to campus for public lectures that drew connections between Ludlow and contemporary issues such as healthcare, social inequality, and the political disenfranchisement of immigrants. These events were available to students and the public alike and drew large, diverse crowds.

In the view of the UMWA, as expressed by Robert (Bob) Butero (see his interview, chapter 3, this volume), the archaeological project had a positive impact on these memorial services. Butero (this volume) also credits the archaeological project for revitalizing interest in Ludlow and exposing the history. He notes a bump in attendance at the memorial services once the CCWAP began. Since the CCWAP began its excavations, Butero (personal communication, 2019, chapter 3, this volume) has included project members as speakers at the memorial services over the years, which he believes has made the event more widely attractive. However, whether this bump in attendance is due to interest in the history and the archaeological project or the fact that project involvement also corresponded with a strike at the CF&I steel mill in Pueblo that occurred at the same time is unclear. Certainly, interest in the archaeological project extended beyond the traditional audience at the memorial service and increased exposure to the history. But the strike in the 1990s also galvanized the local labor community. Butero (personal communication, 2019, chapter 3, this volume) now includes a wide range of scholars in the memorial services each year. The work of the Commission provided a relevant platform to continue and further this outreach while providing Butero with a diverse scholar, author, and artist pool from which to draw.

As noted above, the Commission recognized that multiple descendant communities desired to participate and Commission members felt an ethical obligation to engage and collaborate with these various communities. Some lineal descendants of the striking miners actively participated in the events related to the anniversary of the strike and the massacre. Some also still come to the memorial each year. They are principally professional Anglos; few are miners or members of the working class today. Their primary interest is in a personal and familial memorialization of the strike and the massacre. Some speak on behalf of their family and draw out these direct connections to the past, but most attend to reestablish a connection to the familial heritage and honor their ancestors' roles in the social changes that followed. Many have familial stories to tell about their recollection of the past. As good stewards and collaborators, scholars have an obligation to listen and take the time to evaluate these stories.

Collaborative scholars should also, when appropriate, incorporate descendants' stories into the fabric of our interpretations. Unfortunately, not all "experts" practice collaborative scholarship. One incident during the commemorative events drove this point home in an uncomfortable yet illuminating way. At a lecture given by an invited author of Ludlow history, one of the lineal descendants offered an addition to the story of the "Death Pit" from information that had been passed down orally in her family. According to her family's recollection, her heavily pregnant great-aunt gave birth in that fated cellar just before her death. The historical accounts mention a pregnant woman who died in the cellar that day but do not recount her giving birth. As a result, there is no "historical" or written documentation to either support or refute that version of the story. The author told her flat out that her family's recollection was wrong. The descendant was rightfully offended and angry. She questioned why her family's oral account was not as valid as the official historical documentation. This struck me as a valid question, since the "official" historical documentation is spotty at best. The dismissal of the lineal descendant's account raises important points about the process of collaboration and how scholars and experts position and recognize authority, control narratives, and practice public scholarship. This example provides a cautionary tale. Good collaboration with descendant communities necessitates listening to the descendants' oral histories, evaluating those lines of evidence as equivalent to other historical or archaeological lines, and being willing to share "authority." To advocate for the descendant community, one must actively listen, share authority, and privilege their needs, desires, and knowledge. The Commission intentionally worked to create spaces for equity and diversity of thoughts, perspectives, memories, and ideas. Yet this incident involving the invited speaker drove home the fact that not all public scholars practice collaboration in the same spirit of inclusion and partnership.

How else can the project and scholars aid in stewardship while privileging the descendant communities' needs? The answer is both simple and multifaceted. Scholars should remember to simply ask the descendant communities what they hope to gain, but there is no one solution that will work in every situation. When asked what the UMWA would like the scholars to contribute, Butero (chapter 3, this volume) noted that the main contribution of the academy is to continue to spread education about the importance of the strike and the massacre. Yolanda Romero (UMWA Women's Auxiliary Local 9856) (chapter 2, this volume) stressed the same goal as the driving force behind her efforts to spread the knowledge and importance of the union and the events at Ludlow. They want the next generation to know the history and understand the contribution of unions, labor, and collective bargaining in shaping our current social and political situation. Butero wants scholars to continue to keep Ludlow in the public eye and understand the event's role in our civil rights so that future generations do not lose these rights. This illustrates the importance of stewardship of the past in the service of the present and the future.

These examples offer a glimpse at the successes and failures of our attempts to create a truly collaborative and inclusive public scholarship. While I offer this cautionary tale, overall, the Commission was very successful in its attempts at collaboration. This collaborative nature of the Commission allowed expanded opportunities for advocacy and stewardship. Collaboration during the Commission's work happened on many levels and with diverse communities of interest. Combining collaboration with stewardship means incorporating diverse sources of cultural memory into varied methods of narration creation and widely distributing these narratives to diverse publics.

FOSTERING PUBLIC ENGAGEMENT AND EDUCATION

The Ludlow Centennial Commemoration Commission also brought people of diverse backgrounds and talents together to tell diverse stories, using different mediums in an effort to reach a wider, more varied public. As an academic, I set out during my tenure on the Commission to reach out to new audiences both on and off campus. An important aspect of this work involves education in both the classroom and the community. To create a society of critically thoughtful and politically engaged adults, we need to invest in educating our students as well as the broader public. Being good stewards of the memory necessitates outreach in both familiar and unfamiliar venues. We should seek to educate these multiple audiences first about the past and then about how the past informs their social and political lives. The composition of the Commission and the diverse approach to programming allowed the Commission to reach audiences not traditionally served by academics. At the same time, my position on campus also exposed students who had never heard of the event or pondered its importance to the history and its relevance.

On a university campus, students are an important audience. But in general, a professor's reach is limited to their discipline. The history of the strike and the Ludlow Massacre has far-reaching implications and cross-disciplinary boundaries. Yet when I ask students in class if they have heard of the Ludlow Massacre, only one or two hands shoot up (if I am lucky) despite the fact that at least 75 percent or more have grown up in Colorado and attended school in regions where this history happened. This is appalling and disheartening. I recognize that the history is unsavory and a bit embarrassing for the "powers that be." However, this history marked a turning point in US labor relations that deserves remembrance. To create a society of informed citizens, we need to engage histories like Ludlow that embarrass the establishment and relate them to contemporary social life so we can use those opportunities to learn from this collective memory.

To reach students during the centennial anniversary, I tried both traditional and nontraditional methods. Traditional methods included organizing a campus-wide All Campus Reads that introduced the campus to the history of Ludlow, teaching classes on topics related to Ludlow both in my discipline of anthropology and in the broader humanities program, and guest lecturing in classes across campus. In addition, I tried innovative, immersive, and high-impact teaching practices. One of these involved creating a role-playing curriculum that asks students to engage with and debate various stakeholder positions using both primary and secondary documents (discussed in chapter 8, this volume). This activity was created in collaboration with a history faculty member from Metro State University in Denver. We have both successfully used this lesson plan in classes and made it available and distributed it to other faculty members across the country.

Being a good steward, though, means promoting an understanding for the benefit of all—in other words, reaching outside the academic community to advance the relevance of the archaeology and history to a wider audience. To this end, I spoke at community forums in Colorado Springs, such as the American Association of University Women, the Colorado Springs Pioneers Museum, the UCCS Kraemer Family Library, and local schools. However, these are still lecture-based formats that appeal to narrow slices of the public. Reaching a wider audience often involves stretching out of the academic comfort zone and engaging a variety of different formats. For example, using art, exhibits, literature, poetry, music, and theater are other effective ways of talking about difficult subjects in more accessible ways. To this end, I collaborated with colleagues both on and off campus to instigate a variety of visual and performing art experiences inspired by Ludlow. These included a contemporary art exhibit called *Protest!* at the Galleries of Contemporary Art at UCCS in Colorado Springs, a reading and discussion by David Mason (Colorado's then Poet Laureate) on his verse novel *Ludlow*, a performance related to protest music performed for the public by the UCCS music program, and two plays on Ludlow—one original produced by the university's local professional theatre company and the other a sponsored traveling performance on Mother Jones, mentioned previously.

This interdisciplinary and cross-platform programming and pedagogy was far more impactful than an academic simply delivering lectures on the topic to college anthropology and history majors would have been. This approach reached multiple audiences with multiple learning preferences. It touched on history, archaeology, fiction, art, performance, politics, and ethics to humanize the past through nontraditional collaborations in new and innovative ways that would not have occurred if we had not engaged in public scholarship.

CONTINUED STEWARDSHIP

Working on the Commission as a representative of the CCWAP has permanently altered my practice and perspective related to the importance of memory, stewardship, and collaboration in scholarship. The Commission's structure and methodology simultaneously reinforced and transformed my understanding of these concepts, which I had been pondering during most of my career. The collaborative experience of both the CCWAP and the Commission was unique, but the lessons are widely applicable. These lessons relate to the importance of collaboration, the role of memory and advocacy, and the practice of stewardship in scholarship. Working on the Commission exposed new aspects and lessons of practicing public scholarship that highlight the benefits and importance of long-term collaboration and stewardship. The establishment of the Ludlow Centennial Commemoration Commission (figure 5.2) provided a platform for exploring a different type of archaeological collaboration with multiple stakeholders and facilitated public engagement that extended the reach of traditional public scholarship and stewardship. It was the structure, form, and goals of the Commission that created a synergy that fashioned transformative experiences for those who both organized and participated in the events surrounding the commemoration.

The examples offered here provide insights, lessons, and potential models for practicing stewardship and public scholarship. The Commission spent two years trying to remind people of the importance of Ludlow to our future. Using community outreach, we sought to engage multiple audiences in the construction of knowledge and make these new interpretations of the past relevant to multiple audiences, including descendant communities, unionized workers, scholars, educators, students, policymakers, and the public. The process of practicing this type of public scholarship offered many insights and lessons. I will summarize just a few.

1. Good collaboration and stewardship took creativity, work, humility, and dedication. Creating these types of diverse and inclusive experiences involved a large time commitment and effort by everyone on the Commission and the larger community committee.
2. This work necessitated thinking outside the box and sharing authority and narration creation. At times, this process proved uncomfortable and difficult. But most of the time, the process resulted in wonderfully creative products and opportunities.
3. The unfortunate incident described above suggests that scholars need to recognize other sources of knowledge and evidence. To achieve true collaboration, scholars should approach the process with humility and an open mind. Scholars should share authority and power with descendant communities.

FIGURE 5.2. Governor John Hickenlooper signing the Executive Order establishing the Ludlow Centennial Commemoration Commission in his office with Commission members in the background, Denver, Colorado, April 19, 2013. Commission members pictured include (*left to right*): Thomas Andrews, (Josephine Jones not shown), Dawn DiPrince, Karin Larkin, Maria Sanchez-Tucker, Robert Butero, Dean Saitta, and two local representatives not on the Commission, Leroy Garcia and Ed Vigil from southern Colorado. *Courtesy*, Dawn DiPrince.

4. The relationship should be reciprocal and mutually beneficial. Continued stewardship dictates that our work and collaboration with descendant communities should continue beyond the funding limitations of the project. Collaboration involves developing relationships. These relationships take time to nurture and should not be abandoned when the project concludes. One common complaint from descendant communities about collaboration involves scholars neglecting these relationships when the project ends. However, continued stewardship necessitates continued collaboration.

5. Finally, expanding beyond traditional scholarship and practicing transdisciplinary education and outreach can be extremely impactful.

These reflections on my involvement with the Ludlow Collective of archaeologists and the Ludlow Centennial Commemoration Commission working alongside union representatives, lawmakers, descendant communities, and students have shaped my understanding of the practice and importance of collaboration and stewardship. This platform created a rich tapestry of information sharing, advocacy, and outreach. The Ludlow Centennial Commemoration Commission helped develop interdisciplinary narratives that reached varied audiences not attainable sequestered in the academic realm. This project has proven repeatedly that what we do matters. While the Commission officially ended in December 2014, the members all agreed that we need to continue to work together to be good stewards of the past and help the public remember the important lessons these events taught us. We need to make sure they continue to carry forward into the next 100 years. Let's not forget the lessons of Ludlow: that working collectively—union member, archaeologist, worker, historian, community member, and student—we are more powerful together than divided. Together, maybe we can help continue the important work these striking families started and can carry their stories forward to affect change.

REFERENCES

Alcock, Susan E. 2005. "Monuments and Memory." *Archaeology* 58 (4): 16.

Andrews, Thomas G. 2008. *Killing for Coal: America's Deadliest Labor War*. Cambridge, MA: Harvard University Press.

Blakey, Michael L. 1997. "Past Is Present: In the Realm of Politics, Prospects for Public Participation in African-American Plantation Archaeology—Comments." *Historical Archaeology* 31 (3): 140–145.

Clark, Bonnie J., and Anne Amati. 2018. "Powerful Objects, Difficult Dialogues: Mobilizing Archaeological Exhibits for Civic Engagement." *International Journal of Heritage Studies* 25 (7): 708–721.

Clyne, Richard J. 1999. *Coal People: Life in Southern Colorado's Company Towns, 1890–1930*. Vol. 3. Denver: Colorado Historical Society.

Colwell-Chanthaphonh, Chip, and T. J. Ferguson. 2008. *Collaboration in Archaeological Practice: Engaging Descendant Communities*. Lanham, MD: Altamira.

Connerton, Paul. 1989. *How Societies Remember*. Cambridge: Cambridge University Press.

Dalglish, Chris. 2011. *Archaeology, the Public, and the Recent Past*. Suffolk: Boydell.

Denzin, Norman K., Yvonna S. Lincoln, and Linda Tuhiwai Smith. 2008. *Handbook of Critical and Indigenous Methodologies*. Los Angeles: Sage.

Duke, Philip, and Dean Saitta. 2009. "Why We Dig: Archaeology, Ludlow, and the Public." In *The Archaeology of Class War: The Colorado Coalfield Strike of 1913–1914*, edited by Karin Larkin and Randall H. McGuire, 351–362. Boulder: University Press of Colorado.

Eber, Dena Elisabeth, and Arthur G. Neal. 2001. *Memory and Representation: Constructed Truths and Competing Realities*. Bowling Green, OH: Bowling Green State University Popular Press.

Gaskell, George D., and Daniel B. Wright. 1997. "Group Differences in Memory for a Political Event." In *Collective Memory of Political Events: Social Psychological Perspectives*, edited by James W. Pennebaker, Dario Paez, and Bernard Rimé, 175–189. Mahwah, NJ: Lawrence Erlbaum Associates, Inc.

Halbwachs, Maurice. 1992. *On Collective Memory*. Chicago: University of Chicago Press.

Hobsbawm, Eric J., and Terence O. Ranger. 1983. *The Invention of Tradition*. New York: Cambridge University Press.

Larkin, Karin, and Randall H. McGuire, eds. 2009. *The Archaeology of Class War: The Colorado Coalfield Strike of 1913–1914*. Boulder: University Press of Colorado.

Leone, Mark P. 1995. "A Historical Archaeology of Capitalism." *American Anthropologist* 97 (2): 251–268.

Lonetree, Amy. 2012. *Decolonizing Museums: Representing Native America in National and Tribal Museums*. First Peoples: New Directions in Indigenous Studies. Chapel Hill: University of North Carolina Press.

Mallon, Florencia E. 2012. *Decolonizing Native Histories: Collaboration, Knowledge, and Language in the Americas*. Narrating Native Histories. Durham, NC: Duke University Press.

McGovern, George S., and Leonard F. Guttridge. 1972. *The Great Coalfield War*. Boston: Houghton Mifflin.

McGuire, Randall H. 2008. *Archaeology as Political Action*. Vol. 17. Berkeley: University of California Press.

McGuire, Randall H. 2014. "Won with Blood: Archaeology and Labor's Struggle." *International Journal of Historical Archaeology* 18: 259–271.

McGuire, Randall H., and Karin Larkin. 2009. "Unearthing Class War." In *The Archaeology of Class War: The Colorado Coalfield Strike of 1913–1914*, edited by Karin Larkin and Randall H. McGuire, 1–28. Boulder: University Press of Colorado.

McGuire, Randall H., and Robert Paynter. 1991. *The Archaeology of Inequality*. Cambridge, MA: Basil Blackwell.

Mills, Barbara J., and William H. Walker. 2008. *Memory Work: Archaeologies of Material Practices*. 1st ed. Santa Fe, NM: School for Advanced Research Press.

Montoya, Fawn-Amber. 2014. *Making an American Workforce: The Rockefellers and the Legacy of Ludlow*. Boulder: University Press of Colorado.

Oland, Maxine, Siobhan M. Hart, and Liam Frink. 2012. *Decolonizing Indigenous Histories: Exploring Prehistoric/Colonial Transitions in Archaeology*. Tucson: University of Arizona Press.

Pauketat, Timothy R. 2001. *The Archaeology of Traditions: Agency and History before and after Columbus*. Gainesville: University Press of Florida.

Saitta, Dean J. 2007. *The Archaeology of Collective Action*. The American Experience in Archaeological Perspective. Gainesville: University Press of Florida.

Smith, Linda Tuhiwai. 2012. *Decolonizing Methodologies: Research and Indigenous Peoples*. London: Zed Books.

Society for American Archaeology. 2019. *Principles of Archaeological Ethics*. http://www.saa.org/AbouttheSociety/PrinciplesofArchaeologicalEthics/tabid/203/Default.aspx. Accessed June 2, 2019.

Trouillot, Michel-Rolph. 1995. *Silencing the Past: Power and the Production of History*. Boston: Beacon.

UMWA (United Mine Workers of America). 1918. "The Ludlow Monument." *United Mine Workers Journal* 6 (4): cover.

Van Dyke, Ruth and Susan E. Alcock. 2003. *Archaeologies of Memory*. Chichester: John Wiley and Sons.

Vromen, Suzanne. 1986. "Maurice Halbwachs and the Concept of Nostalgia." *Knowledge and Society: Studies in the Sociology of Culture Past and Present* 6: 55–66.

Walker, Mark. 2009. "Archaeology and Workers' Memory." In *The Archaeology of Class War: The Colorado Coalfield Strike of 1913–1914*, edited by Karin Larkin and Randall H. McGuire, 311–330. Boulder: University Press of Colorado.

Wood, Margaret C. 2002. "Moving towards Transformative Democratic Action through Archaeology." *International Journal of Historical Archaeology* 6 (3): 187–198.

6

Melodies and Memories

Places for Remembrances of Ludlow

FAWN-AMBER MONTOYA

The words from the song "Joe Hill" rang through Pueblo, Colorado's Memorial Hall on the night of April 18, 2014. Perhaps it was fitting that this song was sung here. Woodrow Wilson gave his last public speech on September 25, 1919 at Memorial Hall before he fell ill from a stroke (Knock 1992, 263; Link and Little 1990). Wilson had called out federal forces to quell the violence of the 1914 Colorado Coalfield War. John McCutcheon, the performer of the song, was the final musician of a group of talented artists brought together to commemorate the 100th anniversary of the Ludlow Massacre. The other musicians who shared their talent with an audience of over 200 people included the Fanning Brothers, Inaiah Lujan, and Daniel Valdez. The concert was part of a weeklong series of events that included poetry and book readings, an academic symposium with scholars from all over the United States, and a memorial at the Ludlow Massacre site with visitors from as far away as Greece (Montoya et al. 2016).

During the concert, John McCutcheon (2012) shared a story before his rendition of "Joe Hill." He spoke about a performance he had given in

https://doi.org/10.5876/9781646422289.c006

Melbourne, Australia, years before, sharing that a retired electrician in the audience had requested the song "Joe Hill." As a younger man, the electrician heard opera singer Paul Robeson perform an impromptu concert at the construction site of the Sydney Opera House (Curthoys 2010, 171). Robeson told the workers that after the completion of the Opera House, the world would talk about its greatness and the beauty of the architects' work. Robeson encouraged the workers to remember that they were the ones who built this architectural wonder.

The story resonated with the audience in Pueblo in 2014 and with the memorial events surrounding the Ludlow Massacre. As McCutcheon began to sing, the audience was enthralled. The song in many ways reflected what I felt about my own connection to the Ludlow Massacre. The importance of the labor movement remained relevant in my life and in the lives of the audience because of the sacrifices miners and their families made during the Ludlow Massacre. The audience at the celebration included residents of Pueblo, Colorado, and visitors from around the world. These visitors came to southern Colorado to acknowledge the need to remember the massacre and how it had impacted their lives. The music connected the audience members to each other; regardless of their background, the songs brought history back to life, with the performers connecting the audience to historical figures. Coalminers and steel mill workers, their sons and daughters, grandsons and granddaughters all joined with McCutcheon on the final chorus. The lyrics of this song brought back not just the memory of Robeson's Sydney Opera House visit, the performance allowed the audience to transcend location and time through music.

In the communities around Ludlow, Colorado, survivors of the massacre and members of the United Mine Workers of America (UMWA) have shared and continued to tell the story of the Ludlow Massacre for the past 100 years. They gather at the massacre site to recall the memories of those who died and to tell the stories of the living impacted by the massacre. This tradition of sharing has occurred and still occurs in innumerable ways. The descendants of those present on the day of the massacre at Ludlow, Colorado, and others who came to know this history did so through the continual sharing of stories in an oral form.

My first hearing of the story occurred in an oral format in a third-grade classroom less than 20 miles from the massacre site, followed by my first school fieldtrip to the site in the spring of 1986. At a young age, I learned that the Ludlow Massacre site mattered to the national narrative of the United States.

This experience created a personal narrative for me as well. In formal histories written with an objective view, the personal experience can be easily left out because emotions attached to the event are not generally respected in an academic setting. In an oral telling, however, the perspective of the teller enriches the meaning of the story, and songs and lyrics can be included to illustrate the lasting nature of community memory. The emotions the teller portrays through his or her emphasis on certain words, pauses, and details evoke a meaning beyond just words on a page. Oral tradition may be a brief telling, portions of the story woven into a larger narrative, but it can also be told through music composition. Each telling is unique to the specific moment and to the audience. Lyrics and music composition enable the history of the massacre to be shared with countless audiences through the artists' own voices, lyrics, or melodies.

Perhaps the most famous oral telling of the massacre is Woody Guthrie's "The Ludlow Massacre." His music allows the story to be told in a manner accessible to a wide audience across time. This story sharing allows the listener to repeat the story in their own manner and to listen to the music in addition to the words. By creating an oral and artistic retelling thirty years after the event, Guthrie shares his own version of the Ludlow Massacre (Jackson 2007, 116–118). Guthrie's music about the event introduced scores of people to the Ludlow Massacre. Due to the popularity of his work, this song has lived on in a variety of musical retellings for more than seventy years.

What about songs written from the perspective of those present during the massacre or active in its unfolding? Are there artists whose work possibly did not gain the same notoriety as Woody Guthrie enjoyed, yet had lyrics composed physically or temporally closer to the Ludlow Massacre or whose actions have influenced those present during the massacre? Without the same notoriety as Guthrie, would these words survive for over 100 years?

SONG OF PUEBLO

In the fall of 2008, Deborah Espinosa, then director of El Pueblo History Museum, and her husband, Juan Espinosa, received grant funding from

History Colorado to hire a composer to write music and lyrics for the production *Song of Pueblo: An Oratorio*, focused on the history of southern Colorado. The concept behind the oratorio format focused on the idea that the history of the region could be told through a stage performance that included dance, video, and song. The Espinosas contracted with composer and actor Daniel Valdez to create the piece.

Valdez began his work in performing arts and music while a member of Teatro Campesino during the California farm worker protests in the 1960s. He and his brother Luis worked with Cesar Chavez in portraying the farm workers' plight through *teatro*. Daniel Valdez rose to prominence when he was cast in the 1978 stage production of *Zoot Suit* as one of the main characters, Henry Reyna. After the *teatro* performances ended, he played the same part in the 1982 Hollywood film. In addition, Valdez is known for his work as one of the producers of the film *La Bamba*, in which he also played a supporting cast member. In 2017, he appeared in the revival of *Zoot Suit* at the Mark Taper Forum in Los Angeles, California, for the 40th anniversary commemoration (Los Angeles Theater Works 2017; La Voz 2016).

For the *Song of Pueblo*, the Espinosas compiled primary documents about the Sand Creek Massacre, the Pueblo flood of 1921, the local steel industry, and the region's broad migration and immigration history to share with Valdez to assist him in writing the oratorio. Valdez traveled with the Espinosas to the physical spaces where the history occurred. He and the Espinosas felt that by both visiting the spaces where historical events took place and researching the historical documents, Valdez would capture the emotions of the location and its history to portray to audiences viewing *Song of Pueblo*. His understanding of the emotions connected to spaces where violence and historical trauma had occurred influenced Valdez's creation of the production.

In 2008, at a house party at which he previewed a few of the songs from *Song of Pueblo*, Valdez recounted his visit to the Ludlow Massacre site and how he felt a connectedness to the location. He commented that the last name Valdez was included among the names of the dead and that recognizing his own name made him think about how his family—even though they were not involved—could have been among the victims of the massacre. Like many others with no direct connection to the site, when Valdez found his family name on the memorial, he experienced a more personal view of those who lost their lives. The visit to the site made the people who died at Ludlow relatable and connected to Valdez's own life (Espinosa 2008).

REVISITING LUDLOW FIELD

In 1918, the UMWA held a large memorial at the Ludlow Massacre site to unveil the permanent monument. The monument became the gathering place for survivors and victims of the massacre and their descendants where the Ludlow Massacre could be remembered for generations. For the past 100 years, visitors from throughout the region and the rest of the world have come to Ludlow to pay their respects to those whose lives were lost. The UMWA would come to refer to the Ludlow Massacre site as its Gettysburg, with an annual formal gathering to acknowledge the lives lost and the impact of the massacre on the larger movement. The UMWA leadership uses this site to recognize that the Ludlow Massacre symbolizes more than just a skirmish in Colorado (Rees 2010, 13–14).

In 1918, Frank J. Hayes, UMWA president at the time, composed a poem. Hayes had served as UMWA vice president during the 1913–1914 strike. On the occasion of the memorial, Hayes shared his poem "Ludlow Field." Hayes's poem was recorded in a 1918 issue of the *Trinidad Chronicle*, which I came across in the process of writing my doctoral dissertation (Hayes 1918). I included the poem in one of my dissertation chapters reflecting on the Ludlow Massacre site. Two years later, I was introduced to Valdez and the Espinosas. I shared a copy of the poem along with some other primary documents relating to the Ludlow Massacre with Daniel Valdez.

While visiting the site, Valdez recalled that a melody came into his mind. The tune stayed with him as he sought the right words to match the music. He found none. Valdez said that weeks later he came across the poem "Ludlow Field" that I had given him, and as he recited the lyrics, he realized that the words of the poem fit perfectly with the melody that haunted him. Today, the song is known as "Ludlow Field," with Valdez giving credit for the lyrics to Frank Hayes in 1918 and for the musical composition to himself.

The *Song of Pueblo* performances share Hayes's poem with audiences throughout Colorado. In addition, the song has been recorded for distribution by Valdez and by the Song of Pueblo Ensemble with Tom Munch as the main vocalist. In 2009, Munch performed "Ludlow Field" at the Ludlow Tent

Colony site for the annual memorial, and in 2014, Valdez performed the piece at Pueblo's Memorial Hall for the Ludlow concert.

For me, the sharing of "Ludlow Field" with Valdez made me pay closer attention to how music could link people to the Ludlow Massacre even decades later. This experience opened my mind to think more about the Ludlow Massacre from a personal perspective rather than an academic one. It also caused me to think about the connections across time that only someone living in these spaces might witness, especially if that person understood the historical context.

By opening my mind, I found that living near the massacre site and participating in memorial events allowed me to see connections across time. It allowed me to meet the descendants of those who had been present at the massacre and to realize that my own memories associated with this space were part of a broader narrative.

In 2013, I was elected co-chair of the Ludlow Centennial Commemoration Commission (the Commission). Much of my work on the Commission focused on facilitating a statewide speakers' series and planning an academic symposium that included a concert. During Commission meetings, we often discussed how to highlight the central role music played in the lives of the people who lived at the Ludlow Tent Colony, it had provided a way for individuals of different language groups to communicate with each other and improve morale.

The idea for the concert began in the fall of 2013, when Dr. Madison Furrh shared a songbook English graduate students at Colorado State University–Pueblo had compiled as an assignment for one of the courses he taught. The students had concluded that music was a method of telling the complexities of the history of labor, and the songbook contained many songs that centered on the Ludlow Massacre. In November 2013, Furrh approached Dawn DiPrince, the other co-chair of the Commission, and I regarding how this text could be represented in the centennial commemorations. During these discussions, John McCutcheon reached out to Furrh regarding his plans for the celebration. McCutcheon made it clear that he would be at the Ludlow Massacre site on the morning of April 20. His idea was very simple; he was coming to southern Colorado to commemorate the Ludlow Massacre, and he would sing and play songs that resonated with him, including the "Colorado Strike Song." People were welcome to join him, and, best-case scenario, there would be a small impromptu concert at the Ludlow Tent Colony 100 years to the day that the Ludlow Massacre occurred. McCutcheon's plans and the book of songs started discussions about the potential for a larger concert to be held during the weeklong series of events planned for April 2014 that would culminate with a memorial service at the massacre site.

As I assisted with organizing the concert, I reached out to Daniel Valdez to see if he would be interested in performing "Ludlow Field." At the time, Valdez was artist in residence at Su Teatro, a Chicano theater company in Denver, Colorado. During his residency, Valdez assisted Tony Garcia, Su Teatro's executive director, with the revival of the performance piece *Ludlow: El Grito de las Minas* (figure 6.1). The year prior to the concert, I had met Garcia when he began attending meetings of the Ludlow Centennial Commemoration Commission. As Valdez and Garcia worked on the revival of *Ludlow*, their interest in Latino/a musicians present at the massacre resulted in them finding a reference to a corrido written by Elias Baca, a survivor of the Ludlow Massacre. Garcia and Valdez contacted me in March 2014, asking if I might have any more information about Baca.

I did some research and came across a journal article written by Sarah Rudd (2002). Rudd's piece was based on oral interviews collected by Nancy Taniguchi and David Stanley in the 1980s. The interviews included Baca sharing his history and music, as well as Baca's family sharing their knowledge of his life and music. After reading the article, I reached out to Rudd in early April 2014 to see if she had more information about Baca. She quickly replied, informing me that she had audiotapes of interviews that had not been digitized or transcribed.

The week before the weeklong series of events, I was in Salt Lake City, Utah, for the National Association of Chicano and Chicana Studies Conference. I was able to retrieve the tapes and took them back to Pueblo to be digitized and put on a DVD. The night of the concert, I was able to deliver a DVD of Elias Baca's voice and music to Daniel Valdez.

Elias Baca was born in 1895 in Trinidad, Colorado, and was raised in Aguilar, Colorado. He spent his working life in the coalfields of southern Colorado, Wyoming, and Utah. As a young miner, he joined the UMWA and recalled being at Ludlow. Baca's love of music was fostered as a young child with his father, a fiddle player, teaching him how to play the fiddle

FIGURE 6.1. Poster for *Ludlow el Grito de las Minas: The Cry of the Mines* performance at Su Teatro Cultural and Performance Center, Denver, Colorado, March 2014. *Courtesy*, Anthony Garcia.

and guitar. As he grew, he played at dances in his community and began to write his own music and lyrics. Elias Baca wrote corridos about the massacre, which he shared with family members. His version of the Ludlow Massacre was preserved with his corrido *"Que Viva La Nación."* Baca's corrido rallied Spanish-speaking union miners and created an identity linking his labor with his ethnicity. The corrido lyrics were originally in Spanish, but Rudd transcribed the song and provided the translation in her article.

Baca's corrido of the massacre left an imprint on his life. It was not nationally recognized, and it has not become part of a broader narrative of the Ludlow Massacre from a historical perspective; yet the singing of the corrido retold the story of Ludlow again and again to audiences outside southern Colorado. It also kept the memory of Baca's role in the massacre and his experience as a miner fresh in his mind and became a way to connect people to an event they were unaware of due to their language or origin.

Perhaps Baca was present at the many memorials that occurred after the Ludlow Massacre, with his songs shared more often than has been recorded. The Ludlow Massacre impacted people for their entire lifetimes, and many of these stories have been lost or have only been retained in the family memories of the survivors. The memory of the Ludlow Massacre has lived on in informal spaces and has been shared as a story of a community of workers united in a common cause, far from the official histories.

Hayes and Baca's oral telling of the Ludlow Massacre never gained the popularity of Woody Guthrie's "Ludlow Massacre," but their creativity influenced their audiences; Baca, a corrido singer, shared with Spanish-speaking audiences and Frank J. Hayes's words spoke to union audiences (Rudd 2002). This method of remembering the Ludlow Massacre explains not just how people can remember the massacre but also how the massacre felt in the hearts and minds of those who had embraced its history.

Woody Guthrie's song has been preserved. *Ludlow Field* and *"Que Viva la Nación"* have been saved through oral telling and the recording of the music composition. These songs will continue to allow the history of the Ludlow Massacre to be told across the world. Being a witness to this transfer of knowledge in an oral, musical, and artistic format allowed me to become part of the history. I was the bridge for Frank J. Hayes's and Elias Baca's voices to be heard once again in the spaces they had occupied, allowing the victims of the massacre to live again. John McCutcheon's singing of the "Joe

FIGURE 6.2. Ludlow in Requiem poster, April 18, 2014, Pueblo Memorial Hall. *Courtesy*, Fawn-Amber Montoya.

Hill" lyrics "I never died, says he" reminded me at that concert that it was through the music of the Ludlow Massacre and the oral telling, that the victims were able to live again across space and time.

I sat in that concert hall in April 2014. My son had been born the spring after Daniel Valdez performed *Song of Pueblo: An Oratorio* for the first time (figure 6.2). My daughter was born three weeks before Governor John Hickenlooper signed the Executive Order appointing the Commission. My children have been to Ludlow more times than I can count; they have heard me tell the story and visited the coalmines of southern Colorado. Yet in the early spring of 2019, I brought my children to Ludlow. I played "Ludlow Field" to give them a different telling. For the first time in their lives, it clicked. My son looked at me and said, "that's here. Those children died." My daughter spent the next three weeks requesting the song whenever we got in the car. The following week, on April 18, Daniel Valdez participated in a short concert. He recounted his discovery of the words for "Ludlow Field." Although I had heard it performed a number of times, this was the first time my children heard it in person. The story of the Ludlow Massacre can be told through a lecture, a film, a visit to the site. But for some, the music tells the story in a way no expert can.

REFERENCES

Curthoys, Ann. 2010. "Paul Robeson's Visit to Australia and Aboriginal Activism, 1960." In *Passionate Histories: Myth, Memory, and Indigenous Australia*, edited by Frances Peters-Little, Ann Curthoys, and John Docker, 163–184. Canberra: Australian National University Press.

Espinosa, Juan. 2008. *Making of Song of Pueblo*. DVD in author's possession.

Hayes, Alfred, and Earl Robinson. 1936. "Joe Hill." http://www.folkarchive.de/joe hill.html. Accessed September 24, 2019.

Hayes, Frank J. 1918. "Beautiful Monument to Ludlow Victims Unveiled on Site of Tent Colony Today." *Chronicle News* (Trinidad, CO), May 30.

Jackson, Mark Allan. 2007. *Prophet Singer: The Voice and Vision of Woody Guthrie*. Jackson: University Press of Mississippi.

Knock, Thomas. 1992. *To End All Wars, New Edition: Woodrow Wilson and the Quest for a New World Order*. Princeton, NJ: Princeton University Press.

La Voz Staff and Deborah Espinosa. 2016. "Song of Pueblo." *La Voz*. http://www .lavozcolorado.com/detail.php?id=8574. Accessed September 13, 2019.

Link, Arthur S., and J. E. Little, eds. 1990. *The Papers of Woodrow Wilson*. Vol. 63. Princeton, NJ: Princeton University Press.

Los Angeles Theater Works. 2017. "Daniel Valdez." https://latw.org/artist-public-profile/daniel-valdez. Accessed September 13, 2019.

McCutcheon, John. 2012. "Joe Hill (live)." https://www.youtube.com/watch?v=pUEmmTVNcsk. Accessed September 2, 2019.

Montoya, Fawn-Amber, Dawn DiPrince, Karin Larkin, Thomas Andrews, Robert Butero, William Convery, Victoria Miller, Adam Morgan, Jonathan Rees, Dean Saitta, Maria Sanchez-Tucker, and Josephine Jones. 2016. "Report to the Governor of the State of Colorado Concerning the Ludlow Massacre Centennial Commission." Submitted to Governor John Hickenlooper, August 1, 2016. Denver.

Rees, Jonathan H. 2010. *Representation and Rebellion: The Rockefeller Plan at the Colorado Fuel and Iron Company, 1914–1942*. Boulder: University Press of Colorado.

Rudd, Sarah M. 2002. "Harmonizing Corrido and Union Song at the Ludlow Massacre." *Western Folklore* 61 (1): 21–42.

PART III
Teaching Ludlow

The story of the Ludlow Massacre has been used to teach lessons for over a century. Whether those lessons are learned around a dinner table, in a union hall, or in a classroom, the history becomes both a cautionary tale and a rallying point. The primary goal of the stewards of Ludlow has been and remains to educate the public about this history and the importance of these events in shaping the present. Linda Linville, Robert Butero, and Yolanda Romero all express the importance of educating the public about this history. The Ludlow Centennial Commemoration Commission (the Commission), starting with the statewide grassroots committee, embraced the goal of education in the spirit of collaboration.

The language of the Executive Order establishing the Commission emphasized education. To paraphrase, the Executive Order outlined the mission of the commission as to (1) engage in efforts to raise awareness of, (2) explore the social and political issues that underscored, and (3) examine the impact of the events surrounding the strike and the massacre. We interpreted all this to mean educating a multifaceted audience broadly about this history and its relevance.

https://doi.org/10.5876/9781646422289.p003

This effort was begun decades before the work of the Commission and has taken many forms. Various parties have participated in these efforts, ranging from historians to archaeologists to lineal descendants to union officials and members. In their interviews in this volume (chapters 2 and 3), Bob Butero and Yolanda Romero discuss some of these efforts by the union and the local community. Butero discusses how his father, grandfather, and uncle would sit around the table and discuss the history of union workers in the region and the role of the union over time in shaping policy and workplace benefits. Every year at the memorial service, the United Mine Workers of America (UMWA) utilizes the lessons of this history to inform attendees about current social and political affairs. Butero describes the union's use of labor history at the memorial services. Romero adds a different perspective. She discusses how the work of Mother Jones inspired her to work with a group of coalminers' wives to start a Women's Auxiliary for the local union in the 1970s. Since then, she and the Women's Auxiliary have been working to support the union's efforts of education and commemoration. These stewards have been doing the heavy lifting around educating their local communities for decades. They also played pivotal roles in facilitating and supporting scholarly efforts.

When asked what scholars can do to further the overall goals of the UMWA, Robert Butero answered that he would like to see labor history (particularly Ludlow) be a regular part of the curriculum in US and Colorado history (see his interview, chapter 3, this volume). He requests that we teach the next generation about labor history. This includes the role of unions and collective bargaining in shaping and maintaining workers' rights. He likens the importance of the Ludlow Massacre to the Civil and Revolutionary Wars and notes that it played a big role in civil rights history (see his interview, chapter 3, this volume). Sadly, this episode in history rarely makes it into the textbooks or the curriculum. Butero, in his interview, laments that of the fifty-six students who visited the site as part of a service learning project, not one had heard the history of Ludlow prior to the visit. In fact, those of us who teach at the college level in Colorado have had similar experiences. Larkin likes to conduct informal surveys at the beginning of every class period during which she talks about the Ludlow Massacre. At least 75 percent of her typical classes comprise students who have grown up and attended schools in southern Colorado. Yet during these surveys, when she asks students if they have heard of the Ludlow Massacre, only one or two hands shoot up. This sobering and appalling fact underscores the observations by Butero and Romero that students are not learning about this history before entering college.

In a chapter of *The Archaeology of Class War* titled "Why We Dig," Philip Duke and Dean Saitta (2009, 357) note that the project "made two substantive and, by all accounts, successful efforts to bring knowledge of the Colorado Coalfield War into both schools and the public consciousness." They go on to describe Summer Teacher Institutes they developed through a grant from Colorado Humanities (later, Colorado Endowment for the Humanities). During these institutes, they worked with K–12 educators to imagine ways "Colorado's rich labor history could be incorporated into the public schools' American history curriculum" (357). It was one of these institutes that Linda Linville references in the prologue to this volume. These institutes resulted in several tangible products designed to provide tools for educating students about this history through archaeology in the classroom. They include a traveling education trunk and exhibit, lesson plans, and an article about the project in a public history reader intended for college students (Duke et al. 2005). Even though the article was intended for college students, Duke and colleagues (2005) note that it would also be appropriate as a supplement for high school teachers discussing labor history in Colorado. The traveling trunk and exhibit contained historical photographs and excavated artifacts with accompanying interpretive text and lesson plans to facilitate discussion and activities in a school classroom. These materials were designed for fourth grade through high school levels. The Summer Teaching Institutes also produced several lesson plans shared by teachers for other teachers to incorporate into their own classrooms. A few of these can still be found on the University of Denver's Ludlow Archaeology webpage (du.edu/Ludlow/). The work of both the Colorado Coalfield War Archaeological Project (CCWAP) and the Commission focused efforts on educating students. While the anecdotal stories above suggest that students are still not exposed to this history in the typical curriculum, Larkin notes that she has seen more hands raised by her students in the past few years, suggesting that the work of the Commission had an impact.

Butero's comment was not limited to K–12 but was also referring to educating college students in the classroom. He did not differentiate whether that should occur in a history or a business classroom. In his opinion, either discipline would benefit from incorporating this history into the college curriculum. However, the question remains, How often is this material referenced? Duke and Saitta (2009, 356) note anecdotally that "in two popular Colorado history books pulled at random from the shelves of the Durango Public Library, Ludlow is describe[d] in one page of text with an accompanying photograph in one of the books . . . it is not even mentioned in the other." They go on to note that the subject is only briefly touched on (three pages worth) even in the left-leaning Howard Zinn's (2005) *A People's History of the United States*. This omission is disheartening but not entirely unexpected. There are other, better-known examples of labor unrest in the United States, some of which get more mention in the history books. However, this does raise questions of how often Ludlow is included in college-level history books and how college professors can incorporate this history into their classroom in engaging and impactful ways.

The following chapters address these questions. Robin Henry's chapter surveys college-level history textbooks to identify how and if labor history is included. Her results suggest that labor history continues to be marginalized in college-level survey textbooks. She explores the causes and effects of these omissions. Recognizing that this history is often omitted, individual faculty members have worked to reintroduce the topic in a variety of ways and at differing levels. For instance, Duke and Saitta (2009, 357) describe a high school teacher in Durango who uses Ludlow as a case study to explore the wider issue of union-company conflict in late nineteenth-century Colorado. Bonnie Clark and Eleanor Conlin Casella (2009) offer a trans-Atlantic comparison of their efforts to use the history and archaeology of the Colorado Coalfield War in their undergraduate classrooms in both the United States and England. They also discuss successes and challenges as well as lessons learned when attempting to incorporate this history and archaeology. In this section, Larkin and Maher describe their efforts to create an immersive role-based curriculum that focuses on the strike and the Ludlow Massacre. They describe the curriculum and its impact in their history and humanities classrooms at the college level.

Butero's statement also alludes to scholars' efforts at community outreach and at including the history of Ludlow in public discourse. Mark Walker, the first project director of the Colorado Coalfield War Archaeology Project,

FIGURE 7.1. Interpretive Trail at Ludlow monument, created by the Colorado Coalfield War Archaeological Project and funded by History Colorado State Historical Fund and UMWA. *Courtesy,* Karin Larkin.

conducted an informal survey of visitors at the site in 1998 to determine what they knew of the history. His survey revealed that nearly 60 percent of the visitors at the site thought the sign "Ludlow Massacre Memorial" referred to a memorial dedicated to the American Indian Wars and not to an industrial labor war (Duke and Saitta 2009, 357). The CCWAP shared these results with the UMWA. Butero (chapter 3, this volume) admits that these results initially surprised him. This sobering fact led to the development of more robust interpretive efforts at the Ludlow Massacre Memorial site (figure 7.1). The CCWAP collaborated with the UMWA to develop interpretive signage at the site of the Ludlow Massacre to educate site visitors. While the archaeological project was working at the site, the CCWAP offered a variety of public outreach programming associated with the project's grant-funded activities (Ludlow Collective 2001, 2007, 2018; Duke and Saitta 2009; Duke et al. 2005; McGuire and Reckner 2002).

The union Local 9856 and the Women's Auxiliary, headed by Mike and Yolanda Romero, worked for decades to both preserve the monument site and interpret the labor history for the public in southern Colorado, to the local community and visitors alike. Since 2012, the Romeros have worked tirelessly to create a museum in Trinidad to help interpret coal mining history and the Ludlow Massacre for the community and visitors to the area. They opened the Southern Colorado Coal Miners' Memorial and Museum in 2016 with a Coal Miners Memorial, exhibits, and educational spaces for adults and children. This space has furthered the goals of education in several ways, including providing tours and educational outreach to schoolchildren in the region, offering a meeting space for union members to discuss current issues and plan, and providing the public with interpretive materials that connect Ludlow to the present.

The work of the Commission also expanded educational outreach efforts beyond Trinidad and its surrounding areas by providing transdisciplinary experiences for the public throughout Colorado through art and history exhibits, music performances, plays, poetry readings, and more. In his chapter, Michael Jacobson also describes his public outreach effort of creating a digital atlas that allows virtual visits to the site. He explains how a digital atlas can take the story into a virtual space, breaking down physical barriers to access. His chapter offers both a description of how to use ArcGIS to create a StoryMap and words of advice for applying this method more broadly. This platform can transcend time and space to reach students and the public alike.

To create a society of critically thoughtful adults, we need to invest in educating our students as well as the broader community, first about this history, then about how this history informs their social and political lives. These chapters highlight our efforts to educate students and the public about Ludlow surrounding the centennial commemoration. They focus on the importance, successes, and challenges of teaching and learning from the story of the Ludlow Massacre.

REFERENCES

Clark, Bonnie, and Eleanor Conlin Casella. 2009. "Teaching Class Conflict: A Trans-Atlantic Comparison Using the Colorado Coalfield War Archaeological Project in Undergraduate Curricula." In *The Archaeology of Class War: The Colorado*

Coalfield Strike of 1913–1914, edited by Karin Larkin and Randall H. McGuire, 331–350. Boulder: University of Colorado Press.

Duke, Philip, Randall McGuire, Dean Saitta, Paul Reckner, and Mark Walker. 2005. "The Colorado Coalfield War Archaeology Project: Archaeology Serving Labor." In *Preserving Western History*, edited by Andrew Guilliford, 32–43. Albuquerque: University of New Mexico Press.

Duke, Philip, and Dean Saitta. 2009. "Why We Dig: Archaeology, Ludlow, and the Public." In *The Archaeology of Class War: The Colorado Coalfield Strike of 1913–1914*, edited by Karin Larkin and Randall H. McGuire, 351–362. Boulder: University of Colorado Press.

Ludlow Collective, ed. 2001. *Archaeology of the Colorado Coal Field War 1913–1914*. Archaeologies of the Contemporary Past, edited by Victor Buchli and Gavin Lucas. London: Routledge.

Ludlow Collective, ed. 2007. "Colorado Coalfield War Archaeological Project Website." University of Denver. https://www.du.edu/ludlow/. Accessed July 6, 2019.

Ludlow Collective. 2018. "Teaching Ludlow CO." Teach Ludlow. http://www.teachludlowco.com/dotnetnuke/. Accessed June 20, 2018.

McGuire, Randall H., and Paul Reckner. 2002. "The Unromantic West: Labor, Capital, and Struggle." *Historical Archaeology* 36 (3): 44–58.

Zinn, Howard. 2005. *A People's History of the United States, 1492–Present*. New York: Harper Perennial.

7

Can We Teach US History without Ludlow?

ROBIN C. HENRY

One of the responsibilities of US history professors is teaching US history courses to incoming freshman. These courses, known as the US survey, are divided into two separate courses. This can be a daunting and at times frustrating task. One particular challenge with teaching the second half of the survey is how to cover the complexity of US history and still deal with the infinite stretch of "to the present." While periodization differs among universities, most history departments divide their introductory-level US history courses at either 1865 or 1877. It is up to the instructors, textbook writers, and editors to decide what gets included and how much coverage subjects receive each semester. Considering that survey courses are often the only history course non-majors take, it is important to both cover significant changes over time, such as world wars and civil rights movements, while also introducing students to lesser-known moments, people, and perspectives in history that they may not have considered in previous history classes. Bound by the finality of the semester, introductory course instructors typically have between twelve and sixteen weeks to cover approximately 150 years of history.

https://doi.org/10.5876/9781646422289.c007

Of course, there is no single answer; each instructor must determine the right balance of information and coverage for themselves. However, one of the determining factors in what is taught is the choice of textbooks. In 1979, Jean Anyon (361) observed that textbooks are "social products that can be examined in the context of their time." Instructors, school officials, and professional curricular developers have typically overemphasized the power, and thereby the importance, of dominant groups. Even in 2019, when textbooks had evolved to include more marginalized groups, actions, and decisions, dominant groups remained the focus. The eleven textbooks examined for this chapter indicate a significant amount of similarity and reflect positive changes since 1979. However, in the area of labor history, they also reveal two important points: labor history is not prioritized, and the Ludlow Massacre—an event the novelist Wallace Stegner (1982, xvii) once called "one of the bleakest and blackest episodes of American labor history"—appears in only two of the eleven textbooks. While individual instructors can, and probably do, supplement the textbooks with lectures, primary documents, and supplemental monographs, not placing Ludlow as a pivotal moment in both labor and US history continues to skew the focus of introductory courses (Johnson 2009). As a result, a complex narrative on the industrial American West in which radical workers defy mythological visions of rugged individualism remains elusive. Although Ludlow remains one of the lesser-remembered labor strikes, Ben Mauk (2014), writing for the *New Yorker*, argues that its memory continues to reverberate throughout US history. It has been memorialized in song, poem, and sculpture, but it is also time to make it a focal point in textbooks. Shouldn't we understand more about why it has been left out?

LABOR IS MISSING

Labor history is one area of study that textbooks and the larger historical profession continue to marginalize. Historian Roy Rosenzweig (1987) found that between 1959 and 1987, the 2,000 articles published and the approximately 10 million words dedicated to history yielded only thirty-seven references to labor leaders and their actions (table 7.1). If we contrast that with the number of references to capitalists and entrepreneurs, the number is alarmingly low.

While other marginalized social groups, in particular African Americans and women, have taken a more prominent place in textbooks, Rosenzweig

TABLE 7.1. References to US labor leaders in historical articles, 1959–1987 (Rosenzweig 1987, 51)

Labor Leader	Number of References
Samuel Gompers	13
John L. Lewis	8
Bill Haywood	8
Emma Goldman	3
Walter Reuther	2
William Z. Foster	2
Terrance V. Powderly	1

concluded that labor history and labor leaders remained on the margins in academic publishing. In textbooks, this uneven coverage translates into a focus on three major strikes: the Great Railroad Strike of 1877, the Homestead Strike in 1892, and the Pullman Strike in 1894; Haymarket in 1886 sometimes makes a fourth. The American Federation of Labor (AFofL) is the most cited labor union, followed by the Knights of Labor. In total, these strikes and labor unions receive an average coverage of 6 pages out of 7,344 pages total in the eleven textbooks I examined, with an average of 667 pages for each textbook (Rosenzweig 1987, 51–52). While historically there is no moment between the Great Railroad Strike in 1877 and the passage of the Taft-Hartley Act in 1947 that did not see some agitation on behalf of labor, that fact is not reflected in most textbooks. Instead, it appears that labor agitation disappeared after the Pullman Strike and does not reappear until the 1930s. This narrative structure and coverage of labor skews readers' understanding of the labor movement in two fundamental ways.

First, this approach leads readers to focus almost solely on strikes that result in labor failure or in the limited government-enacted workplace reforms that working- and professional-class employees enjoy today.[1] Though these strikes remain important, this approach denies the legitimacy of more radical methods and ideology that drove labor unions and leaders but did not result in changes. By marginalizing more radical critiques of capitalism and management, textbooks emphasize approaches of limited government intervention in the economy as reasonably progressive measures without developing a conversation on less successful ways of fundamentally reshaping the economy as the solution to disagreements between labor and management.

Second, by isolating labor activism to between 1877 and 1896 and to major cities such as New York, Chicago, and Pittsburgh in the Northeast and the upper Midwest, textbooks relegate labor concerns to only certain times, certain regions, and certain people in a way that tends to isolate the experience as not a wholly American one, in either place or time. This isolation means that most western agitation, the presence and contributions of the Western Federation of Miners, and the violence of the Ludlow Massacre, for example, remain almost absent from the master narrative of US history. With the sizable impact of social and cultural history on the profession, textbooks have changed to include more in-depth discussions of the contributions and histories of women, African Americans, Native Americans, and immigrants from Asia, Europe, and the Americas. Textbooks not only demonstrate these peoples' continued presence and contributions but also remind readers that the experience of living and working in the United States is complicated, not always the same, and that the white middle-class narrative is not the only or even the main narrative in US history.

While more than thirty years have passed since Anyon's and Rosenzweig's initial studies on labor history in textbooks, the coverage has changed to add some of the western and rural strikes, but Ludlow, for example, is covered in only 18 percent of textbooks. For this chapter, I examined the eleven most frequently adopted textbooks used for college, Advanced Placement, International Baccalaureate, and concurrent/dual enrollment courses that cover the second half of the introductory level of US history: 1865–1877 to the present day. I examined textbooks such as Howard Zinn's *A People's History of the United States* (2015) and David M. Kennedy and Lizabeth Cohen's *The American Pageant* (2015) that have over ten editions and five textbooks—mostly newer contributions—that have five or fewer editions. The textbooks' most recent editions ranged between 2013 and 2017.

Initially, I looked for two levels of coverage: (1) the coverage of labor history overall and (2) the coverage of the Colorado Coalfield War and the Ludlow Massacre of 1913–1914. Within the first point, I examined whether the coverage of labor history (1) moved beyond the time frame of 1877 to 1896, (2) included more than the three of the aforementioned strikes, and (3) moved outside the Northeast/upper Midwest regional preference identified in previous investigations. For a better presentation and understanding of the Ludlow Massacre, I argue that these changes are important to see Ludlow in the context of western mining agitation and radicalism, as well as the growing use of state militias to perpetrate government and capital-sanctioned violence against striking workers. In the case of Ludlow, this violence also affected the families—wives and children—of the striking workers, resulting in the deaths of eleven children and two women.

In general, textbooks have remained limited in their coverage of labor history (table 7.2). All of the textbooks I studied, however, had increased their coverage, in particular the social context of the three main strikes—Railroad, Homestead, and Pullman—from previous editions. For example, in the seventh edition of Carol Berkin and others' *Making America: A History of the United States*, the authors divide their coverage of labor between two chapters: 17 and 19. In chapter 17, they discuss the origins of labor unions—the Knights of Labor and the AFofL—in relation to the Great Railroad Strike, Homestead, and Haymarket and discuss the different organizing philosophies of significant labor leaders Terrance Powderly, Eugene Debs, and Samuel Gompers. In chapter 19, the authors address the development of labor's political wing and the rise of the Socialist Party USA, as well as the influence of the Industrial Workers of the World (IWW) and the United Mine Workers (Berkin et al. 2015, 455–464, 509). This additional information helps readers contextualize the rising discontent over worker safety, hours, and compensation and presents the struggle for union recognition and the right to collective bargaining from both a political and a more radical perspective. However, this expanded discussion of labor remains relegated geographically to the Northeast and upper Midwest regions.

Other textbooks have expanded to include brief discussions of western mining strikes, most frequently strikes in Coeur d'Alene, Idaho, in 1892 and Cripple Creek, Colorado, in 1894. Mary Beth Norton and colleagues' *A People and a Nation* (2014) dedicates seven pages to late nineteenth- and early twentieth-century labor unrest and includes a separate section titled "Labor Violence in the West." This addition is a brief discussion of the Cripple Creek Strike and the presence of the Western Federation of Miners and the IWW (476–480). Norton and colleagues' book is one of the few that recognizes western agitation and connects Cripple Creek workers' demands to the common labor issues of work hours, safety, and compensation. However, this standalone approach potentially guides readers to see the strike as a singular issue and not the beginning of years of labor conflict in the Rocky Mountain and Inter-Mountain West regions that radicalized industrial workers, significantly contributing to overall labor gains in the late nineteenth and early twentieth centuries.[2]

TABLE 7.2. Table of US history textbook coverage of the Ludlow Massacre

Author	Textbook	Publication Date	Edition	Ludlow Massacre Mentioned	Pages	Ludlow Massacre Indexed	Index Reference
Berkin	*Making America: A History of the United States*	2015	7	No	None	None	None
Brand et al.	*American Stories: A History of the United States*	2014	3	No	None	None	None
Davidson et al.	*Experience History: Interpreting America's Past*	2013	8	No	None	None	None
Foner	*Give Me Liberty! An American History*	2017	5	No	None	None	None
Henkin/ McLennan	*Becoming American: A History for the Twenty-First Century*	2014	1	No	None	None	None
Kennedy/ Cohen	*The American Pageant*	2015	16	No	None	None	None
Norton et al.	*A People and a Nation*	2014	10	No	None	None	None
Roark et al.	*The American Promise*	2014	6	No	None	None	None
Schaller et al.	*American Horizons: U.S. History in a Global Context*	2017	3	Yes	696, 711	Yes	Ludlow Massacre
Shi/Tindall	*America: A Narrative History*	2016	10	No	None	None	None
Zinn	*A People's History of the United States*	2015	20	Yes	355–357	Yes	Ludlow Massacre

COVERING LUDLOW OR COVERING UP LUDLOW?

While the coverage of western labor agitation has improved since Anyon and Rosenzweig conducted their research, I discovered only two textbooks that discuss Ludlow and the Colorado Coal Wars: Michael Schaller and others'

American Horizons: US History in a Global Context (2017) and Howard Zinn's *A People's History* (2015). Even these two books are not uniform in their coverage of Ludlow. Both books refer to it as Ludlow, the Ludlow Massacre, or both and index it as Ludlow. Schaller and others' (2017) text, however, includes a brief discussion of Ludlow in a section titled "Mediating the Labor Problem" and contextualizes it in a discussion of the Progressive Era and as part of the United Mine Workers' larger series of strikes that began around 1902. In addition, they juxtapose it with the 1902 strikes that saw President Theodore Roosevelt pressure mine owners to negotiate with coalminers to stop an economically crippling strike (2017). This approach, as Rosenzweig discusses, presents the federal government in a positive role of attempting to mediate the dispute and implies a governmental preference for labor that did not exist.

When Schaller and his coauthors (2014) get to Ludlow itself, they provide a paragraph describing how local deputies and state militia doused the tent camp in kerosene, set it on fire, and then started shooting at the encampment. The death count is listed as fourteen, including eleven children.[3] Although historians consider the higher-end fatality numbers to be exaggerated, the deaths of women and children illicited an outcry from the 1914 public that was so vociferous that John D. Rockefeller Jr. had little choice but to respond. Finally, Schaller and coauthors add that there were violent actions on the parts of both labor and management, but they do not provide more local, contextual information on the strike, working and compensation conditions at Colorado Fuel and Iron Company (CF&I), or the extent and length of the ongoing violence throughout late 1913 and the first half of 1914 or in the larger context of escalating labor violence in the West (696, 711). This two-page coverage represents half of the total coverage of Ludlow. While few labor events receive much more or better coverage in US history textbooks, this event was, according to historian Thomas G. Andrews (2008, 1), "the deadliest strike in the United States."

Howard Zinn's *A People's History of the United States* (2015) provides more expansive coverage of Ludlow and labor history in general. The second of two textbooks to mention Ludlow, Zinn's book provides a detailed description of the events but also gives a brief summary of the reasons for the strike. He places Ludlow in several historical contexts, including its connection to socialism and Americans' challenges with adopting socialism, which reflect Ludlow's complicated but important role in the development of early twentieth-century US history. In addition, Zinn asks questions about general Progressive-Era reforms in relation to the massacre at CF&I and examines the immediate aftermath and national reactions, including CF&I's chief owner, John D. Rockefeller Jr.'s, and CF&I's role in changes in labor relations and corporate management structures—especially the creation of the Employee Representation Plan. Finally, he places the Colorado Coalfield War (1913–1914), of which Ludlow is a single event, within President Woodrow Wilson's larger domestic presidency and juxtaposes it with the same-day attack on Vera Cruz, Mexico, that along with rising tensions in Europe, competed for Americans' attention in April 1914 (355–377). In part, this difference in Zinn's textbook can be attributed to his choice of primary sources, including headlines from the local newspaper, the *Trinidad Chronicle*, which covered both of these events in the same days' issues. Thus they read as simultaneous, rather than before-and-after, events.

While Zinn's coverage provides more context than Schaller's, the Ludlow Massacre's coverage in US history textbooks overall remains low. For an event connected to significant changes in labor relations, corporate structure, public relations, and the development of radical social and political movements, it seems poised to be a major event in US history but is not widely covered. The question remains, why not? As historians, we know there is rarely a single answer to this type of question. However, I have developed three possible answers that speak to the particular relationship Americans and the United States have with the Ludlow Massacre, the labor movement, and violence in US history.

First, it is important to consider time and location. Over the past thirty years, US history textbooks have improved significantly in their range of coverage of both geography and the types of people and events that are covered. No longer are they telling the story of white middle-class and wealthy male elites. However, the coverage does continue to have an East Coast, northern, urban bias. Coverage of the American West has become more complicated—dotted with cities as well as ranches and homesteads and populated by Asians, Hispanics, African Americans, and Native Americans in addition to the Anglo minority that formed the region's mythology. However, its placement in textbooks is pretty uniform: 1870s–1890s, usually the chapter after Reconstruction and around industrialization. For textbook editors, writers, and collaborators, this is the height of the region's first wave of American development, and focusing on these twenty years allows students to understand the region in terms of possibility and challenges. After 1890, development of the region emerges again in the 1930s, when refugees migrated from the Great Plains to California during the Dust Bowl, and in the 1940s and 1950s, when people moved to worksites related to the military industrial complex.

The study of the American labor movement follows a similar time line as that of the development of the American West. Most textbooks trace unionization in the 1870s and 1890s and then pick unions up again in the 1930s and 1970s. In general, labor history is presented as an unpopular series of disconnected struggles between labor and management, with occasional government interference for the presentation of state and managerial power. The strike at CF&I and the longer Colorado Coal War (1913–1914) and the Ludlow Massacre (April 20, 1914) do not fit into the time frame either for the development of the American West or for the labor movement in the nineteenth century as presented in US history textbooks. Textbook authors usually situate the labor movement and labor strikes within the late nineteenth-century struggle, roughly from the Great Railroad Strike of 1877 to the Pullman Strike of 1894. This time line focuses on the mounting tensions between a growing industrial and capitalist system and the diminishing autonomy of the American worker in the face of the extraordinary pace and level of change during the second Industrial Revolution. In the textbook chaptering system, while labor does not disappear, it moves to a lower place of importance in relation to the rise of urbanization, imperialism, and the Progressive Era. Even outside this narrative arc, Ludlow took place during a very busy year—1913–1914—as President Woodrow Wilson was more consumed by mounting global tensions, including those with Mexico. While the American West is relevant to this time period, textbooks mostly cover it in relation to development and migration, with the main events frequently narrowed to the California Gold Rush of 1849, the advancement of the railroads, the displacement of Native Americans through military actions, and Anglo settlement. Labor remains optimistic and progressive: frequently successful, individualized, and less industrialized than reality bore out. At the dawn of the Great War, Ludlow—a labor strike that took place nineteen years after the Pullman Strike in southeastern Colorado—feels out of place instead of part of the narrative's continuity and does not have a natural place in the themed chapter on the late Progressive Era and the Great War in most US history textbook.

Second, because US history textbooks are most frequently written by consensus, it is easier to perpetuate certain myths even as they are successful at eradicating others. In particular, textbooks, while promoting a more multicultural region, continue to reduce the presence of the industrial working class from the American West in order to perpetuate the remarkably potent myth of a rural frontier (Schwantes 2001, 2, 11). In addition, the government-sanctioned industrial violence perpetuated by managers and owners not only challenges a positivist narrative of US history but also questions the nature of American capitalism and democracy in a way we are only beginning to grow more comfortable thinking about in regard to the racial violence of enslavement and institutional and systemic racism (Hofstadter 2015). And then, only a little more comfortable. For the most part, by the end of the 1890s, American violence is relegated to two main areas in textbooks: Jim Crow–era lynching and military imperialism against Spain in the Caribbean and the Pacific. Richard Hofstadter (2015, 187) argued that Americans "have a remarkable lack of memory where violence is concerned." He elaborated, stating that even historians favor a narrative of attacks on state power over conflicts between groups of citizens, such as the 1791 Whiskey Rebellion over slave rebellions. Textbooks generally now include the Denmark Vessey's 1822 and Nat Turner's 1830 rebellions, but the larger point remains that a hierarchy of knowledge and favoritism tends toward violence that has "taken the form of action of one group of citizens against another group rather than by citizens against the state" (191). It is not that Americans are incapable of considering violence, but in the case of Ludlow, because it falls outside the more accepted narrative of violence centering the narrative in the East or in other urban areas, post-Pullman western labor violence requires us to reconsider both the place and the timing of the entire first third of the second part of the survey course. By denying events like Ludlow—collective actions turned violent—and their significance as points of larger national conversations on power, we risk allowing them to remain isolated events with limited impact on the narrative of US history. In addition, readers might see state-sanctioned violence as a limited, last-ditch response instead of a more frequent occurrence with limited long-term consequences. This potential to reframe what is important also requires the United States to reconsider how and why it entered into World War I and, more difficult for many Americans, to consider that the United States does not only use force for good.

Finally, the possible connections between industrial violence in the United States to international worker uprisings, socialism, and communism were an even more important part of the postwar narrative than the possibility of showing fractures within the national democratic, industrial capitalism structures. This link between violence in a relatively isolated southern Colorado company town and the early stirrings of the Russian Revolution meant that its history remained local and isolated as well. While the Ludlow Massacre helped in the development of the region, for industrial capital to continue to grow, its local danger needed to remain isolated and the larger populous protected from this isolated violence by the government and militia (Walker 2003, 66–67). At best, these regional histories could serve as seeds of change in the larger narrative of US history. But at the core, capital, alongside a complicit state, typically held the upper hand and was capable of setting the terms both in how labor and industrial violence was managed and, later, in how it matters.

CONCLUSION

There are no simple solutions to how Ludlow is or should be covered in US history textbooks because a long list of events, people, places, and nuanced interpretations are also left out of the master narrative. That is the frustrating work of writing and editing a textbook, as well as putting together a survey course. There is no way to include everything and everyone. As historians, we know this, and yet it is our job to try. Textbook writers have taken their first steps away from the white, male, elite narrative but need to continue to decolonize the narrative and, in the case of Ludlow, to also think more critically about capitalism and its limitations. Finally, if we are willing to recognize that the struggle over power, wealth, and their distributions is universal and timeless rather than isolated, we also must recognize the constant presence of violence in achieving and protecting these powers (Wiebe 1966; Painter 1987). As I have considered why Ludlow remains almost wholly unknown in US history textbooks, I return to unbelievable violence perpetuated on civilians by the long arms of the state that did not lead to easy success. The coal war continued, adding more violence. The American public, notoriously anti-union, chaffed at the deaths of women and children—so much so that the US Congress held hearings and Wilson created the US Department of Labor but the American public refused and still refuses to consider the effects of the broader violence and intimidation perpetrated in southern Colorado in 1913 and 1914 as problematic. The violence continued in the West, as it did in other parts of the county.

The Ludlow memorialization projects have, indeed, complicated the history of Ludlow, Colorado, and the industrial American West in intriguing and necessary ways. Artists, historians, preservationists, archivists, and interested members of the public have worked since the 1930s to introduce, reclaim, and present this important history part of history to the American public (Schwantes 2001, 13; Schulten 2005). More recently, historians have also been invested in connecting the actions of and reactions to the Ludlow Massacre and the Colorado Coalfield War to the larger historical narratives of industrial violence and unionization in the West and in the United States. The songs, sculptures, poems, and reenactments speak of violence that parallels the struggle for workers' rights across the country (Dabakis 1989; Montoya 2014; Walker 2003; Saitta 2004; Green and Jameson 2009). However, these depictions should also make us think more critically about how we teach about laborers in US history and the American West, especially juxtaposed with the more identifiable industrialists, entrepreneurs, and cowboys—the latter-day heroes of post–Civil War American expansionism and imperialism.

The Ludlow Massacre and the Colorado Coal War need to be told somewhere, preferably in a textbook. If violence, and in this case industrial violence, is removed from its isolated, local, action-of-last-resort status and instead placed in the center of the story, we become more honest storytellers. As scholars Paul Lipold and Larry W. Isaac (2009, 168) asserted, "The proliferation of industrial violence into the twentieth century inspired Progressive Era journalists and reformers to seek ways to alleviate market and workplace conditions thought to inspire such strife, as did their successors during the New Deal. With the general cessation of strike-related violence during the post–World War II era, social scientists have increasingly looked to labor's turbulent past in an effort to explain its seemingly moribund present."

As Open Source texts and flipped classroom teaching styles move more into mainstream use in the survey, the opportunity to incorporate a more nuanced narrative about state-sanctioned violence that not only includes Ludlow but also highlights it as a major event in US history appears. However, traditional narrative textbooks remain a staple of this course and, as such, have an enormous impact on how students understand what happened and what is important in US history. It is the inclusion and exclusion that tells them this no matter what supplemental materials or additional narrative a professor provides. National stories are messy, complex, and incomplete; and, by nature, they favor someone. But perhaps if we approach the jelly with a nail gun, we might get it to stick to the wall for just a little while longer.

NOTES

I would like to thank Fawn-Amber Montoya, who continues to ask me to participate in Ludlow discussions and, in turn, shows me that there is still so much more to this historical moment; also to Paul Leeker, who makes me want to be a better historian.

1. Every Labor Day (the first Monday in September in the United States), labor unions and historians tend to remind Americans about the weekend, eight-hour workday, workplace protections, child labor, and many more rights. United Teacher Union–Los Angeles (2017).

2. For further reading on these strikes, consult Elizabeth Jameson, *All That Glitters: Class, Conflict, and Community in Cripple Creek* (Urbana: University of Illinois Press, 1998); George G. Suggs, *Colorado's War on Militant Unionism: James H. Peabody and the Western Federation of Miners* (Detroit: Wayne State University Press, 1972); Melvin Dubofsky, *We Shall Be All: A History of the Industrial Workers of the World* (Urbana: University of Illinois Press, 1969, 2000).

3. Fatality counts for the Ludlow Massacre vary from 14 up to 21 on the day of the Ludlow Massacre (April 20, 1914), but they rise to as high as 199 if we include the subsequent retaliations throughout CF&I properties that are commonly referred to as the Colorado Coalfield War.

REFERENCES

Andrews, Thomas G. 2008. *Killing for Coal: America's Deadliest Labor War*. Cambridge, MA: Harvard University Press.

Anyon, Jean. 1979. "Ideology and United States History Textbooks." *Harvard Educational Review* 49 (3): 361–386.

Berkin, Carol, Christopher Miller, Robert Cherny, and James Gormly. 2015. *Making America: A History of the United States*, vol. 2: *Since 1865*. 7th ed. Boston: Cengage Learning.

Brand, H. W., T. H. Breen, Ariela J. Gross, and R. Hal Williams, 2014. *American Stories: A History of the United States*, vol. 2. 3rd ed. New York: Pearson.

Dabakis, Melissa. 1989. "Formulating the Ideal American Worker: Public Responses to Constantin Meunier's 1913–14 Exhibition of Labor Imagery." *Public Historian* 11 (4): 113–132.

Davidson, James West, Brian DeLay, Christing Leigh Heyrman, Mark Lytle, and Michael Stoff. 2013. *Experience History: Interpreting America's Past.* 8th ed. New York: McGraw-Hill Education.

Foner, Eric. 2017. *Give Me Liberty! An American History*, vol. 2. 5th ed. New York: W. W. Norton.

Green, James, and Elizabeth Jameson. 2009. "Marking Labor History on the National Landscape: The Restored Ludlow Memorial and Its Significance." *International Labor and Working-Class History* 76: 6–25.

Henkin, David, and Rebecca McLennan. 2014. *Becoming American: A History for the Twenty-First Century*, vol. 2: *From Reconstruction*. 1st ed. New York: McGraw-Hill.

Hofstadter, Richard. 2015. "Reflections of Violence in the United States." *The Baffler* 28: 187–215, reprint of the introduction to Richard Hofstadter and Michael Wallace, eds., *American Violence: A Documentary History*. New York: Knopf.

Johnson, Marilynn S. 2009. *Violence in the West: The Johnson County Range War and the Ludlow Massacre: A Brief History with Documents*. Boston: Bedford/St. Martin's.

Kennedy, David M., and Lizabeth Cohen. 2015. *The American Pageant*. 16th ed. Boston: Cengage Learning.

Lipold Paul, and Larry W. Isaac. 2009. "Lethal Contestation and the 'Exceptional' Character of the American Labor Movement, 1870–1970." *International Review of Social History* 54 (2): 168–205.

Mason, David. 2004. "*Ludlow*: A Verse Novel Part I." *Hudson Review* 57 (3): 401–439.

Mauk, Ben. 2014. "The Ludlow Massacre Still Matters." *The New Yorker*. April 18. https://www.newyorker.com/business/currency/the-ludlow-massacre-still -matters. Accessed June 14, 2017.

Montoya, Fawn-Amber, ed. 2014. *Making an American Workforce: The Rockefellers and the Legacy of Ludlow*. Boulder: University Press of Colorado.

Norton, Mary Beth, Jane Kamensky, Carol Sheriff, David W. Blight, and Howard Chudacoff. 2014. *A People and a Nation*, vol. 2: *Since 1865*. 10th ed. Boston: Cengage Learning.

Painter, Nell Irvin. 1987. *Standing at Armageddon: The United States, 1877–1919*. New York: W. W. Norton.

Roark, James L., Michael P. Johnson, Patricia Cline Cohen, Sarah Stage, and Susan N. Hartmann. 2014. *The American Promise*, vol. 2: *From 1865*. 6th ed. Boston: Bedford/St. Martin's.

Rosenzweig, Roy. 1987. "American Labor History: A Conspiracy of Silence?" *Labor Review* 110 (8): 51–53.

Saitta, Dean J. 2004. "Desecration at Ludlow." *New Labor Forum* 13 (1): 86–89.

Schaller, Michael, Robert Schulzinger, Janette Thomas Greenwood, Andrew Kirk, Sarah J. Purcell, Aaron Sheehan-Dean, John Bezis-Selfa, and Christina Snyder. 2017. *American Horizons: U.S. History in a Global Context*, vol. 2: *Since 1865*. 3rd ed. New York: Oxford University Press.

Schulten, Susan. 2005. "How to See Colorado: The Federal Writers' Project, American Regionalism, and the Old New Western History." *Western Historical Quarterly* 36 (1): 49–70.

Schwantes, Carlos A. 2001. "The Case of the Missing Century, or Where Did the American West Go after 1900?" *Pacific Historical Review* 7 (1): 1–20.

Shi, David E., and George Brown Tindall. 2016. *America: A Narrative History*, vol. 2. 10th ed. New York: W. W. Norton.

Stegner, Wallace. 1982. "Foreword." In *Buried Unsung: Louis Tikas and the Ludlow Massacre* by Zeese Papanikolas, viii–xix. Lincoln: University of Nebraska Press.

United Teacher Union–Los Angeles. Facebook post, December 21, 2017. https://www.facebook.com/UTLAnow/photos/a.373269696027831/1907608542593931/?type=3&theater. Accessed October 18, 2019.

Walker, Mark. 2003. "The Ludlow Massacre: Class, Warfare, and Historical Memory in Southern Colorado." *Historical Archaeology* 37 (3): 66–67.

Wiebe, Robert H. 1966. *The Search for Order, 1877–1920*. New York: Hill and Wang.

Zinn, Howard. 2015. *A People's History of the United States*. 20th ed. New York: Harper Perennial.

8

Teaching Ludlow and Reacting to the Past

KARIN LARKIN AND MATTHEW MAHER

The historical events surrounding the Southern Colorado Coalfield Strike of 1913–1914 and the resulting massacre at Ludlow offer a powerful case study for studying and teaching difficult topics and issues related to capitalism, economic and social inequality, gender relations, collective action, and conflict. The complicated and tragic history has been studied by scholars in a wide range of disciplines (McGovern and Guttridge 1972; Saitta 2007; Montoya 2014; O'Neil 1971; Munsell 2009; McGuire and Reckner 2002; Gitelman 1988; Fishback 2011; Clyne 1999; Mason 2010; Martelle 2007; Margolis 1985; Larkin and McGuire 2009; Beshoar 1957; Andrews 2008); however, the subject is rarely taught in the classroom, either at the K–12 or the college level. The reasons for leaving this seminal event out of the history books are varied and political. However, we argue that this omission misses an opportunity to teach "hard history" and to use this history to teach important lessons related to the issues noted above (Van der Valk 2018). Recently, scholars of the event have tried to address this omission by developing curricula that explore the larger social issues of the strike and the resulting Ludlow Massacre using immersive

https://doi.org/10.5876/9781646422289.c008

and engaging methods (McGuire 2008, 219; Maher and Larkin 2015; Clark and Casella 2009; Saitta 2007, 96–97). Using data from the Colorado Coalfield War Archaeological Project (CCWAP), archaeologists have created an on-line interactive digital atlas that spatially ties together archival and archaeological evidence, developed elementary school curricula by and for teachers using funding from Colorado Humanities, contributed to a mock trial curriculum for middle and high school students, and designed websites to offer educational resources (Jacobson 2006; Ludlow Collective 2001, 2018). These resources are all free and accessible to the public. Despite the examples provided here and the importance of the historical event, the subject is rarely included in textbooks on labor or Colorado history. This chapter focuses on one attempt to create a curriculum for the college classroom, employing high-impact teaching practices, that was developed in conjunction with the centennial anniversary of the strike and the massacre. Here we discuss the development of a Reacting to the Past (RTTP) role-playing game and how RTTP fits with high-impact teaching and learning practices, the utility of the format in conveying the importance and complexities involved in the history, and the benefits and limitations of the format.

HIGH-IMPACT TEACHING AND REACTING TO THE PAST

Since the mid-1990s, universities and their faculty have been experimenting with active learning and shifting from lecture-based to student-centered and productive learning (Kuh, Schneider, and AAC&U 2008; White 2018; Carnes 2011; Watson and Hagood 2018). These experiments have been collectively described as "high-impact practices" (HIPs) and touted as having a disproportionately high positive impact on student learning by the Association of American Colleges and Universities (AAC&U) (Kuh, Gonyea, and Williams 2005; Kuh, Schneider, and AAC&U 2008; Hagood, Watson, and Williams 2018). These researchers and others argue that active learning fosters student engagement, positively impacts student learning outcomes, and particularly benefits underserved students (Weidenfeld and Fernandez 2017; Watson and Hagood 2018; Kuh, Schneider, and AAC&U 2008).

The practices outlined by George D. Kuh and the AAC&U are generally instituted at university administrative levels and do not offer practices instructors can implement at the college classroom level, with a few exceptions (Fink 2016, 3). However, other studies have converted the principles of these HIPs for classroom use and combined them with studies on immersive or engaged learning (Fink 2016, 3; Carnes 2011, 2014; Weidenfeld and Fernandez 2017). L. Dee Fink (2016, 3) notes that "in my view as a faculty developer, these HIPs are primarily institutional or curricular practices. That is, most of these are not practices that a professor can incorporate within a specific course that he or she is teaching." Fink (3, original emphasis) argues that there is a parallel to these HIPs in classroom teaching, which he argues should be called "High-Impact *Teaching* Practices," or HITPs. Fink (3) continues: "What are the practices that have this potential for being 'High-Impact Teaching Practices'? Based on my forty years of working in this field, here is my list of HITPs: 1. Helping students become meta-learners 2. Learning-centered course design 3. Using small groups in a powerful way 4. Service-learning/community engagement—with reflection 5. Being a leader with your students." These practices offer interesting pedagogical challenges and opportunities. For instance, helping students become meta-learners through a learning-centered course design encourages interdisciplinary education. However, the service learning/community engagement with reflection and the use of small groups would seem to select for small class sizes. In large public institutions, where large class sizes and student skills and readiness vary widely, employing these HITPs can be more challenging. The challenges that characterize these types of classrooms in large public institutions can be overcome with creative pedagogical practices that facilitate the use of HITPs in all classroom sizes and any makeup of students. For instance, using role-immersion activities can employ small groups in powerful ways even in a large classroom while employing a learning-centered course design and helping students become meta-learners.

Role-immersion games such as Reacting to the Past games allow for pedagogical opportunities while addressing some of the challenges inherent in employing HITPs. Reacting games encourage students to take responsibility for and an active role in their learning through fostering a learning environment in which the student must thoroughly research a topic and apply that knowledge to a problem defined by the game, no matter the class size or makeup. The game format breaks students into small "factions" or working groups that necessitate interaction and collaboration. These factions create small working groups in larger classes. The small-group atmosphere also lends an urgency to perform and not let down their peers (Carnes 2014). As Mark C. Carnes (2011, A72) explains, "Research shows that the strongest gains come from pedagogies that feature teamwork and problem solving." Designing and implementing an RTTP game in the classroom also allows the instructor to motivate and enable students to accomplish high-quality learning: "Experience . . . suggests that teams work harder when they're competing against one another, and that students learn more when they're obliged to think in unfamiliar ways" (2). Even in large classrooms, students working in smaller factions must employ problem-solving and teamwork skills through the RTTP pedagogy. This helps alleviate the problem of employing high-impact teaching practices in larger classrooms.

Role-immersion games emphasize another important element of effective teaching: leadership and relationship building. An effective instructor creates a caring, respectful, and collaborative learning atmosphere. Instructors can accomplish this by motivating students, showing students the instructors care about their learning and the subject, believing in their students' ability to learn, and building trust relationships while giving students power to make decisions about their own learning (Fink 2016, 13–14). Role-immersion games such as RTTP help create a classroom environment in which students are motivated to research the topic based on the competitive nature of the game but that also gives students the power of knowledge building. RTTP game dynamics allow students to control their learning trajectory as the game develops and create an environment that permits them to make decisions about the learning process. These factors combine to create a high-impact learning environment for students while at the same time addressing another element of impactful learning: enjoyment.

Studies that examine the power of emotion and enjoyment in the education process demonstrate that these emotions increase student learning, engagement, understanding, and empathy (Csikszentmihalyi 2014; Weidenfeld and Fernandez 2017; Carnes 2011, 2014, Tatlock and Reiter 2018; Westhoff 2015). Reacting to the Past pedagogy draws students into modes of learning that foster higher-level scholarship by requiring autonomous thinking, engaging with abstract ideas, and practicing effective communication through role play. The role-play or simulated game aspect of RTTP transforms classrooms into spaces in which students are deeply engaged and invested in the process (Weidenfeld and Fernandez 2017; Carnes 2014; Watson and Hagood 2018). Mihaly Csikszentmihalyi, a Hungarian American psychologist, studied motivation and factors that contributed to overall success. He recognized a highly focused mental state conducive to productivity, which he calls "flow," that applies to this type of engagement (Csikszentmihalyi 2014, 132). In this state, students transform the idea of work into an experience of enjoyment that leads them to pursue the activity for their own sake. He outlines several conditions necessary to achieve the flow experience, including clear goals, immediate feedback, skill-challenge match, deep concentration, forgetting irrelevant stimuli, control, the loss of self-consciousness, a sense of altered time, and a feeling that the experience is worth having for its own sake (133). A well-designed RTTP game can lead to a flow experience for students. Students in a flow state take control of their learning and engage with the materials because they want to continue the fulfilling and enjoyable experience. Matthew C. Weidenfeld and Kenneth E. Fernandez (2017, 57) note of RTTP games in their classes that "students are so deeply engaged in their work that they are, quite frequently, shouting, laughing, and debating ideas in a way we had not witnessed before." They further note that "students come to so deeply identify with their roles and victory objectives that they become emotionally invested in the meaning of the texts and the outcome of the course" (48).

Carnes (2004, B7) ties this emotional intensity to liminality, which is "characterized by uncertainty and emotional intensity, by the inversion of status and social hierarchies, and by imaginative expressiveness." This higher level of engagement spurred by students' emotional investment, intrinsic motivation, and enjoyment has additional pedagogical benefits beyond a greater possibility for student learning. This liminal and flow experience allows students to engage more deeply with the nuance and messiness of human history and conflict. Empathy can be a powerful tool in teaching students about negotiation and conflict; and when students are enjoying the learning process through immersive role play, they are better able to engage in empathy. Julie C. Tatlock and Paula Reiter (2018, 17) note of their experience using RTTP pedagogy that "students hone skills in areas of argumentation and public speaking, but also in more hidden skills like negotiation, empathy, critical listening, and building confidence, all of which are necessary in handling any conflict." Weidenfeld and Fernandez (2017, 47) note that students "came to understand the complexities of human agency and politics."

It is very useful to have students deeply engage with complex motivations and political maneuverings when teaching them about conflict. Disciplines such as political science, history, anthropology, and the like would benefit greatly from using liminal experiences to help students engage more deeply. The skills, understanding, and empathy cultivated by RTTP are important for fostering civil discourse and opening students' minds to concepts that may remain controversial. As Tatlock and Reiter (2018, 18) explain, "Students opened their minds to ideas that were, and perhaps remain, controversial. They learned to argue with each other in a nuanced and respectful way." The benefit of RTTP using subjects that are or remain controversial lies in students' understanding and developing empathy for ideas and values that may not be their own and then engaging in compromise and negotiation. Developing these types of skills can help create citizens in our society who engage in problem solving in compassionate, nuanced, and benevolent ways. These skills transcend the subject and even the discipline in which they were learned.

Reacting to the Past pedagogy provides a mechanism for practicing high-impact teaching practices and fostering engagement and empathy. The RTTP curriculum can also cultivate active student learning and engagement in skills that transcend disciplinary boundaries or historical moments. These games use a historical event to impart skills needed to navigate complex and sometimes controversial social and political situations in contemporary society. While other pedagogical techniques can achieve these same goals, here we focus on a RTTP curriculum developed around the strike and massacre at Ludlow as part of the centennial commemoration efforts to show how role-immersion games develop engagement and empathy and employ high-impact teaching practices through small-group work, collaboration, and student-centered learning.

STRIKE! LUDLOW 1913

During the preparations for the centennial commemoration, the authors of this chapter participated in a workshop hosted by the Rocky Mountain Collaboration: Reacting to the Past Project to explore the power of RTTP in our undergraduate classrooms. Because of the approaching anniversary, Larkin, an anthropologist, and Maher, a historian, were drawn to develop a

RTTP game to explore the intricacies of the political, social, and historical contexts surrounding the strike and the massacre. Educating students about the event raises issues that often take them outside their comfort zone and can raise topics that are difficult to discuss or downright controversial. RTTP seemed like an interesting way to approach the topic because of the demonstrated learning outcomes discussed in the previous section. Approaching the topic from different academic disciplines allowed Larkin and Maher to bring an interdisciplinary perspective to the design. To this end, we created an Open-Source interactive classroom activity that uses primary sources, archival records, historical accounts, and archaeological data to examine all sides of the atmosphere leading to and surrounding the strike through role play (Maher and Larkin 2015). We titled this game *Strike! Ludlow 1913*.

The Structure of *Strike! Ludlow 1913*

This game provided students with materials that included primary and secondary sources related to the 1913–1914 Southern Colorado Coalfield Strike and the Ludlow Massacre as well as synthesized background information for both players (students) and moderators (faculty). The game materials consisted of two game manuals (one for students and one for the moderator[s]), role sheets for historical figures or composite figures who played a role in the original historical event, primary documents related to the event, secondary source materials or suggested materials, and an assessment tool for the conclusion of the game. The game manuals provided the historical background as well as instructions for game play. The role sheets outlined biographical information, general motivating factors for the historical figures, and victory objectives. These victory objects both aligned with a group objective and set out personal objectives that may or may not further the goals of the group. These background materials both immersed students in researching the sources and set the stage for the elements included in the game mechanics and objectives. *Strike!* divides students into factions that reflect stakeholders in the original historical event, including Colorado Fuel and Iron (CF&I) company loyalists, United Mine Workers of America (UMWA) union loyalists, workers who must choose to remain loyal to the company or join the union, and indeterminants. Indeterminants were a mixed group, which includes parties such as workers' wives, newspaper journalists, the governor of Colorado, and militia men and women. They did not form a cohesive faction but rather aligned with one or more of the main three factions, which included CF&I, UMWA, and workers. The instructor's manual included additional information on the game mechanics, schedule, assignments, and evaluative materials.

The overall objectives involve decision making around economic, social, and political factors related to negotiating a labor strike. In *Strike!*, the first victory objective asked the company and union factions to influence the miners and their wives to choose whether to, first, join the union and then whether to call a strike or try to negotiate without a strike. Students who are part of either the CF&I or the UMWA faction must use historically accurate means and arguments to convince miners and their wives to either remain loyal to the company or join the union. Once the loyalty lines are drawn, students must then negotiate whether to strike while minimizing loss (of money, power, and lives). Compounding factors such as hidden agendas, unanticipated events introduced by the game moderator(s), or unexpected violent encounters force students to handle problems as they are introduced. For instance, the game forces a strike regardless of whether the workers want one or not. At that point, students need to negotiate the strike.

Even though RTTP is run as a game, assessments during the game are required. Assessment products required in *Strike!* include researched position papers, speeches, newspaper articles, a Greek Orthodox Easter cultural awareness assignment, and more. These assignments are designed to practice high-impact teaching practices, encourage empathy, and, it is hoped, allow students to enter a flow experience while engaging with the materials.

High-Impact Teaching Practices and *Strike!*

The structure of the game was designed to effectively engage students, encourage deeper learning, and impart specific skills and concepts. *Strike!* was developed with several of the five high-impact teaching practices outlined by Fink (2016) in mind, including helping students become meta-learners, employing a learning-centered course design, and powerfully using small groups. The implementation of the game also allowed us, as faculty facilitators, to be a "leader with [our] students." Specific goals and learning objectives included engaging students in understanding the social relations, inequality, and political maneuverings, and presenting them from various perspectives in an attempt to engender empathetic responses to these understandings. We also wanted to teach students about diversity, politics, and conflict resolution. Because our teaching goals focused on the larger concepts and skills outlined above, we were less concerned with the game mirroring "historical reality."

In the RTTP game *Strike!*, we were interested in students developing historical and social understanding of and empathy toward a complex situation and learning the skills to navigate complex negotiations involving gender, class, ethnic, and social conflicts to solve problems instead of memorizing facts related to this historical event. By developing victory outcomes that require students to navigate these complex negotiations, this RTTP game presents clear instructions to students to apply historical information to solve problems. As Fink (2016, 3–4) notes, "A widespread and long-standing lament in higher education is that students do not take a high level of responsibility for their own learning." His review of the recommendations presented in the literature on how to address this lack of responsibility and his own experience have led him to develop the umbrella concept he calls "meta-learning," which he defines as "learning about learning" (4). The general idea is that if students learn *how* to learn and apply the material, they will not only feel more confident in their abilities, but they will also perform better overall.

For students to learn how to learn, they need to first correctly understand the instructor's ultimate expectations within the course's structure. Then they have to believe in their abilities to learn college-level materials. In *Strike!*, all students are given access to the same historical background information and primary and secondary sources, but they are asked to evaluate them with different outcomes and goals. This requires students to research and evaluate the relevant information through their particular lens. All students are working toward the same main goal of resolving the union's demands of the company as outlined in the list of seven demands the UMWA presented to CF&I during the 1913 negotiations and strike. However, depending on the faction's position in the negotiation, students' victory outcomes must be more clearly defined to benefit their position. For instance, the company faction is more interested in preventing workers from joining a union or unionization in general and, secondarily, in resolving the negotiations quickly to avoid a prolonged strike that will impact its profits. In contrast, the union faction wants all workers to rally behind the union to create a strong, united voice supporting the list of seven demands. The union faction also wants workers to vote to strike if negotiations fail to achieve all seven demands (including recognition of the union, which is the sticking point). The workers' victory outcomes include higher wages, a safe work environment, and a better life for their families. These may or may not align with a strike. Outlining specific victory outcomes delineates the expectations for students. Providing students with all the information to achieve these goals and small incremental steps to achieve the victory objectives allows them to succeed, thus instilling confidence in their abilities.

Role-immersion games transform the traditional classroom experience. Typically, instructors identify the major topics relevant to the subject matter, allocate time for each topic as the instructor deems appropriate, and then prepare a series of lectures and exams on each topic. Not surprisingly, this approach tends to bore students and instructors alike, especially if the instructor is not a naturally dynamic lecturer (which most of us are not). Instead of focusing on topics through lectures and tests, RTTP takes a learning-centered approach that entails identifying the learning goals (instead of topics) and then devising the best methods to achieve those goals. For instance, as instructors, we were more interested in students understanding the complicated social, economic, and political factors that led up to the Ludlow Massacre than in memorizing the dates, people, and events. We also wanted students to apply critical thinking skills and empathy in solving complex social, economic, and political problems. The strike and massacre are important in that they can provide a lesson in history's ability to supply tools and insights for navigating contemporary issues and making well-informed decisions. *Strike!* uses this history to teach students these important skills through interactive role play. The game format forces students to evaluate the conflict from various perspectives and historical lenses and apply the information to conflict resolution. As Laura M. Westhoff (2015, 581) notes, "Reacting students do serious intellectual work, both developing 'critical thinking skills,' and learning to think historically about particular content concepts." Tatlock and Reiter (2018, 22) also tout RTTP games as providing students with a "much more nuanced outlook about the nature of human disagreement." These are all important learning goals to us, and RTTP provides a means to achieve these goals.

Dividing students into factions with similar victory objectives allows us to use small groups in a powerful way. Each faction works in coordination to practice guided research, develop arguments, and solve complex problems. The common victory objects foster a team approach as opposed to a group approach in that they tend to become highly cohesive and the members are more concerned with the group than with the individual (Fink 2016, 9). The format of the RTTP game also logically follows the basic sequence of "Team-Based Learning" as developed by Larry Michaelsen and explained and outlined in Fink (9–11). The sequence includes three phases: Preparation Phase, Application Phase, and Assessment Phase. To prepare for the start of the game, students join together in their faction to critically evaluate the game's background materials, primary documents, and secondary sources. They must work together to gather and assemble the relevant information that will support their victory goals. This provides students and their teams with a purpose and direction in their research. Amelia Leighton Gamel (2015) argues that having direction or purpose helps students identify important information and concepts in the texts they encounter. Having a unified goal when students are teamed up allows them to work together to practice purposeful reading of the texts and collaborate on identifying, referencing, and utilizing the information presented. They then must move into the Application Phase to complete the assignment components of the game that include critically evaluating the documents and delivering persuasive speeches and argument-based writing that cite primary and secondary sources. During the RTTP game *Strike!*, student factions spend several class sessions working on solving complex, challenging, and authentic problems that foster team collaboration and critical thinking skills.

In addition to practicing these high-impact teaching strategies, we also felt that this particular historical event provided a vehicle for addressing issues related to diversity, including those of ethnicity, class, and gender. The workers' faction is divided into British, Mexican, and Italian miners. In addition, there is a Greek faction headed by Greek labor organizer Louis Tikas as well as women's roles represented by miners' wives and Mother Jones. These choices mirror the documented tensions between ethnicities and highlight differences in motivations based on ethnicity and gender that are reflected in both the victory objectives and the historical record. Using role play, students must understand and be able to argue for the perspectives of these factions, which are usually outside their own lived experience. In addition, the goals of compromise force students to understand other factions' perspectives so they can engage in negotiation. The goal is to encourage understanding and instill empathy for multiple stakeholders' situations and options (or limitations to those options). We also hoped the complicated political maneuverings related to strained ethnic relations and conflicting economic and social agendas would illuminate the complexities of politics and decision making.

The Successes and Challenges of *Strike!*

With these lofty goals laid out, the question arises as to whether we managed to meet them. Here, we combine data and anecdotal information from our experiences running *Strike!* in the classroom. *Strike!* has been employed in at least two different institutions and numerous classes that range from core humanities (HUM) classes to history courses. Maher teaches at a modified open enrollment university, Metro State University, Denver (MSU Denver), while Larkin teaches at a more traditional university. Class sizes have varied from 25 to 70 students, depending on the university as well as the level of the course. The average class size ranged from 25 to 40. *Strike!* was run in one section of the University of Colorado at Colorado Springs (UCCS) HUM requirement and in two sections of US history taught at MSU Denver in conjunction with the First Year Success program. The UCCS HUM course enrolled 68 students. Most of the students were not history majors (or even in the social sciences or humanities) and were taking the class merely to fulfill this humanities requirement. At MSU Denver in the First Year Success program, the class size was restricted to 25 students, and all of the students were true freshmen. In addition, Maher taught *Strike!* to a more typical student demographic at MSU Denver in the history department, with a class size of 35. Recruiting a colleague, *Strike!* was also run in a world history course of about 45 students. All four of these classes are part of a general studies/multicultural requirement at MSU Denver. Here, we present and discuss feedback received from structured surveys and anecdotal experiences and comments. The majority of this feedback came from the survey we developed to accompany the game materials. The survey was distributed and collected at the end of the game in each class that participated. We also share anecdotal observations as well as provide a critical review of the game structure and efficacy.

Larkin and Maher had similar experiences running *Strike!*, but there were also significant differences. The preparedness and abilities of students vary widely at the two institutions, despite the differences in enrollment policies. Nonetheless, *Strike!* proved to be an effective means of meeting the core learning objectives at both institutions. Specifically, students were compelled to locate sources, to communicate orally and in writing with an awareness of their audience, and to demonstrate historical knowledge. They also learned to use both primary and secondary sources to support convincing arguments and interpretations of events. In all instances, the game was successful in achieving High-Impact Teaching Practice goals. Our results show that engagement in the class was remarkably high (far surpassing the level of engagement in sections where the game was not taught), intensive reading and writing assignments were tackled with more gusto (in part because it was impossible to "win" the game without them) and students became meta-learners, and collegiality and cooperation were evident as faction members worked with each other in their quest to sway indeterminates (players without a faction) to their cause.

Our students need motivation to achieve a learning-centered approach that encourages them to become meta-learners. Larkin ran *Strike!* in a required core HUM course of 68 students. Typically, these HUM courses are reviled because students are forced to take a core humanities course in their junior or senior year as a core requirement, and they are heavily reading- and writing-intensive. However, during the RTTP game, students appeared to be engaged with the material and the practice of team-based learning in their factions. The survey supported these observations. In the survey we asked, "How would you rate your level of participation (circle one)" and gave these options: very active, active, somewhat active, and limited. This question asked students to self-reflect on their level of engagement. Of the 70 students in the class, 68 responded to the survey. Of the 68 responses, 51 students circled either "active" or "very active." Fourteen circled "somewhat active," and only 3 students circled "limited."

The high level of engagement was reflected in the open-ended responses to the question "Do you feel the Reacting to the Past game was an effective way to learn about the Colorado Coalfield War Strike and Ludlow Massacre." Fifty-one said some version of yes. One student noted "yes, I think it was. It got us involved in the learning of roles. People were more invested in sides, got a better perspective into [the] company view." Another student noted "yes, it prompted me to critically think about the event/history," and a third shared "yes, required research to prep the role." These statements reinforce the idea that RTTP presents a learning-centered course design and indirectly indicate that the format teaches students about the learning process. In other words, the format helps them become meta-learners.

Student engagement hit an all-time high in our courses, suggesting that students were achieving a flow experience in the learning process. Student comments also supported this assumption. One student commented, "It was a fun way to learn what happened." Another stated, "It was something fun/different & I will remember it more." Another responded to the question of whether the game was an effective way to learn the history with "Totally! Very interactive, made the class more fun rather than go through slides and tests." This response suggests that students have difficulty engaging with traditional content delivery methods and respond positively to encouraging a flow learning experience.

Empathy for others' points of view was a key and successful outcome. In most cases, students were assigned roles very unlike themselves—different race, class, gender—and were required to advocate for that role. One notable example from a student's evaluation: "I liked my role. My character [an Italian miner] seemed like a pretty nice guy who just wanted to provide for his family the best way possible. During the game I tried my best to come off as one who was genuinely concerned about other workers, and as somebody who was well informed on labor issues."[1] This student was a 21-year-old single Hispanic mother studying to become a computer scientist. His (her) wife in the game was portrayed by a male student, a 37-year-old construction worker who was returning to school to start a new career. An odd parring to be sure (roles were assigned randomly), but he noted: "I felt as if my role lent itself to my own creativity as not much is known specifically about my character. I felt compelled to learn more about working class women around the turn of the [twentieth] century." Other statements indicate that students applied an empathetic lens to the complicated historical past. When asked "Do you feel the Reacting to the Past game was an effective way to learn about the Colorado Coalfield War Strike and Ludlow Massacre," one student noted "Actually yes, it was nice to get the first hand [sic] experience." Another wrote "yes, because it allowed us to be in the shoes of the people involved in

Ludlow to better understand their decisions & actions." Yet another shared, "I do, I feel I can relate to the people better." These comments indicate that the game format in which students must engage with a perspective that differs from their norm effectively provided a safe format for students to engage empathetically with a complicated social and political historical past.

As important as anything, students took away from the course a better understanding of the Ludlow Massacre and of the historical context in which it occurred. One notable testimonial:

> Over the past two weeks we have been conducting a role playing activity where we as students took the roles of coal miners, family members, and company bosses. The scene is set in the coal fields of Southern Colorado during the early 1900s. A business known as the Colorado Fuel and Iron Company lorded over coal miners and their families who lived in tent colonies. This is where the game starts and we were faced with the same problem those miners faced a hundred years ago. Do we go on strike? If we do, what do we want? I believe that because of this it has a very realistic factor and while playing the game I felt fully enveloped in my character. It was never an issue for me to try and get myself in character which I really enjoyed because I was worried at that being an issue beforehand. I believe that by playing this game we gained a new insight into the lives of these workers who lived so many years before us. The events depicted within the game (the tent city, the massacre) are historically accurate to the best of our current knowledge[;] therefore it is an accurate representation of the United States at this time.

Despite the aforementioned successes, the game did present some specific problems and limitations. These limitations are related to both the format and the game mechanics. First, in terms of mechanics, most students felt the speeches were the most effective aspect, according to the survey (42/65 responses). However, they generally felt that bribe cards were confusing and the talent show was less effective (26/65 responses), although many noted that they enjoyed the Easter feast/talent show (14/65 responses indicated that they felt it was one of the most effective aspects). This ambivalence toward the Easter feast/talent show is clearly expressed by these comments in response to the least effective element: "talent show (but it was most fun)" and "eating and feasting but it was still fun." Several noted that they would like more time in their factions to develop strategies and share information, again reinforcing the idea that having students form teams was an effective use of small groups.

Once the game begins, the students take charge of the classroom; the game is dependent on them moving things forward. For the games to be effective, instructors need to allow space for students to engage with the material. Instructors must step away from their previous role as "sage on the stage" and allow mistakes and missteps to happen. While this does present opportunities for instructors to be leaders for their students, for many of the younger students—especially those enrolled in the First Year Success program—that type of independence and responsibility was foreign and even anathema. "What are we supposed to do?" was a consistent refrain. Or, more commonly, the room would be bathed in utter silence. When the game works well, as evidenced above, the results are spectacular. Yet in a class where very few students did the required readings or initiated research and where many had difficulty interpreting primary sources or simply had no immunity to the Siren song of their cell phones, the game ground to a halt. Student apathy can be present, however, whether a game is played or not. The potential benefits and success of *Strike!*—engagement, knowledge, empathy—outweighed the risks.

Another difficulty is the subject matter itself. Students had trouble empathizing with the roles of the company and Rockefeller specifically. One student noted, "Company men didn't have much to do/say . . . felt ostracized by other factions." This comment reinforced an observation made by game leaders during the game play. The factions need better balance and the role sheets need some adjustment so students can better empathize with these roles. For most students, there are simply not "two sides" to the violence at Ludlow. To them and to many Americans at the time, the company was responsible. On a national level, the United States Commission on Industrial Relations endorsed the reforms the unions had been seeking, siding with the striking workers and placing blame for the violence squarely on the shoulders of management, including John D. Rockefeller Sr. In *Strike!*, some students are asked to play roles of company men. They take on a position abhorrent to their own beliefs. It is difficult for some students to maintain empathy for their characters. One student wrote, "I despised my role [Lamont Bowers, vice president of CF&I]. Everyone in class hated me. I could not even take joy in playing the villain. I took no joy in exploiting people for profit, I felt I had no redeeming qualities. Was he some sort of sadist? I also felt I had no choice, as my role dictated my behavior." This was one of the more extreme responses, but it underscores the difficulty of teaching hard history. Subjects like the Holocaust, American slavery, or (in this case) capitalist exploitation are emotionally charged. Because of this, "being a leader for your students" becomes especially important. Debriefing is essential to correct for counterfactuals (that may have occurred during game play), to give students the opportunity to express their feelings, and to provide a space for students to leave their game personas behind.

TYING PAST TO PRESENT

The use of high-impact teaching practices can help students recognize and evaluate the nuance and importance of this event for navigating contemporary social and political structures and policies that still resonate while giving them the skills to solve these contemporary problems. Perhaps this student summed it up best: "The game was a reflection of our society today because it showed the difficulty of organizing [diverse] people and the harsh nature of labor relations. People did not always act on what American values were or what was good for the people, but they instead focused on what would help them achieve their ambitions. It is important that we, as a class, were all exposed to the corruptible nature of business and politics, so that we can be aware when we participate in the real world ourselves."

Overall, the RTTP format for exploring the social and political complexities of the 1913–1914 Southern Colorado Coalfield Strike and the Ludlow Massacre has proven effective for achieving high-impact teaching practices and encouraging empathy for the historical past. RTTP pedagogy allowed instructors to use the past to explore the hard history to better evaluate and understand the current political and social climate. The intent in creating the RTTP game around the Ludlow Massacre was not to show history as the result of inevitability but instead to highlight the importance of human agency and humans' decisions and actions on the course of history. These actions can have both positive and negative consequences that are not always anticipated or intended. The game stresses that the decisions people, corporations, and governments make are based on subjectivity and their positionality and are not black and white or right and wrong. All of these collective decisions and actions have consequences that influence the historical past (sometimes becoming the hard histories) and have shaped the present.

For the Ludlow Massacre, these hard histories are related to labor/capital and gender relations, xenophobia, political power, and their impact on contemporary society. For example, learning about the economic factors and striking miners' list of demands that led up to the 1913–1914 strike highlights the never-ending imbalance between wage and profit and the inequities in access to basic rights such as education and healthcare. Studying history and archaeology can also expose the important social and economic contributions women made in the past and allow students to examine the similarities and differences in women's social, political, and economic roles between then and now. Another lesson this hard history imparts relates to xenophobia and "othering." The practices and policies (both implicit and explicit) of the company as well as of the miners themselves provide important lessons related to the ideas of nativism and the troubling practice of stereotyping "good" versus "bad" immigrant groups. The implicit and explicit racism directed toward miners from Eastern Europe had severe consequences during the Ludlow Massacre. This history provides a clear case study of the problems inherent in creating a culture of fear and intolerance based on race and ethnicity. This lesson seems particularly relevant in light of current political rhetoric.

Finally, the history of the 1913–1914 strike and the Ludlow Massacre as well as the establishment of the Ludlow Centennial Commemoration Commission provides a lesson in political power. The game scenario clearly illustrates the advantage of having access to the political power structure of the governor, the Colorado National Guard, and the police force. However, the format allows students to explore alternative options to address inequities in wealth, power, and freedom. Interestingly, access to political power still impacts the events surrounding the 1913–1914 strike and the Ludlow Massacre. The fact that there was even a governor-appointed statewide commission is the result of access to the right people within the political structure. As explained in chapter 1 of this book, two members of a grassroots committee lobbied their state representative, Angela Giron, to help turn the informal committee into a formal statewide commission. The committee members' professional and personal relationship with Giron paved the way to the governor's appointment. Ironically, this same type of access to the governor's office by company officials of Colorado Fuel and Iron also facilitated the deployment of the Colorado National Guard to police the strike. Both examples illustrate the importance of having access to political power to help achieve the means to an end.

The Ludlow Centennial Commemoration Commission (the Commission) provided the impetus to create the RTTP game around the Ludlow Massacre, while the Rocky Mountain Collaboration: Reacting to the Past allowed this chapter's authors to connect and collaborate. The work of the Commission in providing interdisciplinary, publicly accessible, and open formats for sharing the history of the Ludlow Massacre and its relevance to contemporary issues helped address some of the gaps in awareness. This history matters. Colorado history is American history in this case, in that this event had a lasting and enduring impact on labor reform and basic human rights in this country. The inclusion of the 1913–1914 southern Colorado coal strike and the Ludlow Massacre in the congressional investigations by the United States Commission on Industrial Relations, which published its final report in 1916 (USCIR 1916), elevated this event to national importance. This report triggered labor reform in the United States and sparked the Progressive Era. These reforms set the stage for workers to gain more control over their work environment and set standards for basic workers' rights. The work of the Commission and the use of the RTTP format got students thinking about the big issues surrounding the strike and the massacre and how these issues resonate in contemporary society. The critical thinking skills developed during the RTTP game on Ludlow encourage students to evaluate employers' responsibilities to their employees. Students also begin to think critically about social rights and responsibility in society and to recognize the fact that the United States now affords regulations to protect those rights. The ultimate goal of studying history is to learn from past events and make better-informed decisions moving forward. The format of Reacting to the Past offers one effective means of achieving this goal, as evidenced by the results from *Strike!*

NOTE

1. Student quotations are taken from post-game evaluations submitted by students. Names have been removed to protect students' privacy.

REFERENCES

Andrews, Thomas G. 2008. *Killing for Coal: America's Deadliest Labor War.* Cambridge, MA: Harvard University Press.

Beshoar, Barron B. 1957. *Out of the Depths: The Story of John R. Lawson, a Labor Leader.* Denver: Golden Bell.

Carnes, Mark C. 2004. "The Liminal Classroom." *Chronicle of Higher Education* 51 (7): B7.

Carnes, Mark C. 2011. "Setting Students' Minds on Fire." *Chronicle of Higher Education* 57 (27): A72.

Carnes, Mark C. 2014. *Minds on Fire: How Role-Immersion Games Transform College.* Cambridge, MA: Harvard University Press.

Clark, Bonnie, and Eleanor Conlin Casella. 2009. "Teaching Class Conflict: A Trans-Atlantic Comparison Using the Colorado Coalfield War Archaeological Project in Undergraduate Curricula." In *The Archaeology of Class War: The Colorado Coalfield Strike of 1913–1914,* edited by Karin Larkin and Randall H. McGuire, 331–350. Boulder: University of Colorado Press.

Clyne, Richard J. 1999. *Coal People: Life in Southern Colorado's Company Towns, 1890–1930,* vol. 3. Denver: Colorado Historical Society.

Csikszentmihalyi, Mihaly. 2014. *Applications of Flow in Human Development and Education: The Collected Works of Mihaly Csikszentmihalyi.* Dordrecht: Springer.

Fink, L. Dee. 2016. "Five High-Impact Teaching Practices: A List of Possibilities." *Collected Essays on Learning and Teaching* 9: 3–18.

Fishback, Price V. 2011. *Soft Coal, Hard Choices: The Economic Welfare of Bituminous Coal Miners, 1890–1930.* New York: Oxford University Press.

Gamel, Amelia Leighton. 2015. *Help! My College Students Can't Read: Teaching Vital Reading Strategies in the Content Areas.* Lanham, MD: Rowman and Littlefield.

Gitelman, Howard M. 1988. *Legacy of the Ludlow Massacre: A Chapter in American Industrial Relations.* Philadelphia: University of Pennsylvania Press.

Hagood, Thomas Chase, C. Edward Watson, and Brittany M. Williams. 2018. "Reacting to the Past: An Introduction to Its Scholarly Foundation." In *Playing to Learn with Reacting to the Past,* edited by C. Edward Watson and Thomas Chase Hagood, 1–16. London: Palgrave Macmillan, Cham.

Jacobson, Michael. 2006. *The Colorado Coalfield War Archaeological Project Digital Atlas.* Denver: University of Denver. https://www.du.edu/ludlow/index_001.html. Accessed July 6, 2019.

Kuh, George D., Robert M. Gonyea, and Joan C. Williams. 2005. "What Students Expect from College and What They Get." In *Promoting Reasonable Expectations: Aligning Student and Institutional Views of the College Experience,* edited by Thomas E. Miller, Barbara E. Bender, John H. Schuh, and Associates, 34–64. Hoboken, NJ: Jossey-Bass.

Kuh, George D., Carol Geary Schneider, and Association of American Colleges and Universities (AAC&U). 2008. *High-Impact Educational Practices: What They Are, Who Has Access to Them, and Why They Matter*. Washington, DC: Association of American Colleges and Universities.

Larkin, Karin, and Randall H. McGuire, eds. 2009. *The Archaeology of Class War: The Colorado Coalfield Strike of 1913–1914*. Boulder: University Press of Colorado.

Ludlow Collective, ed. 2001. *Archaeology of the Colorado Coal Field War 1913–1914*. Archaeologies of the Contemporary Past, edited by Victor Buchli and Gavin Lucas. London: Routledge.

Ludlow Collective. 2018. "Teaching Ludlow CO." Teach Ludlow. http://www .teachludlowco.com/dotnetnuke/. Accessed June 20, 2018.

Margolis, Eric. 1985. "Western Coal Mining as a Way of Life: An Oral History of the Colorado Coal Miners to 1914." *Journal of the West* 24 (3): entire volume.

Maher, Matthew, and Karin Larkin. 2015. *Strike! Ludlow 1913*. New York: The Reacting Consortium.

Martelle, Scott. 2007. *Blood Passion: The Ludlow Massacre and Class War in the American West*. New Brunswick, NJ: Rutgers University Press.

Mason, David. 2010. *Ludlow: A Verse-Novel*. 2nd ed. Pasadena, CA: Red Hen.

McGovern, George S., and Leonard F. Guttridge. 1972. *The Great Coalfield War*. Boston: Houghton Mifflin.

McGuire, Randall H. 2008. *Archaeology as Political Action*. Oakland: University of California Press.

McGuire, Randall H., and Paul Reckner. 2002. "The Unromantic West: Labor, Capital, and Struggle." *Historical Archaeology* 36 (3): 44–58.

Montoya, Fawn-Amber, ed. 2014. *Making an American Workforce: The Rockefellers and the Legacy of Ludlow*. Boulder: University Press of Colorado.

Munsell, F. Darrell. 2009. *From Redstone to Ludlow: John Cleveland Osgood's Struggle against the United Mine Workers of America*. Boulder: University Press of Colorado.

O'Neil, Mary Thomas. 1971. *Those Damn Foreigners*. Hollywood, CA: Minerva.

Saitta, Dean J. 2007. *The Archaeology of Collective Action*. The American Experience in Archaeological Perspective. Gainesville: University Press of Florida.

Tatlock, Julie C., and Paula Reiter. 2018. "Conflict and Engagement in 'Reacting to the Past' Pedagogy." *Peace Review* 30 (1): 17–22.

USCIR (United States Commission on Industrial Relations). 1916. *United States Commission on Industrial Relations Final Report and Testimony*. Washington, DC: Government Printing Office.

Van der Valk, Adrienne. 2018. "Teaching Hard History." *Education Digest* 83 (9): 4–10.

Watson, C. Edward, and Thomas Chase Hagood. 2018. *Playing to Learn with Reacting to the Past: Research on High Impact, Active Learning Practices*. Cham, Switzerland: Palgrave Macmillan. doi:10.1007/978-3-319-61747-3.

Weidenfeld, Matthew C., and Kenneth E. Fernandez. 2017. "Does Reacting to the Past Increase Student Engagement? An Empirical Evaluation of the Use of Historical Simulations in Teaching Political Theory." *Journal of Political Science Education* 13 (1): 46–61.

Westhoff, Laura M. 2015. "Reacting to the Past in the Gilded Age and Progressive Era Classroom." *Journal of the Gilded Age and Progressive Era* 14 (4): 580–582. doi:10.1017/S153778141500050X.

White, Allison. 2018. "Understanding the University and Faculty Investment in Implementing High-Impact Educational Practices." *Journal of the Scholarship of Teaching and Learning* 18 (2): 118–135. doi:10.14434/josotl.v18i2.23143.

9

The Story of Making a Story Map

On a February afternoon in New York City in 1915, survivors of the Ludlow Massacre, Mary Petrucci and Margaret Dominiske, testified to the United States Commission on Industrial Relations about their experiences during the Ludlow Massacre and the Colorado Coalfield War (USCIR 1916). Testifying less than a year after losing three children during the massacre was an ordeal for Mary Petrucci. Yet, she, Margaret Dominiske, and United Mine Workers officials followed their testimony with lectures and interviews that brought the experiences of those who survived the attack to a national audience (Huffaker 1915). Most of the national audience that read newspaper stories about the massacre or heard the survivors' accounts had never been to Colorado's southern coalfields and had no material connection with the coal camps or the strikers' colonies. However, with their accounts, the survivors generated a sense of empathy that led audiences to identify with the Ludlow strikers' colony as a place, appropriating it into a larger labor identity and struggle (Jones 2012).

Although with no such trauma, those researching the Ludlow Massacre and the Colorado Coalfield War face issues in translating their historical and archaeological findings to a global audience that, for the most part, has never been to the site of the Ludlow Massacre. Project reports and academic publications help disseminate information to colleagues but often fail to reach a mass public audience and do not have the format or the structure to evoke feeling and meaning in the audience. Admittedly, artifact catalogs and archaeological feature descriptions are not the most riveting readings. Academic publications also lack a sense of flexibility and timing needed to meet the public's interests. The issues of labor, class, ethnicity, and poverty were not just central to the Colorado Coalfield War; they continue to be important issues. Yet people do not readily make a connection between the events of the Colorado Coalfield War and today unless tied to specific times, such as the centennial of the Ludlow Massacre. To keep the Ludlow Massacre in the public's memory, I sought a venue that was more wide reaching and adaptable than traditional publication venues. I also wanted a format that was evocative and engaging. In sum, I needed a way to promote an audience's engagement with the history and experience of the Ludlow Massacre.

The development of digital humanities software has allowed such storytelling to progress. Digital humanities scholars have pushed the use of digital and virtual representations of historical sites and artifacts to promote public outreach, protect threatened sites, and regain access to lost sites and materials (Douglass et al. 2017; Opgenhaffen, Lami, and Kisjes 2018). In such applications, participants engage with 3D scans of monuments and sites, virtual reconstructions, or rendered maps of a landscape (King, Stark, and Cooke 2016; Pedersen et al. 2017; Pietroni and Adami 2014). With these digital reconstructions, audiences can engage with distant locations separated from them by both time and space. This allows for flexible evocative experiences not available from traditional publications. Although virtual and digital representations are reconstructions, models, and simulations-abstractions of material space that might not directly connect an audience with material space, they can still aid in the development of community identity and sense of place. The divide between virtual and actual becomes indistinct in such an engagement, as both formats can shape social identity as it relates to place. The format and messaging tied to these virtual representations can lead people's experiences with these places through storytelling, imagery, and material connection. The audience is experiencing place, if not in the real world, then in a virtual one—and ultimately developing a connection with that place.

This chapter presents a case study of a Geographic Information System (GIS) story map created to help commemorate the Ludlow Massacre's centennial. The story map presented a geographic representation of the area surrounding the Ludlow strikers' colony. It established an engagement with Ludlow's historic landscape by marking the locations related to the events of the Colorado Coalfield War linked to historical photos and other media related to the strike and the massacre. Telling the story of the events and the archaeology at the site with the story map provided a virtual material setting and social relations equating to a place-making activity.

BUILDING THE STORY(MAP)

The development of the GIS story map was an outgrowth of my research on the Colorado Coalfield War. My research focused on the community's use of space, and GIS was a key analytical tool for this work. The ability to compare and analyze various spatial data sets, as well as provide mapping tools, makes GIS an effective tool for archaeologists. My research addressed how the coal companies, the United Mine Workers, and the strikers and their families defined the landscape of southern Colorado's coal camps and strikers' colonies to develop their community identities before, during, and after the Colorado Coalfield War (Jacobson 2006). To accomplish this, I added information from congressional testimonies, strikers' accounts, coal company publications, historical photographs, and the results of archaeological excavations into various databases connected to the GIS. At a basic level, it provided a storehouse for my research data. It also provided a venue to compare various views of the landscape to gain a better understanding of people's perceptions of spaces and places in Colorado's southern coalfields during the early twentieth century.

One key feature the GIS format provided was the ability to track individuals across the landscape or compare different descriptions of the same landmark. By including specific people's remarks on various landscape features in the GIS, I could follow an individual—whether a striker, a striker's wife, a coal camp guard, or a National Guard member—across the landscape, noting how the individual described each landmark or feature. I could also look at one landmark and compare how different people described what the landmark meant to them based on the person's identity. For example, strikers and their wives saw the Ludlow strikers' colony as protective and safe and were fearful of the areas outside of the colony based on repeated attacks and threats from company guards. These guards, in turn, described a hostile threat from the strikers in the form of rifle pits positioned throughout the Ludlow strikers' colony to intentionally fire upon or ambush the National Guard troops. These pits were the tent cellars strikers excavated beneath their tents to shelter and protect their families from company guard attacks (Jacobson 2006). The tracking of people across the coalfields provided an evocative experience. I was also able to track photographers after locating the positions where they took their photographs, identify their preferences for a subject, and determine any messages they were trying to convey through their photographs. All these data sets told the story of the Ludlow Massacre and the Colorado Coalfield War in specific ways but used the landscape as the common medium. In researching these stories, I saw that GIS could effectively tell the story of the Ludlow Massacre to a public audience.

The main obstacle to developing a GIS for a public audience was the difficulty in its use and access. Currently, there are various software solutions for presenting maps and historical data that lead to story maps. These software options include programs specific to mapping—such as ESRI's ArcGIS StoryMap, Google Earth, National Geographic Mapmaker, and Tableau—to less specific options, such as Microsoft's Sway or HTML (hypertext markup language). At the time of my research, I was more familiar with ESRI ArcGIS and HTML. GIS is a useful program for spatial analysis and cartography, but it is not user-friendly or easily accessible to most of the public. In 2006, when I began looking into developing a public GIS platform, it was especially difficult to transition from GIS to an online platform. As a result of these limits, I developed the *Colorado Coalfield War Digital Atlas* using HTML. This was limited by my coding skills and hosting issues. By the time of the Ludlow Massacre's centennial in 2014, ESRI had created tools to bring GIS to the public with its ArcGIS online tools and, more specifically, its StoryMap application. The ArcGIS StoryMap application provided a solution for translating GIS data for a public audience. The story map is ESRI's product to translate geographic data and spatial information into an online narrative by integrating spatial data with text and other media. ESRI's (2019) selling point for the story map is "to harness the power of maps and geography to tell your story." The StoryMap application allowed me to bring my ready GIS materials online in a publicly accessible format. The StoryMap templates required minimal to no coding experience and allowed me to quickly translate my materials for an online venue. The result was the *Centennial of the Ludlow Massacre April 20, 1914–2014 StoryMap*[1] that I published on the centennial of the Ludlow Massacre.

THE STORY MAP

The story map, *Centennial of the Ludlow Massacre April 20, 1914–2014*, presents a virtual experience of the Colorado Coalfield War of 1913–1914 and the Ludlow Massacre. The website provides an online spatial arena that compiles various types of media to tell the history and archaeological research related to the Colorado Coalfield War. Media, including historical photographs, maps, and participants' quotes, as well as the results of the archaeological research—artifacts, maps, and landscape analyses—are linked to geographic locations, allowing audiences to experience the historical landscape of the Colorado Coalfield War. The story map provides an overview of the coalfield war's landscape and history and serves as a compilation of the Colorado Coalfield War Archaeological Project's historical and archaeological research rather than a fully immersive or virtual experience.

I developed the story map using ESRI's StoryMap tour template. The format I used includes three panes on the webpage. The top pane serves as a header that includes basic information about the site, such as the project title, links to related websites, and a social media toolbar allowing users to share the page. The main pane consists of a base map that shows locations of popups. Users can zoom in and out of the map view. The popup windows include media (e.g., photograph, digital image, and video) and descriptive text or captions. A scroll bar was placed along the bottom of the page, which displays thumbnails of the popups and lets users access popups.

The media included in the story map represents various aspects of research into the Colorado Coalfield War. The Colorado Coalfield War Archaeological Project identified numerous historical photographs, documents, and artifacts and produced associated historical and archaeological analyses (CCWAP 2000; Larkin, Gray, and Jacobson 2004; Larkin et al. 2005; Walker et al. 2002). These data sets provide both distinct and shared perspectives of the history of the coalfield war. I integrated data from the various sources to tell that history. I limited the story map to twenty-four popups or media positions within the map. I chose this number to allow enough material to provide an informative experience without overloading the user. Each popup consisted of media (historical photograph, artifact photo, map, or video) as well as an explanatory text providing information on the media and how it related to Ludlow's overall history. The popups were positioned geographically on the map to represent the location of a specific event. I used approximate positions instead of actual locations to help ensure the protection of the cultural resources from looting or vandalism. I numbered the markers chronologically to help provide a linear story beginning with the causes of the Colorado Coalfield War as reflected in the coal camps, continuing through the strike and the Ludlow Massacre, and ending with archaeological finds at the Ludlow strikers' colony.

Although I arranged the slides to follow a linear narrative, the story map's format allows users to engage in two ways: chronologically or spatially. Users can use the scroll bar following the narrative pattern or click on the markers on the map to bring up the media related to specific locations. This allows the user to decide her or his interactive experience within the bounds provided by the story map design.

The geographic positions of the images and text were based on my (Jacobson 2006) landscape study of the Colorado Coalfield War. That study used a classification system to map the remarks concerning spatial features of those involved in the strike (e.g., guards, strikers, strikers' families). These remarks referred to the landscape, large features or sites (strikers' colonies or coal camps), and small features (tent cellars, rifle pits). This allowed for the interpretation of a sense of place within the Colorado coalfields that was transferable to the story map.

I also identified the locations of historical photographs to help identify the locations of features within the Ludlow strikers' colony. The Denver Public Library and the Steelworks Center of the West served as the main sources for the historical photographs of the Colorado Coalfield War and the Ludlow Massacre used for this project. By overlaying the negatives of historical photographs over the present terrain, I determined the photographers' positions and shooting angles as well as the locations of features. The photographers' positions allowed for the mapping of historical photographs in the story map. The locations of the photographs link to a popup that, when clicked, shows the historical photograph along with a caption with relevant text. Together, the assorted media from multiple data sets provided users with an interactive platform to engage with the history and archaeology of the Colorado Coalfield War.

APPLICATIONS

The online publication of the *Centennial of the Ludlow Massacre April 20, 1914–2014* story map coincided, as the name implies, with the Ludlow Massacre's centennial. I disseminated the story map by sharing it on my own and ESRI's social media accounts (i.e., Twitter and Facebook). Following shares on social media, institutions became interested in using the story map as part of their commemoration of the Ludlow Massacre's centennial. El Pueblo History Museum in Pueblo, Colorado, included the story map on the museum's tablets as part of its presentation of the Colorado Coalfield War. This was followed by promotion and use by the Ludlow Centennial Commemoration Commission and Colorado Public Radio (Dawn DiPrince, personal communication, April 6, 2014). In these and other venues, the story map engaged audiences with the history and archaeology of the Colorado Coalfield War. In addition to reaching the general public, the story map has also led to specific applications related to education and memorialization.

Educational outreach is the main application related to the story map. The inclusion of historical documents and material culture in conjunction with historical themes, such as labor history and ethnicity, makes the story map useful in college history and archaeology courses. Faculty at the University of Colorado at Colorado Springs used the story map to instruct their students in at least two courses. The first course was a large humanities course co-instructed by an archaeologist and a historian and curator at the Colorado Springs Pioneers Museum. The course involved an interdisciplinary approach to address a historic topic, in this case, the Ludlow Massacre and its impact on the Progressive Era. The instructors used the story map during class exercises as an aid for students to visualize and engage with the region's history (Karin Larkin, personal communication, April 8, 2020). The instructors also used the story map as an example in lectures on archaeology and the Colorado Coalfield War Archaeological Project and, more specifically, on how to use historical photographs from the Denver Public Library's catalog in research and outreach.

In addition to providing historical background, the story map has also served as a lesson for students in museum studies and public humanities. One of the previously mentioned instructors also used the story map in a museum education course. The story map served as an example of alternatives to public outreach that went beyond traditional exhibits. In one activity, the instructor used the story map, along with a series of interpretive panels made for the Ludlow Massacre monument, as examples of nontraditional outreach materials (Karin Larkin, personal communication, April 8, 2020). The story map served as a template for students to develop their own virtual or online projects for public outreach. Similarly, Binghamton University professors Shiobhan Hart and George Homsy from the Anthropology and Public Administration Departments, respectively, used the story map as a lesson in their course and the related Neighborhood Heritage and Sustainability research project. Using the story map as a guide, students developed their own story maps to present the cultural heritage of a neighborhood in Binghamton, New York. Students interviewed neighborhood residents, focusing on the residents' memory of the neighborhood and the effects of heritage preservation on their community identity (Hart and Homsy 2020). Students added historical maps, photographs, and other documents into their story maps to develop a long-term context for the neighborhood, how it has changed demographically, and how heritage may help residents sustain a sense of community.

The story map also provides an alternative venue for memorialization and remembrance of the Colorado Coalfield War and the Ludlow Massacre. The United Mine Workers of America owns and maintains the site of the Ludlow strikers' colony and promotes the site's identity as a memorial. Since the union purchased the property in 1916, it has continued to hold an annual memorial for those who died during the Ludlow Massacre. The union also maintains a memorial complex occupying a small section of what was the Ludlow strikers' tent colony. The complex consists of a monument, a pavilion, the remains of the tent cellar named the "Death Pit," and some historical markers. Artifacts scattered across the surface of the cattle fields surrounding the memorial complex mark the remains of the strikers' colony. The absence of tents, cellars, and other features in the landscape tells the massacre's story and highlights the colony's destruction. As part of the monument, the lone open tent cellar, the "Death Pit," helps present the story of the colony's destruction. Most of the massacre's victims, including Mary

Petrucci's children, died in this cellar. The union's use of the Death Pit and the rest of the memorial promotes a story of Ludlow as absence, destruction, and loss. It is a story of the strikers' and their families' sacrifice for a larger labor conflict. For many engaged in the continuation of this labor struggle, Ludlow has become a site of pilgrimage, with attendance at the annual remembrance or throughout the year.

The story map provides a different perspective and, as such, serves an alternative way to memorialize the Ludlow strikers' colony. While absence marks the destruction of the colony and memorializes it, the story map shows the experience of strikers and their families while living in the colony. It enlivens the colony in a way that does not replace the story of loss but highlights what the strikers and their families sacrificed by showing life before the massacre and its effects. Historical photographs, curated artifacts, and archaeological analysis tell the story of place not presented in the massacre's story. This story is also open to a larger audience. With the story map, those unable to travel to Ludlow can be part of a virtual pilgrimage to the site and access the memory of the strikers and their families at any time from any place.

LESSONS LEARNED

In creating the *Centennial of the Ludlow Massacre April 20, 1914–2014* and subsequent story maps, I have learned some lessons on making story maps more accessible to the public. The foundation of these lessons is that the public is primarily interested in story; therefore, the materials that go into a story map and its structure must ultimately serve the story. This section presents some overall guidance in developing a story map.

Do not overwhelm the audience: It can be easy to add numerous data or locational points that add detail to the story. As researchers, we have lots of information that we are excited about and want to share with the public. However, the idea of more details creating a more engrossing story does not follow into practice. Multiple points and data layers begin to overlap and merge; the user loses the ability to compare and contrast. The story becomes a forest of data in which the audience gets lost. Many story map visitors will visit with superficial interest. If they are welcomed by a mass of data, they may quickly move on, or if they are daring, may lose interest.

To better engage with an audience, limit the number of points or data layers. Make your story map clean and efficient. See data points and layers as plot points for your story. Determine which ones you need to progress the story and which ones serve as tangents that you can leave out. It is important to remember that GIS can serve as a data storehouse that allows an analyst to turn layers on and off for comparison. However, the story map is the interpretive story of data for public use and not a data storehouse. Limit the points within a story map to about fifteen to twenty. Keep in mind that each map should say just one or two things, and the data layers used should be directly connected to this message. If you want to say something else, then add another map. Use simplicity, cleanliness, and efficiency as the guiding principles in making a story map.

Know your audience: As with all storytelling, you need to shape your story to your audience. When developing your story map, ask yourself who you want to reach. Will it be an academic research audience or an audience with in-depth knowledge of the subject? If so, you can provide more detail and rely less on the background. Will it be for a casual public or K–12 school audience? You may need to provide more background and less detail. Make the text age-appropriate, and address any educational guidelines so the text fits into educators' lesson plans.

It may also help to determine how people will engage with the story map. Will they be doing so on their home or office computer? Will they be using it in the field on a mobile device, such as a smartphone or tablet? Websites made for computer online viewing are not often formatted for mobile devices and can be difficult to view on such devices. Make sure the story map is formatted for viewing on such devices and that the media used does not require large data downloads. Such large downloads could slow the audiences' experience and require charges for using excessive data.

Plan how you want to reach your potential audience: Setting up a story map does not mean people will find it. After identifying an audience, reach out to them using social media or working with groups (e.g., schools, museums, preservation groups) that can connect to your audience. An effective marketing and dissemination strategy is the best way to get people to see a story map.

Need to update your site: If the story map is stagnant, audiences will lose interest over time. The story map format allows for flexible and continuous updating. As the Ludlow Massacre's centennial is years in the past, I have updated the story map with new layouts and additional materials to continue the engagement with current and new audiences.[2]

Also, consider new venues. I am interested in developing a more mobile version of the story map accessible on tablets and smartphones. The mobile application would include tagged geographic locations to direct visitors to specific landmarks within the site of the Ludlow strikers' colony. This should provide a more evocative experience for visitors to the site, as they could use the app and stand in the same place where a historical photograph was taken. The visitor could see that a family's tent once stood near where they were standing and how the destruction of the massacre impacted that space. The mobile application would return a material connection to the story map's experience while also reflecting on the loss of material using the historical media that is presently best experienced with a digital application.

DISCUSSION

In the years since I developed the Ludlow Massacre story map, there has been a growth in digital humanities. This growth has not just been within academia but in public media as well. The online news platform Slate.com continuously offers interactive maps to discuss topics ranging from the loss of Native American lands (Onion and Saunt 2014) to the African slave trade (Kahn and Bouie 2015). The *New York Times* Magazine 1619 Project marking the 400th anniversary of the first enslaved Africans brought to the Virginia colony has brought historical analysis and traditional journalism together in a digital venue to discuss the 400-year history of slavery and race in the United States. As part of this series, Anne Bailey's (2020) article on identifying lost or hidden slavery auction sites merged historical documents and present-day photographs with location information to show the ways slave auction sites were hidden in the landscape following the Civil War. These examples show how visuals and an interactive platform can effectively engage with a public audience on some of our nation's forgotten and tragic events.

Digital humanities, specifically story maps, can help the public reengage with historic events or themes that are hidden or forgotten. Sites that are erased by acts of demolition, events that are not taught or discussed, or themes that are difficult for people to conceptualize and are therefore not discussed can all be brought back into public discourse in digital venues. This is the case with the Ludlow strikers' colony. The coal companies' guards burned down the colony in an attempt to end the community the strikers, their families, and the union had established. After more than 100 years, the events of the Colorado Coalfield War have left public discussions. Although the concerns of strikers and their families (i.e., wages, work safety, job security) remain with us today, the public discourse often does not include a mention of the Ludlow Massacre. With story maps, we can work to bring historic events, such as the Ludlow Massacre, back into the public's memory. By blending historical images, the materials of daily life, and our analysis in a flexible and accessible format, we can continue what Mary Petrucci and Margaret Dominiske did with their testimonies and speaking tours—make distant sites local and relevant to the public.

NOTES

1. The website address for the story map is http://arcg.is/1mDTeb.
2. For the latest update, see https://arcg.is/18yCKD.

REFERENCES

Bailey, Anne. 2020. "They Sold Human Beings Here." *New York Times Magazine*, February 12. https://www.nytimes.com/interactive/2020/02/12/magazine/1619 -project-slave-auction-sites.html. Accessed February 22, 2019

CCWAP (Colorado Coalfield War Archaeological Project). 2000. *Archaeological Investigations at the Ludlow Massacre Site (5LA1829) and Berwind (5LA2175), Las Animas County, Colorado: Report on the 1998 Season.* Denver: Colorado Historical Society.

Douglass, Matthew, Dennis Kuhnel, Matthew Magnai, Luke Hittner, Michael Chodoronek, and Samantha Porter. 2017. "Community Outreach, Digital Heritage, and Private Collections: A Case Study from the North American Great Plains." *World Archaeology* 49: 5623–5638.

ESRI. 2019. *Story Maps.* https://storymaps.arcgis.com/en/. Accessed February 22, 2019.

Hart, Shiobhan M., and George C. Homsy. 2020. "Stories from North of Main: Neighborhood Heritage Story Mapping." *International Journal of Historical Archaeology* 24: 950–968. https://doi.org/10.1007/s10761-019-00529-4. Accessed April 27, 2020.

Huffaker, Lucy. 1915. "That the Sacrifice of Her Three Children's Lives May Count for Workers' Betterment . . ." *New York Tribune*, February 4. https://

chroniclingamerica.loc.gov/lccn/sn83030214/1915-02-04/ed-1/seq-7/. Accessed April 27, 2020.

Jacobson, Michael. 2006. "The Rise and Fall of Place: The Development of a Sense of Place and Community in Colorado's Southern Coalfields, 1890–1930." PhD dissertation, Binghamton University, Binghamton, NY.

Jones, Thai. 2012. *More Powerful than Dynamite: Radicals, Plutocrats, Progressives, and New York's Year of Anarchy*. New York: Walker and Company.

Kahn, Andrew, and Jamelle Bouie. 2015. "The Atlantic Slave Trade in Two Minutes." *Slate*, June 25. http://www.slate.com/articles/life/the_history_of_american_slavery/2015/06/animated_interactive_of_the_history_of_the_atlantic_slave_trade.html. Accessed April 27, 2020.

King, Laura, James Stark, and Paul Cooke. 2016. "Experiencing the Digital World: The Cultural Value of Digital Engagement with Heritage." *Heritage and Society* 9 (1): 76–101.

Larkin, Karin, Anna Gray, and Michael Jacobson. 2004. *Archaeological Investigations at the Ludlow Massacre Site (5LA1829) and Berwind (5LA2175), Las Animas County, Colorado: Report on the 2001 and 2002 Seasons*. Denver: Colorado Historical Society.

Larkin, Karin, Mark Walker, Michael Jacobson, Anna Gray, Dean Saitta, Randall McGuire, Andrea Zlotucha Kozub, April Beisaw, and Erin Saar. 2005. *Archaeological Investigations at the Ludlow Massacre Site (5LA1829) and Berwind CF&I Coal Camp (5LA2175), Las Animas County, Colorado: Final Synthetic Report*. Denver: Colorado Historical Society.

Onion, Rebecca, and Claudio Saunt. 2014. "Interactive Time-Lapse Map Shows How the U.S. Took More than 1.5 Billion Acres from Native Americans." *Slate*, June 17. http://www.slate.com/blogs/the_vault/2014/06/17/interactive_map_loss_of_indian_land.html. Accessed April 27, 2020.

Opgenhaffen, Loes, Martin Revello Lami, and Ivan Kisjes. 2018. "Pottery Goes Public: Performing Archaeological Research amid the Audience." *Open Archaeology* 4 (1). doi.org/10.1515/opar-2018-0004.

Pedersen, Isabel, Nathan Gale, Pejman Mirza-Babaei, and Samantha Reid. 2017. "More than Meets the Eye: The Benefits of Augmented Reality and Holographic Displays for Digital Cultural Heritage." *Journal on Computing and Cultural Heritage* 10 (2): Article 11.

Pietroni, Eva, and Andrea Adami. 2014. "Interacting with Virtual Reconstructions in Museums: The Etruscanning Project." *Journal on Computing and Cultural Heritage* 7 (2): Article 2.

USCIR. 1916. *United States Commission on Industrial Relations Final Report and Testimony*. Washington, DC: Government Printing Office.

Walker, Mark, April Beisaw, Daniel Brookman, Phil Duke, Randall McGuire, Paul Reckner, Dean Saitta, and Margaret Wood. 2002. *Archaeological Investigations at the Ludlow Massacre Site (5LA1829) and Berwind (5LA1829), Las Animas County, Colorado: Report on the 1999 Season*. Denver: Colorado Historical Society.

CONCLUSION

Looking Back and Moving Forward

KARIN LARKIN, FAWN-AMBER MONTOYA, AND
THE LUDLOW CENTENNIAL COMMEMORATION COMMISSION MEMBERS

The 100-year anniversary of the Southern Colorado Coalfield Strike and the Ludlow Massacre presented an opportunity to reflect on the importance of the Ludlow Massacre to Colorado and US history. During the work of the Ludlow Centennial Commemoration Commission (the Commission), we took this opportunity to look back on the history of both the events and our own scholarly work. More important, it allowed an opportunity to transform our scholarly work into a truly collaborative public scholarship and partnership with stakeholders. The creation of the Commission provided both a platform for reflecting on the contemporary impacts of this history and a mechanism for collaborating with a wide range of stakeholders while partnering with descendant communities. Our goal here was to share the successes and challenges we encountered during this process and offer a model for how to practice collaboration, relationship building, and impact in public scholarship. We hoped to illustrate the benefits of creating lasting partnerships in collaboration. In other words, we were interested in developing a roadmap moving forward for participatory scholarship that shifts from collaboration to true partnership.

https://doi.org/10.5876/9781646422289.c010

FIGURE 10.1. Repaired Ludlow monument statues, Ludlow, Colorado. *Courtesy*, Randall McGuire.

We also acknowledge that this model for collaboration has been inspired by the United Mine Workers of America (UMWA), miners and their families, and communities throughout Colorado, which they have practiced over the past 100 years. The desecration of the monument acted as a rallying point to

reinvigorate collaborative efforts around the scholarship and memory making of the Ludlow Massacre (see figure 1.1). The violent beheading of the
statues represented an act of desecration within a sacred and hallowed space
for laborers and unions. This desecration was met with equal measures of
outrage and action. People from around the world donated money to restore
the damaged monument (figure 10.1). The vandalism also raised concerns
about future protection for the site, leading to a discussion about applying for
National Historic Landmark status through the National Park Service. The
desire to apply for this status brought together scholars and their research
to advocate for this status (Green and Jameson 2009). The National Historic
Landmark nomination integrated the historical and archaeological research
and illustrated their compatibility. The process also connected scholars, politicians, and union leaders—laying the foundation for the centennial commemoration collaboration.

Elizabeth Jameson's (chapter 4, this volume) concept of re-membering
carries many meanings. She notes that the process of literally repairing the
dismembered statues represents one form of re-membering. She also points
to the power of memory to inspire people. The establishment of the monument, the annual Ludlow Memorial Service, the testimonies of visitors who
sign the registry at the site, and the recounting of the stories around dinner
tables and in union halls are all acts of remembering of events that continue to have a profound impact on people's lives. The nomination process
and the Ludlow Centennial Commemoration Commission and committee
also connected (or re-membered) a dismembered community of advocates
to rally around this memory. The National Historic Landmark nomination
connected scholars, politicians, and union leaders with each other, creating
a cohesive body of advocates who could quickly re-member or join together
to create a meaningful centennial commemoration event. This "community of interest" (to borrow Robert Butero's phrase [chapter 3, this volume])
united to create a partnership that was based on the previous collaborative
efforts for advancing the memory of the Ludlow Massacre. This book also
serves to remember the work of the Commission and the statewide committee and can serve as a model for sparking ideas around collaborative partnerships and stewardship of the past. Here, we have asked members of the
Commission to offer some thoughts on the Commission's history and work,
as well as on how this work might move forward. Some members recount

personal reflections, while others reflect the role their institutions played. These thoughts are shared in the following sections.

LOOKING BACK

Commission members' reflections on their experiences touch on multiple levels of influence, including the role of Ludlow in understanding history and contemporary society, the role of institutions in commemoration, to how their personal history or experience interacted with the commemoration. Josephine Jones representing Colorado Humanities notes, "Colorado Humanities supports national, state, and local commemorations to help fulfill our mission to engage Coloradans in ideas and exploration of our diverse culture and heritage. We are proud of the commemorations at the Ludlow Memorial site and around the state. This lasting resource will inform an ever more inclusive Colorado history." During this time of social upheaval around racial and social inequity, Ludlow can offer lessons on inclusion and collective action.

Jonathan Rees

Jonathan Rees reflected on the significance of his Commission work for advancing historical memory and stewardship:

> When I first began visiting Ludlow in the early twenty-first century, I heard from multiple people that they had encountered tourists who had left the highway to visit the site who were disappointed that it wasn't the site of an Indian massacre. I think the work of the Commission makes it far less likely that any Coloradan will ever make that mistake again. Because of the attention that the whole coalfield war received over an extended period of time, more citizens know what happened at Ludlow in 1914 and more schoolchildren will know what happened there for decades to come. For a commemorative commission, this would be the ultimate success story.

In his role as an educator at Colorado State University (CSU)–Pueblo, he recognizes the importance of educating the public about the events and their impact. He highlights the work of the Commission in furthering stewardship efforts around community education at all levels, from schoolchildren to adult visitors at the site.

Victoria Miller

Victoria Miller describes the impact of her time on the Commission on her professional work in the following statement:

> As the curator of the Steelworks Center of the West (the repository for the Colorado Fuel and Iron [CF&I] collection), I am constantly challenged by sources created during the pre-, during, and post-Ludlow era from the company point of view. The documentation housed in the archives with which I work was written by the company, for the company. Sitting on this Commission allowed me to meet and work with others who have worked with or have knowledge and insight of other documentation that tells an all-encompassing view of the events that surrounded the strike. I have been able to use these other sources in my work of interpreting the event to our museum visitors and researchers, as well as creating new lesson plans for our secondary students of what (I hope) is a more fair and balanced viewpoint of the event(s).

Here, she describes how the collaboration on the Commission has allowed her access to different perspectives and knowledge bases that have, in turn, enhanced her ability to interpret her collection for visitors.

Maria Sanchez-Tucker

Maria Sanchez-Tucker combines her personal and professional experiences in her statement. She describes her personal connection to the Ludlow Massacre as well as how she was able to use her position to advance public knowledge of this history. She states:

> Working on a statewide commission to commemorate the Ludlow Massacre was professionally and personally rewarding. My great-grandfather was a Greek immigrant and my grandfather was a longtime steelworker; both gen-erations worked for the Colorado Fuel and Iron Co. The importance of the Ludlow Massacre is part of my heritage and [of] many others who have family roots in southern Colorado. To be able to bring this nationally significant aspect of labor history to the local level through my role as manager of the Special Collections and Museum Services at the Pueblo City-County Library District was extremely important. [The] public library programs, community dialogue, and the exhibit *"Reports from the Field": Newspaper Coverage of the*

Ludlow Massacre that was designed specifically for the commemoration helped bring greater access to history for the public. The accessibility of the Public Library broadened the reach of the project and provided a very open place for learning, dialogue, and engagement. My son who was born in spring of 2014 was given the middle name Tikas in honor of Louis Tikas and to remember this important year where we commemorated a great tragedy and brought greater public awareness to this aspect of our shared history.

She discusses the role of public libraries in partnering with other stakeholders to create opportunities for greater public access and awareness. As academics, we tend to partner with museums, but libraries offer another accessible space that can complement public outreach efforts.

Dean Saitta

Dean Saitta, University of Denver, nicely summarizes the ways the Commission's work was gratifying. He also reflects on how his work on the Commission has informed his scholarship and influenced his current research endeavors. He explains how this history and archaeology can inform contemporary social issues. He notes:

The Ludlow Commission's work was gratifying in ways too numerous to mention. But two ways stand out. First, it gave me many opportunities to tell Ludlow's story around the state. These accounts also validated the importance of archaeology to creating better and more comprehensive social histories. Second, it gave me an opportunity to know my colleagues at other institutions. It was inspiring to have people from different disciplines and backgrounds pulling together in a common cause.

One example of the Commission's impact is relevant to my current research interest in urban anthropology, specifically, the challenges facing the intercultural city. In his award-winning book *Killing for Coal*, fellow commission member Tom Andrews reports documentary evidence suggesting that the Ludlow strikers nicknamed their tent colony the "White City" because of the "gleaming canvas facades" of the tents and "as an ironic reference to the dreamlike buildings that had housed the 1893 Chicago World's Fair" (Andrews 2008). The moniker could also refer to Belgrade, the capital of Serbia, whose name translates as "White City." Strikers of Serbian identity were almost certainly present at Ludlow. Whatever the case, the important fact is that the Ludlow strikers lived side by side in an ethnically diverse settlement. They overcame their various differences to maintain a long strike in a makeshift community under conditions of serious economic deprivation, systematic corporate harassment, and one of the worst winters in Colorado history. What particular shared values and identities allowed Ludlow's diverse immigrant groups to come together in such a remarkable way? What sort of material symbols and meanings reinforced these shared values and identities and promoted cross-cultural solidarity? What does Ludlow teach us about principles and strategies for managing the inclusive city in an Urban Age plagued by racial and ethnic unrest? Is there anything that modern-day bureaucrats—especially mayors, city councilors, and community planners—can learn from Ludlow's experiment in "tactical urbanism"?

Thomas Andrews

Thomas Andrews both reflects on the work of the Commission and recognizes the continued significance of the strike and the massacre not just for working-class citizens but for our democracy as well:

The Ludlow centennial now seems like it happened eons ago. So much has changed—so many local and world-historical transformations that I failed to foresee (the recall of several state legislators over gun rights, the 2016 election, COVID-19, and so forth) have made 2013–[20]14 seem like some distant epoch. What I most appreciated and enjoyed was the spirited collaboration between folks with different backgrounds, specialties, and takes on the massacre and the 1913–[19]14 coalfield war. I found it gratifying beyond words to see just how important this history remained for so many people in and beyond southern Colorado's former coal mining communities. I happened to miss some of the more contentious exchanges during the year, so perhaps my view is a bit rosier than others'; from my more distant standpoint, though, even these disagreements seemed productive and necessary. I felt a great deal of convergence in 2014, and it gave me hope. Six years on, I find myself wishing—indeed, hoping—for more fruitful times, as well as for further opportunities to bring working-class history to bear on the current problems that are threatening to destroy our democracy and set us back on a collision course for the resumption of injustices much like those that Colorado's coal mining families were seeking to redress more than a century ago.

These reflections from Commission members on the impact and importance of their synergistic collaborations illustrate the many ways the Commission not only fulfilled the goals laid out in the original Executive Order but exceeded them and resonated in both personal and professional areas. All Commission members agree that this work needs to continue.

MOVING FORWARD

Where to go from here? How do we continue to remember and re-member the importance of the Ludlow Massacre over the next 10, 20, 50, and 100 years? Here, we offer suggestions from the Commission members as presented in the final report as well as through their reflections five years later.

Jonathan Rees

Jonathan Rees offers suggestion for re-imagining how history is taught when he reflected:

> I see the recognition of the Ludlow Massacre as the beginning of an entire reimagining of Colorado history. Instead of arranging the narrative around governors and settlement, I can see the history of the state as a continuing story of economic development, complete with all its consequences, good and bad alike. Start with Native Americans, continue with Spanish agricultural settlements in the south, then fur trading and the arrival of Americans to mine and farm. The Ludlow Massacre would fit in as the worst example of economic exploitation associated with the industrialization of these processes. The story would continue on through the growth of tourism and lead to the debates over natural resources that persist down to today. Because the massacre itself had such obvious broader implications, its commemoration can help us understand all of Colorado history in the same way.

His reimagining of how to present this history places the events related to the Ludlow Massacre into the larger context and offers a way scholars could integrate it into the classroom to continue the education around a topic that is so often omitted from the textbooks, as noted in Henry's chapter (chapter 7, this volume).

Victoria Miller

Victoria Miller offers another suggestion for continuing education efforts about the subject:

> The events that happened at Ludlow a century ago forever altered labor and management interactions in the United States as well as played a significant role in the history of Colorado. Because of the importance of this event, I hope that scholarly annual academic symposia will continue in an academic setting in which scholars and students can share ideas and allow historians of all levels—whether professional, undergraduate, and graduate level—to exhibit their talents. In addition, I would also like to see a published platform come from these academic symposia (i.e., published book, journal, website) of papers and presentations for the benefit of those not able to attend and for future reference, research, and citation.

These suggestions also address how we could integrate this history into scholarship and preserve the ideas and information that are generated to pass along to future generations.

Maria Sanchez-Tucker

In reflecting on her successes as part of the Commission, Maria Sanchez-Tucker looks forward to expanding this story's geographic reach in her new position as Library Division Director at the Santa Fe Public Library. She explains:

> The work of the Ludlow Commission was collaborative, and events took place throughout the state. Bringing national speakers, film screenings, exhibits, and community discussions to the public library was important because libraries serve as centers of civic engagement and learning. Public libraries remove barriers for participation and are open to diverse audiences. In addition to public programs, the library is [a] place where a community can archive the work of the commemoration for future generations. I have a vision to continue to bring presentations and scholarship centered on the

Ludlow Massacre to the Santa Fe Public Library where I am now the director. Libraries are the center and heart of a community, and they should continue the work to serve as a place of learning and discussion where even difficult topics can inspire inquiry and public engagement.

Dean Saitta

Dean Saitta remains active in connecting his archaeological work to contemporary issues. His active involvement in using archaeology to advocate for change in contemporary society has driven much of his work since initiating the Colorado Coalfield War Archaeological Project. His vision for that project helped shape the careers of people associated with it. Much of the work of the Commission would not have been possible without his involvement and vision in developing an archaeological project that collaborated with the UMWA. This involvement is evident in his statement. We also believe he echoes the sentiment of many Commission members when he notes:

> Going forward, I obviously would like the Ludlow story to remain alive in our collective consciousness. The episode remains relevant to discussions of workplace rights, immigration, and the challenge of how as a nation we achieve broader and more inclusive economic justice and prosperity. Although I've moved into urban anthropology, I will never refuse an invitation from civic groups to talk about Ludlow and its lessons for contemporary society. Using archaeology to help achieve National Historic Landmark status for the Ludlow Tent Colony remains the single most gratifying accomplishment of my scholarly career. It will likely never be topped. In collaboration with UCCS [University of Colorado at Colorado Springs], we will continue to house the project archeological collections at the University of Denver for as long as necessary. We will welcome students from any institution who are interested in working on these collections. Ideally, some students might even return to the site for more fieldwork, armed with new research questions and methodologies that will enhance our understanding of this extraordinarily consequential historical event.

Butero shares Dr. Saitta's interest in continuing archaeological research related to the collections and the site, as indicated in his interview in chapter 3 of this volume. The National Park Service is currently working on stabilizing the cellar known as the Death Pit at the time of writing this book, conducting additional archaeological testing and monitoring. New areas of inquiry could further explore the issues of ethnicity and inequity to inform contemporary social issues.

Robert (Bob) Butero

Bob Butero shared how the work of the Commission motivated individuals and organizations to participate in commemorating the event and how this work will be necessary in the future:

> A look back especially over the last ten years, the work everyone put forward I believe will have a major impact on how Ludlow will be looked at. The work that the Commission put into the events leading up to Ludlow was tremendous. They held events, but they managed to motivate many individuals and groups to also step forward to participate. A lot of times an organization can shut out others by how they conduct business. I believe people's participation is still occurring, and I believe it relates back to the Commission and what they did.
>
> Being a part of the senior labor group, I believe Ludlow will always be a part of what we do. However, with some of the younger labor group and the public in general, we must still hand out to the spirit of the Ludlow Commission and encourage participation and education of what Ludlow was, the effect it had on America life, and the saddest part of the lessons it taught us and that we have those lessons we let slip away. Ludlow is a landmark in how we live and in how we must fight for both social and economic justice in our great country.

The fact that he, as a representative of the UMWA, feels that the work of the Commission was impactful and inclusive speaks to the success of the model developed and the collaborative nature of the work we all accomplished together.

Collectively, Commission members agreed on some ideas moving forward. In the report presented to the governor upon the Commission's sunset, the members offered these suggestions. Commission members agreed that the next 100 years should focus on the continued preservation of the site, maintaining the collaborative partnerships around Ludlow, and creating more diverse outlets to tell the story, including books, lectures, music, theater, art,

FIGURE 10.2. Small child remembering the victims of the Ludlow Massacre during the centennial commemoration memorial service. *Courtesy*, Dawn DiPrince.

poetry, dinner table stories, and visits. The Commission members felt strongly that each member should continue to support the work of new scholars, new activists, new artists, and new descendants to tell the story with. All agreed that the most important goal is the continued collaborative relationship among scholars, the UMWA, local organizations, musicians and artists, descendants, and community members. Some specific areas of focus included:

- Preservation and stabilization of the tent cellar. The Commission members felt that preservation efforts should guarantee that the cellar is intact for the 200th anniversary of the massacre. The integrity of the concrete in the cellar has become compromised over the past several decades. The establishment of the site on the National Register and as a National Historic Landmark has allowed for some funding to help facilitate this restoration. These efforts began in 2013 and 2014 with an initial assessment and temporary stabilization of the cellar through collaborative efforts of the UMWA and the National Park Service, and they continued in 2018.

- The state of Colorado should provide continued training for education. Commission members felt this was important to recommend; however, we fully recognized that this would be more difficult to accomplish with the sunset of the Commission. Educational efforts do continue through the Southern Colorado Coal Miners' Memorial and Museum in Trinidad, the UMWA, the Steelworks Museum, and the scholars who continue to educate students, teachers, and the public about this history and its importance.
- Gather and include educational resource sets. Begin other annotated resource sets.
- Recognizing the importance of maintaining and expanding dialogue around labor history. The power of our collaborations relies on the ability for the story to live on beyond the storytellers, through a multitude of venues, and to get passed along and shared.

The partnerships we created and the inclusive model of scholarship we designed for the centennial commemoration will frame our work moving forward. We hope this book can contribute to that transfer of ideas and knowledge and continue the memory of the Ludlow Massacre (figure 10.2).

REFERENCES

Andrews, Thomas G. 2008. *Killing for Coal: America's Deadliest Labor War*. Cambridge, MA: Harvard University Press.

Green, James, and Elizabeth Jameson. 2009. "Marking Labor History on the National Landscape: The Restored Ludlow Memorial and Its Significance." *International Labor and Working-Class History* 76: 6–25.

Appendix 1

Executive Order B 2013 003

STATE OF COLORADO

OFFICE OF THE GOVERNOR

136 State Capitol
Denver, Colorado 80203
Phone (303) 866-2471
Fax (303) 866-2003

JOHN W. HICKENLOOPER

GOVERNOR

B 2013 003

EXECUTIVE ORDER

CREATING THE LUDLOW CENTENNIAL COMMEMORATION COMMISSION

Pursuant to the authority vested in the Office of the Governor of the State of Colorado and, in particular, pursuant to Article IV, Section 2, of the Colorado Constitution, I, John W. Hickenlooper, Governor of the State of Colorado, hereby issue this Executive Order creating the Ludlow Centennial Commemoration Commission.

I. Background, Need and Purpose

In September of 1913, the Great Coalfield War began when striking miners were evicted by the Colorado Fuel & Iron Company (CF&I) from their company-owned homes and moved into tents along the Colorado plains. At

---

https://doi.org/10.5876/9781646422289.c011

the height of this conflict, on the morning of April 20, 1914, a skirmish broke out between striking miners and the Colorado National Guard. This event, labeled the Ludlow Massacre, ended with the death of over 20 people, which included a National Guard soldier, miners and their wives and children. The death of children at the Ludlow Tent Colony thrust the Coalfield War into the media spotlight, with national scrutiny focused on the Rockefellers, who were majority shareholders in CF&I. In the aftermath of this tragedy, the Rockefellers and CF&I developed an employee representation plan that trans-formed industrial worker-company relations.

For over 18 months, a diverse group—including historians, scholars, union members, Colorado National Guardsmen, archeologists, tourism representa-tives, among others—have gathered along the Front Range to plan activities, exhibitions, curriculum, lectures, and events to commemorate the 100-year anniversary of these tragic events.

II. Mission and Scope

The mission of the Commission shall be to engage in efforts to raise aware-ness of the tragedy at Ludlow and the events surrounding it; to explore the themes that underscore the Ludlow Massacre and the Colorado Coalfield War, including: economy, immigration, labor, energy, culture, geography, geology, and violence. In addition, the Commission shall examine how this localized history impacted national and international labor relations and energy pro-duction, and continues to have modern-day relevance; and to make available the historical and archaeological resources from the events of 1913–1914. Also, to expand community outreach so that the stories of the individuals involved in these incidents can be heard and finally to reconcile the past and reflect on its relationship to the State of Colorado and the United States today.

Ludlow Centennial Commemoration Commission

B2013 003

III. Membership

The Commission shall be comprised of the following members:

Thomas George Andrews, PhD of Denver, Colorado, to serve as a repre-sentative of the University of Colorado, appointed;

Robert D. Butero of Trinidad, Colorado, to serve as a representative of the United Mine Workers of America, appointed;

William J. Convery III, PhD of Englewood, Colorado, to serve as a representative of History Colorado, appointed;

Dawn Marie DiPrince, of Pueblo, Colorado, to serve as a representative of El Pueblo History Museum, History Colorado, appointed;

Karin Tonya Larkin, PhD of Colorado Springs, Colorado, to serve as a representative of the University of Colorado, Colorado Springs, appointed;

Victoria Ann Miller of Pueblo, Colorado, to serve as a representative of the Bessemer Historical Society, appointed;

Fawn-Amber Montoya, PhD of Pueblo, Colorado, to serve as a representative of Colorado State University–Pueblo, appointed;

Adam Aaron Morgan of Colorado Springs, Colorado, to serve as a representative of the Colorado National Guard, appointed;

Jonathan Hugo Rees, PhD of Pueblo, Colorado, to serve as a representative of Colorado State University–Pueblo, appointed;

Dean J. Saitta, PhD of Denver, Colorado, to serve as a representative of the University of Denver, appointed;

Maria Sanchez-Tucker, of Pueblo, Colorado, to serve as a representative of the Pueblo City-County Library District, appointed;

Josephine A. Jones of Centennial, Colorado, to serve as a representative of Colorado Humanities, appointed.

Ludlow Centennial Commemoration Commission
B2013 003

IV. Duration

This Executive Order shall continue in existence until December 30, 2014, unless it is either terminated or extended beyond that date by further Executive Order of the Governor.

GIVEN under my hand and the Executive Seal of the State of Colorado, this nineteenth day of April, 2013.

John W. Hickenlooper
Governor

Appendix 2

Ludlow Centennial Commemoration Commission Bylaws

Name: Ludlow Centennial Commemoration Commission

Purpose: The mission of the Commission shall be to engage in efforts to raise awareness of the tragedy at Ludlow and the events surrounding it; to explore the themes that underscore the Ludlow Massacre and the Colorado Coalfield War, including: economy, immigration, labor, energy, culture, geography, geology, and violence. In addition, the Commission shall examine how this localized history impacted national and international labor relations and energy production and continues to have modern-day relevance; and to make available the historical and archaeological resources from the events of 1913–1914. Also, the Commission aims to expand community outreach—including statewide monthly meetings—so that the stories of the individuals involved in these incidents can be heard and finally to reconcile the past and reflect on its relationship to the state of Colorado and the United States today. As per the Governor's executive order 2013–003, this commission was established April 19, 2013 and will sunset on December 31, 2014.

https://doi.org/10.5876/9781646422289.c012

Membership Distribution List:

Thomas Andrews, PhD, University of Colorado

Robert Butero, United Mine Workers of America

William Convery, PhD, History Colorado

Dawn DiPrince, El Pueblo History Museum, History Colorado

Karin Larkin, PhD, University of Colorado, Colorado Springs

Victoria Miller, Bessemer Historical Society

Fawn-Amber Montoya, PhD, Colorado State University–Pueblo

Adam Morgan, Colorado National Guard

Jonathan Rees, PhD, Colorado State University–Pueblo

Dean Saitta, PhD, University of Denver

Maria Sanchez-Tucker, Pueblo City-County Library District

Josephine Jones, Colorado Humanities

Voting:

All members are allowed to vote

A quorum is required for a vote

Email votes are allowed; a record will be kept of the votes

Election of Officers:

Officers will be elected by a majority vote

Officers shall be elected by July 30, 2013

Elected officers shall remain throughout the term of the commission

Officers:

The Chair(s) shall:

1. Call regular meetings

2. Create agendas

3. Distribute agendas and draft minutes of previous meeting[s] elec-
    tronically to all commission members no less [than] 24 hours prior to
    each scheduled meeting

4. Preside over meetings

5. Attend meetings regularly

6. Other duties as assigned

The Vice Chair (s) shall:

7. Perform duties of Chair(s) if Chair(s) is/are unable

8. Preside over the meetings if the Chair(s) is/are unable

9. Attend meetings regularly

10. Assist Chair(s) as needed
11. Other duties as assigned

The Secretary shall:

12. Take accurate minutes (including attendance records) of each committee meeting
13. Submit draft of minutes to committee chair no less than 48 hours prior to the meetings
14. Ensure and verify electronic distribution of agendas and/or approved minutes
15. Other duties as assigned

The Treasurer

16. Give financial report to commission at each regular meeting or as needed
17. Report may be submitted 24 hours prior via email if needed
18. Act as liaison between commission and fiscal agent

Meetings:

The Ludlow Centennial Commemoration Commission will meet monthly

Special meetings can be called if needed

A quorum consists of at least one third of members

Meetings can be held via email including agenda, attendance records, and minutes

All meetings are open to the public

Meeting times and agendas will be posted publicly at least 24 hours prior

Attendance:

Each member is expected to attend meetings and to participate in commission activities

Commission members should not miss more than three consecutive meetings

Subcommittees:

Standing subcommittees will be established

Subcommittees may be of any size, but will usually include three or four members

Subcommittees will elect their own chairs

Members of the public are invited to join subcommittees

Finances:

>   Colorado Humanities will act as fiscal agent for [the] commission

>   Commission decisions for allocation of funds will be made based on a majority vote and communicated in writing to Colorado Humanities Executive Director

>   Disbursements of funds will be made within 10 days upon receipt of treasurer form signed by treasurer

Amendments:

>   These bylaws can be amended by a majority vote of the Commission members

Appendix 3

Statewide Committee Members, 2012–2014

Dylan Addington, Pueblo County Government

Beverly Allen, Colorado State University–Pueblo

Tom Andrews, University of Colorado Boulder

Robert Butero, UMWA

Elaine Callas-Williams, Assumption of the Theotokos, Denver, CO

Mary Chamberlain, Fremont County Heritage, Florence, CO

William Convery, History Colorado Center, Denver

Laura Cuetara, University of Colorado Denver

Dawn DiPrince, El Pueblo Museum, Pueblo, CO

Daneya Esgar, Colorado Progressive Coalition/Jobs with Justice, Pueblo

Madison Furrh, Colorado State University–Pueblo

Tim Hawkins, Steelworks Center of the West (Bessemer Historical Society), Pueblo, CO

Dan Hiester, Denver, CO

Suzane Hultin, History Colorado Center, Denver

Pamela Jacobson, St. John the Baptist Greek Orthodox Church, Pueblo, CO

https://doi.org/10.5876/9781646422289.c013

Kate Johnson-Silva, La Veta Public Library, La Veta, CO

Josephine Jones, Colorado Humanities, Denver

Elaine Kusulas, Assumption of the Theotokos, Denver, CO

Karin Larkin, University of Colorado at Colorado Springs

Dianne Layden

Paula Manini, Trinidad History Museum, Trinidad, CO

Tara Marshall, Trinidad/Las Animas County, Trinidad, CO

Loretta Martin, Trinidad State Junior College, Trinidad, CO

Victoria Miller, Steelworks Center of the West (Bessemer Historical Society), Pueblo, CO

Julie Mondot, Mother Jones reenactor

Fawn-Amber Montoya, Colorado State University–Pueblo

Juan Morales, Colorado State University–Pueblo

Adam Morgan, Colorado National Guard, Colorado Springs

Carolyn Newman, Walsenburg Mining Museum, Mother Jones reenactor, Walsenburg, CO

Stan Obrey, Southern Colorado Repertory Theater, Trinidad

Brian Orr, University of Colorado at Denver

Denise Patrick, Mt. Carmel Wellness and Community Center, Trinidad, CO

Fr. Stephen Powley, St. John the Baptist Greek Orthodox Church, Pueblo, CO

Jonathan Rees, Colorado State University–Pueblo

Julie Rodriguez, Black Hills Energy, Pueblo, CO

Dean Saitta, University of Denver, CO

Kim Schultz, Mt. Carmel Wellness and Community Center, Trinidad, CO

Ken Scott

Katherine Sturdevant, Pikes Peak Community College, Colorado Springs

Maria Tucker, Pueblo City-County Library District–Rawlings Library, Pueblo, CO

James Walsh, Romero Trope, Denver, CO

Karen Wilson, Huerfano County Tourism Board, Walsenburg, CO

Millie Wintz, Fremont County Rockers, Florence, CO

Barbara Yule, Spanish Peaks International Celtic Music Festival, La Veta, CO

Appendix 4

Report Narrative to the Governor of the State of Colorado

The following is a reprint of the report submitted to the governor of the state of Colorado concerning the Ludlow Massacre Centennial Commission. The report was prepared by Fawn-Amber Montoya with feedback from Commission members and submitted to Governor John Hickenlooper on August 1, 2016. Commission members included:

- Thomas Andrews, PhD, University of Colorado
- Robert Butero, United Mine Workers of America
- William Convery, PhD, History Colorado
- Dawn DiPrince, El Pueblo History Museum, History Colorado
- Karin Larkin, PhD, University of Colorado, Colorado Springs
- Victoria Miller, Bessemer Historical Society
- Fawn-Amber Montoya, PhD, Colorado State University–Pueblo
- Adam Morgan, Colorado National Guard
- Jonathan Rees, PhD, Colorado State University–Pueblo
- Dean Saitta, PhD, University of Denver

https://doi.org/10.5876/9781646422289.c014

- Maria Sanchez-Tucker, Pueblo City-County Library District
- Josephine Jones, Colorado Humanities

BACKGROUND

Asking for the enforcement of [the] Colorado Mine Safety law, in September of 1913 miners and their families went on strike in southern Colorado. Their demands included a desire for safer working conditions, the ability to be paid in US currency rather than company scrip, the desire to shop at whatever store they chose and the recognition of the union. In response, their employer, the Colorado Fuel and Iron Company[,] evicted them from their company owned homes. The families moved onto the plains of southern Colorado and lived in a tent colony supplied by the United Mine Workers of America, UMWA. In October of 1913, the Governor of Colorado, Elias Ammons, responded to the strike by committing the Colorado National Guard as a security force. A week later, the governor instructed the National Guard to escort replacement workers to the mines, which undercut the aims of the strikers. Through the winter of 1913/1914, one of the worst winters in recorded history, there were a series of abuses inflicted upon the miners by the National Guard troops[,] often referred to as the militia by the miners and their families. Through the winter of 1913/14, the National Guard and the strikers engaged in insults and a number of confrontations defined the relationship between these two groups. There were threats to the military from the strikers and their families, as well as intimidating, harmful, and sometimes fatal actions upon civilians by the strikers as well. There was a mutual loss of respect between troops and strikers, but many civilians were threatened. One of the most notorious exchanges occurred in Trinidad in January of 1914, when a group of women, organized to protest the imprisonment of Mary Harris (Mother) Jones, violated a pre-coordinated route by rushing towards her place of detainment to free her. General Chase ordered his men to block the way, falling off his horse in the process. Frustrated and embarrassed, he ordered his troops to "Ride down the women." The women responded by hurling stones at the troops, while the troops swung the flat sides of their sabers to deter the protesters. Minor injuries were sustained by both sides.

In the spring of 1914, the National Guard began to withdraw troops from the region because of a lack of funding. On Sunday April 19, the striking miners engaged in a game of baseball with some celebrating Orthodox Easter with the Greek miners in the encampment. On the morning of April 20, 1914, the Colorado National Guard and striking miners engaged in gunfire that ended with the National Guard setting fire to the encampment. The fire resulted in the deaths of 11 children and 2 women in a tent cellar below one of the tents. The cellar had been used as a maternity chamber. Before the end of the skirmish[,] over 20 people were killed. The Ludlow Massacre set off a war throughout southern Colorado that raged for ten days and only ended when President Woodrow Wilson dispatched federal troops to the region to quell the violence.

THE COMMISSION

On April 2013, Governor John Hickenlooper appointed the Ludlow Centennial Commemoration Commission to commemorate the 100th anniversary of the massacre. The commission was part of a larger statewide committee that had been meeting on a regular basis for nearly two years before the appointment from Governor Hickenlooper. The idea for the statewide committee emerged from a series of annual events that had been occurring statewide for a number of years[;] these included CSU-Pueblo [Colorado State University–Pueblo] commemorations of the massacre held every April in collaboration with organizations in Pueblo and southern Colorado, such as the Steelworks Center for the West, and the Rawlings Public Library. In addition to the events in April, the United Mine Workers of America has held an annual memorial at the site for nearly a century. Organizations and individuals that had supported these efforts have been part of an informal dialogue about the importance of the Ludlow Massacre and how best to inform the community of Colorado and the nation about the impact these events, that happened in 1914, had on shaping contemporary society. This long-term acknowledgement of the events of the Colorado Coal Field Strike and the Ludlow Massacre has occurred on a national level with the establishment of the Ludlow Tent Colony as a National Historic Landmark in 2009.

The appointment of the Commission was possible largely because of the advocacy of then State Senator Angela Giron who met with members, Dawn DiPrince and Fawn-Amber Montoya of the statewide committee at her home in early January of 2013. Ms. Giron contacted Romaine Pacheco in the Governor's office to discuss the need for the commission and how the commemoration would impact the state. Members of the statewide committee communicated with the Governor's office to put together the language for the executive order.

On April 19, 2013, Governor Hickenlooper appointed 12 commissioners to serve from April of 2013 to December of 2014. Appointed commissioners included individuals from History Colorado, University of Colorado at Boulder and Colorado Springs, Colorado State University–Pueblo, The Colorado National Guard, Rawlings Public Library, The Steelworks Center of the West, and The United Mine Workers of America.

After their appointment, the Commission members met with the state-wide committee on a monthly basis for the remainder of 2013, and on a regular basis throughout 2014. The Commission established bylaws, an organizational structure, a webpage, and a presence on social media. While the Commission was the official organizing body of the commemorations, the Commission members did not see themselves as being the gatekeepers or the central clearing agency for all commemoration events. The statewide committee included interested individuals and organizations from throughout the state. As the committee and the Commission met, they discussed upcoming events and coordinated a calendar that would enable the events at Ludlow to be shared in multiple venues, to diverse audiences, and in a variety of formats. The Commission focused on a Speakers Bureau that brought scholars from throughout the United States and Canada to discuss their research on labor history and reform in Colorado and on the effects of the Ludlow Massacre and its aftermath on the nation. Other events included: an award-winning exhibit—*Children of Ludlow*—housed at El Pueblo History Museum, an exhibit and speakers' series at the Colorado Springs Pioneers Museum, a Memorial Service at the Ludlow Massacre site on the anniversary of the massacre (sponsored by the Greek Orthodox cathedral in Denver), an academic symposium in Pueblo, and the UMWA commemoration in May with over 1000 people in attendance. Some members of the audience traveled great distances to attend the centennial ceremony. In particular, George Stavroulakis, a great nephew of Louis Tikas, who came in from Athens, Greece. Manuela Ciaghi came all the way from Italy. Manuela's grandfather, Giovanni Ciaghi, operated a general store in Hastings in 1914 and personally witnessed the murder of his friend Louis Tikas.

With the dissolving of the Commission, according to the sundown laws of the State of Colorado, the Commission official[ly] ended in December of 2014. The group met in April of 2015, to discuss how they felt the commemoration events went. At the meeting they discussed what they felt had been triumphs of the year-and-a-half long commemoration. Among the triumphs, Commission members included the collaboration among all of those on the Commission and the statewide committee. Commission members felt that the conversation with the various descendants of those that were present enhanced the events. The diversity in meeting locations and attendance throughout the eastern portion of the state, also contributed to the success. The Commission felt that the changes in venue were appropriate and that it [sic] showed respect to multiple organizations. It also allowed for greater participation. This enabled smaller organizations to participate and feel that their work was acknowledged and appreciated by larger organizations. The committee participation was also diverse in region, gender, ethnicity, and age. Another success was the wide variety of formats for events—speakers, theatrical performances, poetry readings, concerts, and exhibits in both history museums and contemporary art galleries. The events reached audiences outside of Colorado and included national and international voices and attendees. The commission especially highlighted that this wide range of programming was accomplished with no direct state monies set aside for the memorial events. Additionally, Commission members were struck by the fact that given the horrific nature of the massacre, attendance had been high and audiences held a genuine desire to learn about Colorado's history. The committee highlighted that social media, specifically Facebook, was an effective means of reaching a larger audience. The commission wanted to acknowledge the leadership of Dawn DiPrince and Fawn-Amber Montoya and other commission members as being collaborative, supportive, and a model for future commissions.

Despite the many successes of the Commission, some improvements could have been made. The Commission felt that a stronger website presence that was updated constantly could have helped improve communication. Additionally, this website could have provided summary reports on events, and links to historical resources.

At the conclusion of the meeting, the commission agreed to continue to meet twice a year in September, at the beginning of the strike, and in April, the month of the Massacre, to discuss how to continue to tell the story of the Massacre. Plans for future commemorations include: writing and submitting National Park Service Grants for interpretation at the site, installing a permanent plaque at the site to record the names that were not include[d] on the 1918 memorial, establishing a conservation plan with funding for the site, monument, artifacts, changing 4/20 to LUDLOW Day[,] thereby establishing an official day of remembrance at the State level, the development of a museum dedicated to the history, continued education related to the history at K–12 and higher education levels, and to continue to record and preserve oral interviews with descendants.

In all, we felt that the commemoration activities were very successful in informing Coloradoans and others in the United States and abroad about the Ludlow Massacre. We felt that communities across the state of Colorado were able to come together to take part in a variety of commemoration events, and that the outreach was successful.

Suggestions for the State of Colorado in the future include:

- The tent cellar. Preservation efforts should guarantee that the cellar is intact for the 200th anniversary of the massacre. State of Colorado should provide continued training for Education.
- Commission members to continue to meet.
- Gather and include educational resource sets.
- Beginning of other annotated resource sets.
- Recognizing the importance of maintaining and expanding dialogue around the labor history
- State resolution incorporated at the Ludlow Site.
- Issuing a formal apology for what occurred at Ludlow
- The following study groups formed with purpose of producing a comprehensive and official publication of the commission:
- In depth study of strike tactics employed by strikers
- In depth study of oppressive tactics employed by mine guards
- In depth study of militia committal and field orders issued to the soldiers
- In depth study of the Regular Army committal by President Woodrow Wilson, and their field orders
- In depth study of the state department reaction to the 15-month ordeal

Appendix 5

Calendar of Events and Attendance

Events for the centennial celebrations began in April 2013 and ended in December 2014. The official kickoff for the memorial events was in September 2013.

Month/Year	Date	Event	Sponsor
April–Nov. 2013		Various presentations by Victoria Miller (Attendance: 452)	Steelworks Museum and CF&I Archives
Sept. 2013–May 2014		All Campus Reads focused on *Ludlow: A Verse Novel* and *King Coal* at UCCS (Attendance/Participation: 350)	University of Colorado at Colorado Springs
Jan.–Nov. 2014		Various commemoration events and programs at Steelworks Museum or by museum staff (Attendance: 754)	Steelworks Museum and CF&I Archives
June 2013		Two-day event celebrating the region's coal mining history	Mt. Carmel Church, Trinidad, CO
Jan.–March 2014		*Protest!* exhibit at Galleries of Contemporary Art (Attendance: 450)	University of Colorado at Colorado Springs

continued on next page

https://doi.org/10.5876/9781646422289.c015

CALENDAR—*continued*

Month/Year	Date	Event	Sponsor
April–May 2014		*Reports from the Field* museum exhibit (Attendance: 4,165)	InfoZone Museum, Rawlings Library, Pueblo, CO
September 2013			
	9/5	Lecture by Thomas Andrews on *Killing for Coal* (Attendance: 135)	Rawlings Library, Pueblo, CO
	9/12	"The Colorado Coal Field War," lecture by Dr. Dean Saitta (Attendance: 35)	Erie Community Library, Erie, CO
	9/14	Coal camp tours of Ludlow and Berwind (Attendance: 15)	Bessemer Historical Society
	9/15	"Ludlow Debates" (1904), pre-Ludlow Victorian debate and social, Theatre in the Round (Attendance: 312)	Florence Art Council, Florence, CO
	9/19	Opening reception for *Children of Ludlow: Life in a Battlezone 1913–1914* exhibit (Attendance: 150)	El Pueblo Museum, Pueblo, CO
	9/21	Free public program: Strike! The Fiery Laborer Activist, Mother Jones, Rallies the Coalminers! (Attendance: 50)	Trinidad History Museum, Trinidad, CO
	9/21	"Commemorating the Coal Mine Strikes of 1913–1914," lecture with author Zeese Papanikolas (Attendance: 90)	Hellenic Community Center, Assumption of the Theotokos, Greek Orthodox Church, Metropolis Cathedral, Denver, CO
	9/22	UMWA 100th anniversary of start of the strike (Attendance: 900)	UMWA Ludlow memorial site, near Trinidad, CO
	9/22	"Strike Vote Remembrance at the Ludlow Memorial" annual event; speakers Zeese Papanikolas and Dawn DiPrince (Attendance: 200)	UMWA Ludlow memorial site, near Trinidad, CO
	9/26	"The Colorado Coal Field War," lecture by Dr. Dean Saitta (Attendance: 55)	Dowd Eisenhower Public Library, Broomfield, CO
October 2013			
	10/1	Panel discussion of the Ludlow Massacre (Attendance 85)	Regis University, Denver, CO

continued on next page

CALENDAR—*continued*

Month/Year	Date	Event	Sponsor
	10/8	"Ludlow: A Verse Novel," Kraemer conversation with David Mason (Attendance: 105)	Kraemer Family Library at University of Colorado at Colorado Springs
	10/25	Maria Montoya presentation "Industrial Healthcare and Mining" (Attendance: 50)	University of Colorado at Colorado Springs
	10/26	"2013 Union Highland Cemetery Crawl. A 2nd Ludlow Event" (Attendance: 86)	Florence, CO
	10/27	Maria Montoya presentation "Industrial Healthcare and Mining" (Attendance: 10)	Trinidad State Junior College, Trinidad, CO
	10/28	Maria Montoya presentation "Industrial Healthcare and Mining" (Attendance: 35)	El Pueblo Museum, Pueblo, CO
November 2013			
	11/14	"The Ludlow Tragedy, a Colorado Militia Retrospective," Major Adam Morgan, Colorado National Guard (Attendance: 20)	El Pueblo History Museum, Pueblo, CO
January 2014			
	1/31	*Protest!* exhibit opening reception and artist talk at Galleries of Contemporary Art (Attendance: 55)	University of Colorado at Colorado Springs
February 2014			
	2/25	"Who Are the Children of Ludlow?" lecture by Dr. Fawn-Amber Montoya (Attendance: 100)	El Pueblo History Museum, Pueblo, CO
March 2014			
	3/5	"The Ludlow Tragedy, a Colorado Militia Retrospective," Major Adam Morgan, Colorado National Guard (Attendance: 25)	Colorado Springs Pioneers Museum, Colorado Springs
	3/8	"Women and Children of Ludlow," lecture for Pikes Peak Regional History Lecture Series by Dr. Karin Larkin (Attendance: 75)	Colorado Springs Pioneers Museum, Colorado Springs
	3/13	"The Ludlow Tragedy, a Colorado Militia Retrospective," Major Adam Morgan, Colorado National Guard (Attendance: 75)	Lafayette Library, Lafayette, CO

continued on next page

CALENDAR—*continued*

Month/Year	Date	Event	Sponsor
	3/13–30	*Ludlow: El Grito de las Minas* performance (Attendance: 200)	Su Teatro, Denver, CO
	3/15	"Unearthing Ludlow," lecture for American Association of University Women by Dr. Karin Larkin (Attendance: 25)	AAUW, Colorado Springs
	3/15	"Louis Tikas Night," *Ludlow: El Grito de las Minas* (Attendance: 50)	Su Teatro, Denver, CO
	3/15	Denver Mayor declares Louis Tikas Day	Denver, CO
	3/18	"Memories of Ludlow," lecture by Dr. Fawn-Amber Montoya (Attendance: 75)	History Colorado Center, Denver
	3/20	"Excavating and Remembering Ludlow," lecture by Dr. Dean Saitta (Attendance: 50)	El Pueblo History Museum, Pueblo, CO
April 2014			
	4/2	"Ludlow in Requiem: Labor and Coal Mining Concert" (Attendance: 30)	Pueblo City-County Library District, Pueblo, CO
	4/13	"Freedom Fighters or Corporate Victims? The Ludlow Massacre and Class War in the American Southwest," lecture by Scott Martell (Attendance: 60)	Denver, CO
	4/14	"Excavating and Remembering Ludlow," lecture by Dr. Dean Saitta (Attendance: 35)	Colorado Archaeological Society
	4/14	"Freedom Fighters or Corporate Victims? The Ludlow Massacre and Class War in the American Southwest," lecture by Scott Martell (Attendance: 65)	University of Colorado at Colorado Springs
	4/15	"Southern Colorado Reading Series Presents David Mason, Author of *Ludlow*" (Attendance: 50)	Colorado State University–Pueblo
	4/15	"Re-Collecting Ludlow," lecture by Dr. Dean Saitta (Attendance: 75)	Norlin Library, University of Colorado, Boulder
	4/16	"Freedom Fighters or Corporate Victims? The Ludlow Massacre and Class War in the American Southwest," lecture by Scott Martell (Attendance: 50)	La Veta, CO

continued on next page

CALENDAR—*continued*

Month/Year	Date	Event	Sponsor
	4/16	Film viewing: *Matewan* (Attendance: 16)	InfoZone News Museum, Rawlings Public Library, Pueblo, CO
	4/17	"Excavating-and Remembering-Ludlow," lecture by Dr. Dean Saitta (Attendance: 75)	Colorado Archaeological Society
	4/17	Lecture by Scott Martelle, author of *Blood Passion* (Attendance: 65)	InfoZone News Museum, Rawlings Public Library, Pueblo CO
	4/18	Exhibit opening *Reports from the Field* (Attendance: 53)	InfoZone News Museum, Rawlings Public Library, Pueblo, CO
	4/18	"Ludlow in Requiem: Labor and Coal Mining Concert" (Attendance: 350)	Memorial Hall, Pueblo, CO
	4/18	Ludlow symposium (Attendance: 25)	Pueblo City-County Library District, Pueblo, CO
	4/18	Lecture by Scott Martelle, author of *Blood Passion* (Attendance: 50)	Bread and Roses
	4/19	Exhibit opening *Memories of a Massacre: Perspective on Ludlow* (Attendance: 150)	Colorado Springs Pioneers Museum, Colorado Springs
	4/19	LaborFest academic symposium (Attendance: 45)	El Pueblo History Museum and Colorado State University–Pueblo
	4/19	"Creative Response to History" with Daniel Valdez and Tony Garcia (Attendance: 75)	El Pueblo History Museum, Pueblo, CO
	4/20	Memorial service and Greek Orthodox Agape service at Ludlow monument (Attendance: 200)	Metropolitan Isaiah from Assumption Greek Orthodox Metropolis Cathedral of Denver, Ludlow, CO
	4/21	"Remembering Ludlow Today," panel discussion including Thomas Andrews, Adam Morgan, Bob Butero, Bill Convery, and Fawn-Amber Montoya (Attendance: 150)	History Colorado Center, Denver

continued on next page

CALENDAR—*continued*

Month/Year	Date	Event	Sponsor
	4/22	Resolution HR-1005 Proclamation read by Representative Garcia in Colorado State House of Representatives	Colorado State House of Representatives, Denver
	4/22	*Pilgrimage* magazine "Labor" release (Attendance: 50)	Bessemer Historical Society and Steelworks Museum, Pueblo, CO
	4/25	"Excavating and Remembering Ludlow," lecture by Dr. Dean Saitta (Attendance: 25)	Molly Brown House, Denver, CO
	4/26	Mt. Carmel Wellness Center's second annual run/walk for the fallen coal miners, started and ended at Ludlow memorial site (5k/10k/½ marathon)	Mt. Carmel Wellness Center, Trinidad, CO
May 2014			
	5/1	"The Road to Ludlow: Breaking the 1913–1914 Southern Colorado Coal Strike," lecture by Dr. Anthony DeStefanis (Attendance: 97)	InfoZone Museum, Rawlings Public Library, Pueblo, CO
	5/4	"The Road to Ludlow: Breaking the 1913–1914 Southern Colorado Coal Strike," lecture by Dr. Anthony DeStefanis (Attendance: 25)	La Veta Public Library, La Veta, CO
	5/5	"The Road to Ludlow: Breaking the 1913–1914 Southern Colorado Coal Strike," lecture by Dr. Anthony DeStefanis (Attendance: 65)	University of Colorado at Colorado Springs
	5/10–17	Theater Play, Kaiulani Lee: *The Story of Mother Jones* (Attendance: 1,360)	Denver, CO; TheatreWorks, Colorado Springs; El Pueblo History Museum, Pueblo, CO; Trinidad, CO
	5/16	Night of remembrance (Attendance: 50)	Mt. Carmel Wellness Center, Trinidad, CO
	5/17	Family day at Ludlow Memorial National Historic Landmark (Attendance: 900)	United Mine Workers of America, Ludlow, CO
	5/17	Bicycle ride from Cokedale to coal camps and Ludlow (Attendance: 50)	United Mine Workers of America, Cokedale and Ludlow, CO

continued on next page

CALENDAR—*continued*

Month/Year	Date	Event	Sponsor
	5/18	100th anniversary of Ludlow Massacre at Ludlow Memorial National Historic Landmark (Attendance: 1,500)	United Mine Workers of America, Ludlow, CO
	5/20	"The Ludlow Massacre: History and Reconciliation," lecture by Dr. Fawn-Amber Montoya (Attendance: 50)	Pikes Peak Chapter of Colorado Archaeological Society, Colorado Springs
	5/22	"Unearthing Ludlow," lecture at Kraemer Family Library by Dr. Karin Larkin (Attendance: 65)	University of Colorado at Colorado Springs
	5/24	Ludlow Art Poster Contest (Attendance: 93)	Bell Tower Cultural Center, Fremont County, CO
June 2014			
	6/14	"Remember Ludlow, Remember Victor: Persecution and Memory in the Victor Labor War of 1904," lecture by Katherine Sturdevant (Attendance: 50)	Colorado Springs Pioneers Museum, Colorado Springs
July 2014			
	7/21	"Social Life in Western Mining Camps," lecture by Dr. Fawn-Amber Montoya (Attendance: 50)	Lafayette Public Library, Lafayette, CO
September 2014			
	9/11–28	*Ludlow, 1914*, the Lida Project, original play by TheatreWorks (Attendance: 550)	University of Colorado at Colorado Springs
	9/18	"Moving Mexican Descent Women to the Center," lecture by Sarah Deutsch (Attendance: 20)	CSU-Pueblo
	9/18	"Moving Mexican Descent Women to the Center," lecture by Sarah Deutsch (Attendance: 25)	Pueblo City-County Library District, Pueblo, CO
	9/18	"Moving Mexican Descent Women to the Center," lecture by Sarah Deutsch (Attendance: 65)	Metropolitan State University, Denver, CO
	9/19	"Moving Mexican Descent Women to the Center," lecture by Sarah Deutsch (Attendance: 50)	University of Colorado at Colorado Springs
	9/25	"Heroes of Ludlow," lecture for First Year Experience by Dr. Karin Larkin (Attendance: 125)	University of Colorado at Colorado Springs

Index

About the Contributors

ROBERT (BOB) BUTERO is regional director of United Mine Workers Region 4. Butero comes from a coal mining family in southern Colorado. After beginning as a coalminer, Butero worked his way up the ranks, then began to work for the United Mine Workers of America (UMWA). Butero organizes the annual memorial service at the Ludlow Tent Colony and Massacre site. Butero served on the Ludlow Centennial Commemoration Commission as the UMWA representative.

ROBIN C. HENRY is associate professor of history at Wichita State University. She is the author of the book *Criminalizing Sex, Defining Sexuality: Sexual Regulation and Masculinity in the American West, 1850–1927*. Henry completed her PhD at Indiana University. Her research interests include legal, gender, and sexuality issues in the American West.

MICHAEL JACOBSON is research and development specialist in the Public Archaeology Facility at SUNY Binghamton. Jacobson completed his PhD at Binghamton University in 2006 and wrote his dissertation on landscape analysis of the Ludlow Tent Colony and Massacre site. Jacobson also acted as crew chief during excavations for the Colorado Coalfield War Archaeological Project. He has published numerous articles and book chapters on the archaeological project.

ELIZABETH JAMESON is professor emerita of history at the University of Calgary. She is coauthor of the article "Marking Labor History on the National Landscape: The Restored Ludlow Memorial and Its Significance," which recounts the Labor and Working-Class History Association's effort to have the Ludlow Tent Colony declared a National Historic Landmark. She is also the author of *All That Glitters: Class, Conflict, and Community in Cripple Creek* and *Building Colorado: The United Brotherhood of Carpenters and Joiners of American in the Centennial State.* She co-edited the books *The Women's West* and *Writing the Range: Race, Class, and Culture in the Women's West.*

KARIN LARKIN is assistant professor and curator for the Department of Anthropology, University of Colorado at Colorado Springs. Larkin received her PhD in anthropology and master's in museum studies from the University of Colorado at Boulder. Larkin acted as crew chief and the second project director of the Colorado Coalfield War Archaeological Project at the University of Denver, funded through the History Colorado State Historical Fund. In 2009, she co-edited the book *The Archaeology of Class War* with Randall McGuire, SUNY Binghamton, published by the University Press of Colorado.

LINDA LINVILLE is a retired high school history teacher. She is the granddaughter of Nicola and Luigia Costa. Her grandparents lived in the Ludlow Tent Colony, leaving before the massacre. Her great-aunt and great-uncle, Cedilena and Charlie Costa, along with their three children, Onofrio, Lucy, and an unknown infant, were victims of the Ludlow Massacre. A fourth child, Tony, died from complications of the flu while living in the Ludlow Tent Colony.

MATTHEW MAHER teaches in the Department of History at Metropolitan State University in Denver and is adjunct faculty in history at the University of Denver. Maher teaches US and world history. He works to incorporate "hard histories" into his teaching and utilizes high-impact teaching practices in his classes.

FAWN-AMBER MONTOYA is the Honors College Associate Dean of Diversity, Inclusion, and External Engagement and professor of history at James Madison University. She is the editor of *Making an American Workforce* and coauthor of *Practicing Oral History to Connect University to Community.* From 2007 to 2019, Montoya was professor of history at Colorado State University–Pueblo.

YOLANDA ROMERO is a lifelong resident of Las Animas County. She is married to Michael (Mike) Romero, a former coalminer and Local 9856 president. The Romeros were caretakers of the Ludlow Tent Colony and Massacre site. Yolanda Romero cofounded the Women's Auxiliary of UMWA Local 9856 and researched and contributed to a book on its history. She is a member of the Trinidad Hispanic Las Animas

County Chamber of Commerce and a business owner. She and her husband founded and run the Southern Colorado Coal Mining Memorial and Museum to honor the history of coal mining in southern Colorado. They are also actively involved in the implementation of fundraising efforts and are primarily responsible for the Southern Colorado Coal Miner's Scholarship Fund, The Romeros were honored by the Trinidad Community Foundation with the City of Champions Award for 2018–2019.